Yellowstone Ecology:
A Road Guide

Sharon Eversman
and
Mary Carr

Mountain Press Publishing Company
Missoula, Montana — 1992

Library of Congress Cataloging-in-Publication Data

Eversman, Sharon, 1940-
    Yellowstone ecology : a road guide / Sharon Eversman and
Mary Carr
        p.   cm.
    Includes bibliographical references and index.
    ISBN 0-87842-278-1 : $12.00
    1. Natural history—Yellowstone National Park. 2. Natural
history—Wyoming—Grand Teton National Park. I. Carr, Mary,
1949-. II. Title.
QH105.W8E84   1992   92-4392
508.787'5—dc20   CIP

Mountain Press Publishing Company
P.O. Box 2399
Missoula, Montana 59806

To Tom, Jennifer and Jay, and my
mother, Louise (S. E.)

To my dad who helped me to love the
out-of-doors and Chuck, who has
helped me to understand it better (M. C.)

Table of Contents

Preface

A car ride between scheduled points of interest can be interesting or trying, a chance to catch up on reading and sleeping, or an opportunity to gain a different perspective on familiar or unfamiliar terrain. The thermal features of Yellowstone are easy to see because they tend to not move around. Animals are more elusive because their most active part of the day is often when humans are least active.

A whole other world exists. Learning to read the landscape can be an enjoyable activity that, besides being something to do in the car, leads to understanding the big picture of the entire rock-soil-plant-animal web.

This book is mostly a guide to what can be seen from a car. We have intentionally not included professional photographs of the wildlife; one has to be incredibly lucky or diligent and have excellent camera lenses to get pictures like that, and many beautifully illustrated books are already available. Our intent is to discuss features of the landscape that are interesting in themselves and that allow animals to exist here. Roadside geology guides are wonderful travel companions; we hope roadside ecology guides like this will be the same.

We gratefully acknowledge the assistance of many people in the writing of this book. Graduate students from Montana State University and elsewhere over the years have written many theses that were very helpful. We made frequent use of the scholarly papers regularly produced and made available to the public by Yellowstone and Grand Teton national park personnel. Numerous published works, listed in the bibliography, addressed pieces of our topics and provided both inspiration and information. We thank Mary Bateson, Calvin Kaya, William Locke, Robert Moore, Jan Nixon, Harold Picton, and David Ward of Montana State University for checking the accuracy of portions of the manuscript. Don Despain of Yellowstone National Park helped with manuscript review and information shared from much experience in the Yellowstone country, as did Rick Wallen of Grand Teton National Park. The Greater Yellowstone Coalition shared background information and maps. We thank Tom Eversman for his excellent animal drawings, and Steve Winslow for his efforts at printing quality photographs from sometimes questionable negatives. And we thank Chuck Gibilisco for helpful suggestions and invaluable "road tests." All remaining errors of fact or interpretation are ours alone.

Sharon Eversman and Mary Carr

Introduction

Say the word ecology and everyone who hears you probably will conjure up a different image. Some will think of plants and animals, some of soil and rain. A number will focus on pollution or the plight of endangered species. Perhaps a few will think of their homes.

Home? It's no coincidence. The word ecology came from the Greek word *oikos* which means home, and it refers to the study of the relationships of organisms to their environment and to one another.

Your home is a building, a physical structure, your environment. It's also a group of people who live in or visit the building. At any one time some of the people in your home may be related, some may not be. The people fight, talk, love, compete, share, and otherwise interact with each other and even with other species, their pets. The people interact with the physical structure, too: they sweep and repair and use the rooms of the home for eating, resting, and staying out of the rain.

The study of ecology explores the same kind of patterns and connections in the relationships among plants and animals and their physical environment. Soil, water, sunlight, rain, mountains and valleys, and rivers are some of the physical features that create the physical space within which plants and animals fight, communicate, mate, compete, and otherwise interact with each other and with their surroundings. The essence of their ecology is how all these relationships work and connect to each other.

The word ecology is sometimes confused with the word environment. The latter word does refer to the physical surroundings of any organism; your home and the meadow where an elk feeds are parts of the environment. But the word environmental today usually refers to political, economic, and social issues, like pollution control and endangered-species protection, which have at their root a concern for how the ecology of an area might be affected by certain human activities. Solving environmental problems requires an understanding of the underlying ecological relationships, but the two are not the same.

In this book, we point out some of the complex environmental issues currently being debated in the area. But we concentrate on describing some of the ecological connections among the region's plants and animals—including people—and their surroundings, particularly those features visible from the major roadsides. The Greater Yellowstone ecosystem is a big place, though—some 14 million acres, about the size of Rhode Island, Connecticut, and Delaware combined. You can see but a glimpse from the roads, so whenever possible, get out of your car and take a closer look. We use the symbol of the magnifying glass to mark a few particularly notable opportunities for closer looks. The essence of ecology is the way things work, and you can best see how things work if you take the time to sit quietly and watch them happen.

What does a ribbon of green trees winding along a dry sagebrush flat tell you about where water is to be found? What does the presence of trees and water tell you about where and what kinds of animals you might find? Can you figure out what kind of soil is beneath your feet by looking at the vegetation? Try to imagine the hundreds of threads that connect the visible and invisible pieces of the picture before you.

How to Use the Roadside Guide

Road guides in this book are presented, with a few exceptions, in the directions of north to south, and west to east. Within Yellowstone and Grand Teton national parks, the roads are in loops; the guide follows a clockwise direction around each loop. Occasional outstanding side trips are noted; these generally are on good gravel roads or less traveled paved roads that are worth the extra time to explore. Topics are presented in a narrative fashion and not generally geared to specific stops or mileages, so routes may be easily followed in reverse should your own travel direction differ from the book's.

National park roads have no official highway numbers. For state and federal highways, official highway numbers are listed at the beginning of the route.

Ecology is the story of connections and relationships, and roadside ecology is but a few of these caught at a moment in time as you travel along a tiny sliver of space. We hope this book will provide not only a guide to some of the connections within the Greater Yellowstone ecosystem, but also a guide to thinking about and searching for connections in the world in and around your own home, wherever that may be.

GENERAL ECOLOGY

Ecosystems and Other Eco-lingo

The term ecosystem refers to all the living and nonliving components of a system—the plants, animals, and microorganisms as well as the soils, rocks, water, climate, and topography. The definition includes not only these biological and physical parts, but also their ecology—how these various elements interact, and how they keep functioning.

Usually an ecosystem is a large area with substantial energy flow, cycling of nutrients, water systems, geological processes, and many layers of biological interactions among the living inhabitants. An ecosystem can also be as small as an elk's stomach, where dozens of species of bacteria interact within their own small world, receiving and transferring energy, processing minerals and nutrients, carrying on like any larger system.

In between the giant and the miniature sizes are nested and interlaced layers of other ecosystems, such as the alpine or forest or lake ecosystems found within Greater Yellowstone. Surrounding any ecosystem are thousands of others, connected by water, energy, migrating animals, people, and countless other threads.

This Bone's Connected to That Bone. . .

We've all heard the jingle about the leg bone connected to the thigh bone connected to the hip bone. . . and the same concept of connectivity holds for the pieces of an ecosystem. The geology and rock layers underneath and near an area, for example, help determine the soil characteristics of a particular system, which can be further affected by climate, which is determined in part by elevation and nearness to an ocean. The plant communities or associations of various kinds of trees, shrubs, grasses, and flowers provide food and habitat for animal life. In turn, the animals eat, pollinate, fertilize, disperse seeds and fruits, bed in, and otherwise affect the vegetation. They also eat, chase, mate with, or somehow interact with other animals.

Changes constantly occur. Vegetation grows and, sometimes, gives way to other kinds of plants; fires and disturbances sweep through; wildlife species move in and out and evolve into other species. It's impossible to think about an ecosystem without taking into account all of these factors, and many others. That's why it's so difficult to define where one ecosystem begins or ends, either in space or in time.

The Ecological Onion:
Layer After Layer After Layer. . .

Because an ecosystem is so complex, ecologists often focus on selected parts of a system for study. The ecology of individual organisms, for example, includes the extremes of environmental conditions such as

Carbon and Nitrogen Cycles

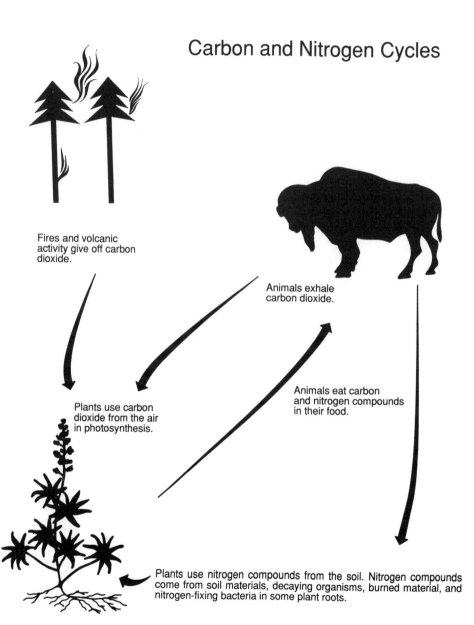

Fires and volcanic activity give off carbon dioxide.

Animals exhale carbon dioxide.

Plants use carbon dioxide from the air in photosynthesis.

Animals eat carbon and nitrogen compounds in their food.

Plants use nitrogen compounds from the soil. Nitrogen compounds come from soil materials, decaying organisms, burned material, and nitrogen-fixing bacteria in some plant roots.

moisture, heat, and light that they can tolerate. It takes into account the scarce factors that might limit their existence in a certain area, such as the amount of usable nitrogen available. Ecology involves how much energy organisms require and pass on, how the individuals behave, how and where they select their habitats, how and where they move around.

Individual plants or animals of the same species living in the same place make up a larger unit called a population, which has its own set of ecological characteristics. Birth and death rates are components of how fast and sharply a population grows and how soon it reaches the limits of available resources. How dense a population is, how it regulates its size, how predators and prey relate to each other, how populations compete, how populations go extinct. . . all these subjects relate to population ecology.

On an even larger scale, communities are made up of populations of various species, generally interacting with each other. Communities have their own level of ecology. The environment of temperature, wind, light, humidity, fire, or soil moisture acts on the whole community. An intense fire, for example, will affect not only the individuals in its path, but the very nature of the community of plants or animals it burns. The reaction to the fire might include the growth of a completely new and different community of plants, at least temporarily, and the appearance of a whole new set of animals; or it might spur plants that were present but inconspicuous before the burn to grow in greater abundance.

At the ecosystem level we also look at how energy and nutrients flow, how water cycles through a system, and how entire landscapes are molded and constantly changed by climate, bedrock and all the interacting factors that work at all ecological levels.

THE GREATER YELLOWSTONE ECOSYSTEM

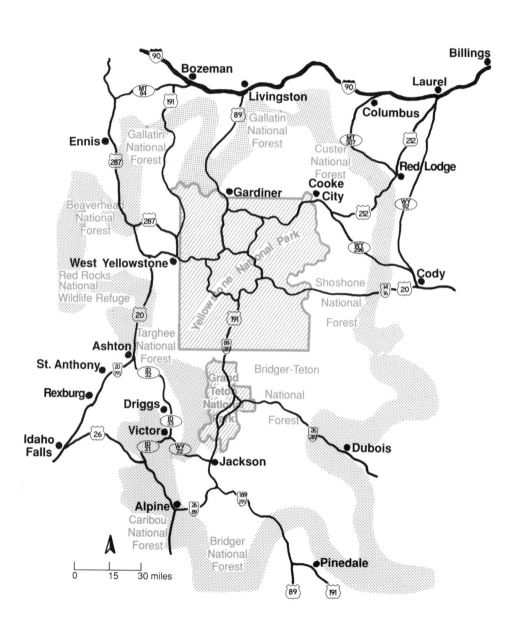

The Greater
Yellowstone Ecosystem

Yellowstone and Grand Teton national parks are in the northern Rocky Mountains. The parks have official boundaries, but the rocks, soils, plants, and animals pay little attention to them. In fact, the parks are only part of the story; they form the core of a much larger, intricately woven region known as the Greater Yellowstone ecosystem (GYE). The Greater Yellowstone ecosystem comprises some 14 million acres of some of the most pristine landscape in North America, and is one of the earth's largest essentially intact temperate ecosystems.

Greater Yellowstone: Which Way is the Border?

The boundaries of the Greater Yellowstone ecosystem are loosely drawn, generally following one or more criteria. Yellowstone Park, for example, is on a high plateau averaging 8,000 feet. It is adjacent to several mountain ranges and to another series of high plateaus known as the Beartooths. This high country and the adjacent valleys are the core of the ecosystem.

The original definition of the Greater Yellowstone ecosystem focused on the known range of the region's grizzly bear population. Other definitions include the low-elevation migration paths and winter ranges of elk and other wide-ranging wildlife. The combined watersheds of the major river systems that begin in the Yellowstone region — the Snake, the Yellowstone, and the Green — provide yet another way to draw a somewhat porous line around the ecosystem. Combining all of these characteristics together probably comes closest to describing where the flexible boundaries lie.

This Land is. . . Whose Land?

The Greater Yellowstone ecosystem under any definition crosses numerous political boundaries, including: three states, two national parks, seven national forests, three national wildlife refuges, an Indian reservation, other federal lands, and nearly a million acres of private land.

1

Roughly 90 percent of the ecosystem is federally owned public land, under the jurisdiction of numerous governmental institutions each with its own history and mission. For example, the National Park Service, an agency of the Department of the Interior, manages Yellowstone and Grand Teton national parks with a mandate to preserve natural processes and provide for public enjoyment. Many forms of recreation are allowed within the parks, but other activities are restricted, including collecting, hunting, logging, grazing, oil and gas extraction, mining, and most kinds of development.

On the other hand, the U. S. Forest Service, an agency of the Department of Agriculture, manages the seven national forests that surround the parks, mostly for multiple use. These areas are used for extraction of resources, such as timber, oil, and minerals, as well as for recreation, wildlife habitat protection, and watershed protection. Roads, vehicles, and a variety of human activities are allowed in most parts of the national forests. But about 40 percent of the national forests here are managed as Wilderness, where the goal is to preserve and protect natural conditions. Activities within Wilderness areas are tightly restricted.

Three wildlife refuges exist within the ecosystem. These are managed by the U. S. Fish and Wildlife Service, primarily for the protection or recovery of particular wildlife species. Red Rock Lakes National Wildlife Refuge in Montana was established to protect the rare trumpeter swan; Grays Lake National Wildlife Refuge in Idaho is the site of an intensive effort to bring back the endangered whooping crane; and the National Elk Refuge in Jackson Hole, Wyoming, is self-explanatory.

Another federal agency, the Bureau of Land Management, owns or manages scattered portions of the ecosystem, devoted primarily to range management for grazing animals. Wyoming, Montana, and Idaho have individual fish and game agencies, which regulate fishing and hunting in the region outside the national parks.

Of these public lands, 44 percent is open to grazing at least part of the year. Forty percent is open for mineral exploration. About 19 percent of the forested land is identified as suitable for commercial timber harvest. Interspersed with the public lands are privately owned parcels. They range from individual dude ranches, to blocks of land owned by timber companies, to entire towns and communities.

No wonder that disagreements about how to manage parts of the system arise, often obscuring the broader goal of managing and protecting the entire ecosystem. Whether the issue is fire control or the reintroduction of the wolf or the installation of a snowmobile trail, differing perspectives and interests are at stake. This mosaic of resources, political jurisdictions, and human pursuits is sometimes difficult to sort out. This is a land of tremendous diversity in topography, climate, vegetation, wildlife, and people.

GEOLOGY AND CLIMATE

The Greater Yellowstone ecosystem is in high plateau and mountain country rising 3,000 to 5,000 feet above surrounding valleys and plains. This is a geologically active region. The Yellowstone Plateau was built in two episodes of volcanic eruptions. The first happened about 50 million years ago when the Absaroka volcanoes were active. Those rocks exist mainly in the northern and eastern parts of Yellowstone Park. They form parts of the Absaroka and Gallatin mountain ranges. The famous petrified forests in the northern parts of Yellowstone Park were buried in volcanic mudflows then.

The current episode of volcanic activity started about two million years ago. Enormous explosive eruptions have happened about every 600,000 years since. They produced the pale volcanic rocks of the Yellowstone Plateau, which look quite different from the much darker Absaroka volcanic rocks. The great explosive eruptions of the past two million years opened great collapse basins called calderas, which then filled with lava. The Yellowstone volcano shows every sign of being active. Most geologists expect more great eruptions in the future.

The series of plateaus known as the Beartooth, east of Yellowstone Park, was raised along a series of nearly vertical faults during Eocene time, about 50 million years ago. The tops of the plateaus are amazingly flat and rolling; some unique alpine communities have developed on them.

All of this region is within the Rocky Mountains, which include many ranges and intervening valleys such as the Teton and Wind River ranges in Wyoming, the Absaroka range of Montana and Wyoming, the Madison and Gallatin ranges in Montana, the Centennial Range on the border between Montana and Idaho, and the Snake Range in Idaho and Wyoming.

High Up on the Divide

Most maps also show the Continental Divide. Water from west of the Divide drains into the Snake River, which runs into the Columbia River, then to the Pacific Ocean. Water east of the Divide runs into the Madison, Gallatin, and Yellowstone rivers, which flow to the Missouri River, then to the Mississippi, then to the Gulf of Mexico.

The Continental Divide affects climate and precipitation, which in turn influence what grows and lives in the ecosystem. Prevailing winds are from the west; the large storms that bring the most rain and snow usually blow in from the Pacific Ocean. As air rises to get over this high country, it cools and drops its moisture as rain or snow, which falls most heavily on higher elevations. The proportion that falls as snow increases with elevation; the highest peaks receive as much as 200 to 400 inches per year. After the moist air masses are past the highest peaks, they sink to the plains east of Yellowstone country. That air is relatively dry because it dropped most of

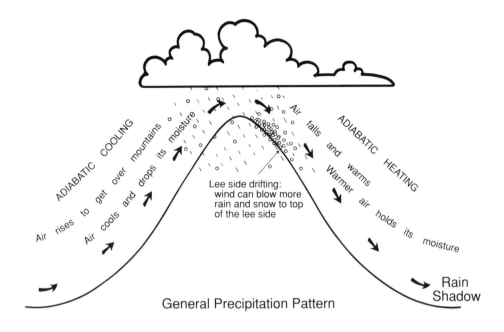

General Precipitation Pattern

ADIABATIC COOLING
Air rises to get over mountains
Air cools and drops its moisture

Lee side drifting:
wind can blow more
rain and snow to top
of the lee side

Air falls and warms
ADIABATIC HEATING
Warmer air holds its moisture

Rain
Shadow

its water on the high country. It warms as it descends, and warm air can hold large amounts of moisture. So the air soaks up moisture out of the valleys like a sponge, creating dry areas east of the plateaus and mountain ranges. These drier areas are in the rain shadow of their respective mountain range.

As a general rule, air temperature drops 3.5 degrees for every 1,000 feet increase in elevation, basically because there is less air and less water vapor at higher elevations to absorb and trap solar heat. Up high, temperatures drop drastically at night because heat escapes readily through the thin air, and cold winds and storms can blow up during the day.

Snow is much lighter than rain. While it depends somewhat on the temperature, a general estimate is that 10 to12 inches of snow, melted, makes one inch of precipitation; 200 inches of snow is the equivalent of about 20 inches of rain. Winter snows in this region are very light and powdery, wonderful for skiing. Wind and warm temperatures, however, compact the snow into very heavy, dense masses. Avalanche danger can be high.

VEGETATION PATTERNS

The broadest patterns of vegetation are woven by elevation, soil, and climate. In general, the lowest, driest locations have grassland-sagebrush plant communities. As you climb in elevation, you see a progression of different kinds of forests, until you reach conditions too harsh for trees to grow; then you are above timberline, in alpine meadows dominated by grasses and tiny flowering plants.

Although approximately 1,700 species of vascular plants grow in the Greater Yellowstone region, they include very few species of trees compared to the complex forest types of the Pacific coast or the eastern parts of the country. The kinds of plants are closely tied to such factors as the bedrock, soil, moisture, wind, fire history, and grazing pressure. Once you recognize about 10 different kinds of plants here, you know quite a lot about the location. And since vegetation provides food and habitat for wildlife, the plant communities in turn will tell you a lot about what animals to expect.

Grassland-sagebrush

The arid West is predominantly a land of grass and sagebrush. No matter from which direction you approach the Yellowstone region, you must drive through grassland and sagebrush country. For those unused to such broad treeless vistas, the vegetation, especially in summer, may look parched, hot, and perhaps lifeless. But these communities support a wide variety of plants and animals.

About 160 species of grass grow in Yellowstone Park alone, the particular species varying considerably with the location. The largest stands of grasses grow primarily in floodplains and meadows, but some grow in almost every habitat, at every elevation.

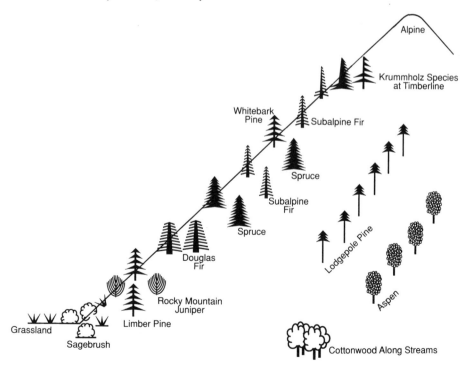

Generalized pattern of tree distribution in the Greater Yellowstone Ecosystem. Precise elevations depend on temperature, wind, moisture, direction the slope faces, available soil, and other factors. Aspen and lodgepole pine grow at many elevations.

5

General vegetation pattern: sagebrush grassland to mountain forest to higher alpine meadows above timberline.

The major grasses are bunchgrasses such as Idaho fescue (*Festuca idahoensis*) and bluebunch wheatgrass (*Pseudoroegneria spicata*). These species, along with other grasses and wildflowers or forbs, are the preferred food for most grazing animals. Most grasses grow best in full sun and have deep roots, so they can resprout almost immediately after a fire or other disturbance and thrive in the sunny conditions.

The most commonly seen sagebrush is big sagebrush (*Artemesia tridentata*); the species name *tridentata* refers to the three lobes at the tips of the leaves. Big sagebrush varies in size from about one foot in height to seven or eight feet. It's easily recognized by its soft grey-green color all through the year; tall spikes of very small yellowish flowers bloom in late August and early September and often persist on the plant even in winter above the snow. The pungent aroma of sagebrush is due to organic compounds called terpenoids. Stop and walk through a sagebrush flat for an aromatic treat.

Deer and elk will browse on big sagebrush to survive the winter, but they prefer grass and woody plants such as willow, aspen, or even junipers and pines. Sagebrush is nutritious, but evidently has a detrimental effect on bacteria in the rumen, the specialized stomach of ungulates. Sagebrush also provides food and shelter for dozens of smaller species, from the sage grouse, which depends almost entirely on this aromatic plant for food and shelter, to small mammals, reptiles, and insects.

Big sagebrush.

Many grazing animals winter in the sagebrush grasslands because less snow lies on these low-elevation communities than on the higher elevation forests. This puts pressure on available food resources when large numbers of hungry animals congregate on the winter ranges. Mammoth Hot Springs and Tower Junction in Yellowstone Park, and the National Elk Refuge in Jackson are three places where you might see the results of intensive winter grazing and browsing.

Conifers

Conifers bear cones instead of flowers; they are evergreen and keep their needles for several years. In fact, because needles are sensitive to air pollution, one way to check the air quality is to count the number of years that the needles hang on. In the Yellowstone region, the pines keep their needles generally from six to twelve years, depending on the species and the hospitality of the site. Ponderosa pine in southern California may have only two years of needle growth, sometimes only one.

Conifers are well adapted to dry, cold conditions. Their narrow needles covered with a thick waxy cuticle help conserve water and give conifers an early start on photosynthesis in spring. Conifers depend on wind, an abundant commodity on the Yellowstone Plateau, to blow pollen grains from male to female cones.

Conifers are also well adapted to the relatively poor soils of the Yellowstone region. Keeping their leaves for several years means they need fewer minerals, nutrients, and water than do deciduous trees that have to develop new leaves every spring. And conifers even have built-in injury and disease protection: their sticky resins tend to ooze at points of injury where insects and fungi attack, hardening into yellowish-brown amber that exudes and traps the attackers and seals the wound against further damage.

Juniper and limber pine. At the upper edge of the sagebrush and grassland zone, more water is available for tree growth. Rocky Mountain juniper (*Juniperus scopulorum*) and limber pine (*Pinus flexilis*) are the dominant trees in this region. You might confuse this juniper with cedar, which also has small scale-like leaves, but cedars have small woody cones while junipers have soft blue cones that look more like berries.

Limber pine gets its name from its flexible branches. It has a look-alike, the whitebark pine. Both have five needles in a bunch, but the limber pine has larger, resiny cones and grows at lower elevations than the whitebark pine.

Limber pine needles in bundles of five. Whitebark pine also has needles in bunches of five.

Rocky Mountain juniper, with short overlapping scales and blue berries.

Ponderosa pine. The ponderosa pine (*Pinus ponderosa*) abounds throughout the West, except in most of the Yellowstone area. For some undetermined reason it doesn't grow as a native in an area that roughly matches the boundaries of the Greater Yellowstone ecosystem. This might be due to the undependable springs, or the possibility of frost at any month of the year, or unfavorable soils. It is a puzzle, because ponderosa pine does grow in protected areas in the ecosystem where it has been planted.

You can see ponderosa pine at a few locations, near Billings or Red Lodge, Montana, for example. You will recognize it by its extremely long needles (up to eight inches) in bunches of two or three, its enormous woody cones with spikes on the scales, and its orangy-brown bark that smells like vanilla when you stick your nose close to it.

Ponderosa pine, with very long needles in bundles of two or three.

Douglas fir.

Douglas fir. In areas of the West where ponderosa pine does grow, it usually grows just above the juniper-limber pine zone. But in most of the Yellowstone region with its lack of ponderosa pine, a different forest type grows in this zone, the Douglas fir (*Pseudotsuga menziesii*). Douglas fir is actually more closely related to hemlock than to the true firs, but old names stick.

Douglas fir can be a majestic tree, economically important for timber on private and national forest lands. Older trees have thick, fire-resistant bark that enables them to withstand most fires. The largest Douglas firs in the ecosystem are at Pine Creek Campground in a cold-air drainage on the west side of the Absaroka range. Other places to watch for Douglas fir include the roads near Tower Junction, along the Teton Pass road, and along the Snake River.

Spruce-fir. Above the Douglas fir zone, you enter a spruce-fir zone where two species, spruce (*Picea*) and subalpine fir (*Abies lasiocarpa*) grow together. Spruce is generally more abundant than fir along streambanks, but the two species usually mingle. They extend together to timberline.

Subalpine fir is a graceful tree of higher elevations; it is a true fir, so its needles are flat and friendly. The winter buds are rounded, unlike the pointed winter buds of Douglas fir. You won't see cones under a

Subalpine fir, with short, flat needles.   *Spruce, with short, pointed needles.*

subalpine fir tree; as the cones mature the scales harden and fall off the cone, leaving bare spikes sticking up from the branches like tiny chewed corn cobs.

Spruces can be distinguished from Douglas fir and subalpine fir by the spruce's papery cones and sharp pointed needles, which are not flat and friendly. When the needles of a spruce fall off, which they seem to do readily, they leave little bumps on the branches. Spruces in the region include Engelmann spruce (*Picea engelmannii*) and white spruce (*Picea glauca*); most are hybrids between the two. In this book, we simply call them all spruce. Colorado blue spruce is widely planted as an ornamental tree, but it is native to the region only in parts of Grand Teton National Park.

Spruce needs a moister site than Douglas fir, so at lower elevations spruce will be found along the streambanks while Douglas fir is higher and drier on the hillsides. At higher elevations, where there is more precipitation, spruce forms extensive stands with subalpine fir.

Lodgepole pine. This pine species, *Pinus contorta*, is another widespread conifer of western forests from Arizona to Alaska, California to South Dakota. Nowhere in the United States, however, does it grow in as large a continuous expanse as it does in the Yellowstone region. Nearly 80 percent of the forested parts of Yellowstone Park are stands of this one pine species. Lodgepole pine grows at all elevations, from just above the grasslands to upper timberline. The species name, *contorta*, comes from the wind-beaten form of this tree on the Pacific coast. Its common name, lodgepole, refers to its growth form in the mountains, where it grows in dense stands of tall, straight trees perfect for teepees and contemporary log homes.

10

Lodgepole pine sprouts quickly and in great numbers after a fire, in part because some have a number of serotinous or closed cones that require the heat from a fire, or intense sunlight, to open. Even a burned tree may contribute thousands of tiny seeds to reseed a burned area, which has the open and sunny conditions that lodgepole seedlings prefer. But lodgepole pine trees also have regular cones that open without heat, enabling them to be the first on the scene after other kinds of disturbances, like

Lodgepole pine with long needles in bundles of two.

wind throws, logging, or road building. Lodgepole is the conifer you most often see growing along the open roadside.

Whitebark pine. This pine (*Pinus albicaulis*) gets its species and common names from its smooth, light-colored bark. Like limber pine, it has five needles in a bunch, but it grows higher than limber pine, just below and at timberline. It doesn't have a hard woody cone like limber pine, but a soft cone that birds and squirrels can readily raid for its large seeds; this means the cone is quickly destroyed and hard to find intact on the forest floor. Whitebark pines are at the center of an intricate and intriguing network of wildlife thieves and tricksters. We will explore that in more detail where the trees are abundant and visible along the road over Mount Washburn in Yellowstone Park.

Deciduous Trees

Deciduous trees, which lose their leaves in autumn, contribute to the spectacular autumn colors throughout the region — not quite like the Eastern maple forests, but dramatic all the same. Yellow colors are the aspens, cottonwoods, and willows; Rocky Mountain maple and serviceberry shrubs turn vivid red. These bright colors against the dark conifer forests and golden brown grass make memorable fall scenery.

Aspen. Quaking aspen (*Populus tremuloides*) grows across much of North America. Its white bark is very thin and contains chlorophyll, so the trunk can photosynthesize as well as the leaves — a very unusual characteristic that makes the bark a nutritious browsing food for elk. This

11

Quaking aspen leaves.

is not so good for the aspen, which responds to browsing pressure by developing thick dark furrows at its base; you'll see these dark marks where elk abound. Aspen also depends on fire for much of its regeneration, both to stimulate growth of suckers from the roots and to create open sunny areas where seedlings can grow well. Fire suppression over the years along with intense browsing by elk have been discussed as reasons why aspen seems to be declining in number.

Aspen requires abundant water. Vast stands indicate that the water table is close to the surface. Aspen also grows in pockets on hillsides and open areas where water is available.

Cottonwoods and other aspen relatives. Cottonwoods are larger relatives of the aspen that grow along streams and in soggy areas. Narrow-leaf cottonwood (*Populus angustifolia*) is the species most commonly found in this region, with thick, dark brown, furrowed bark on older trunks.

Willows (*Salix* species) are among the most abundant shrubs and small deciduous trees in the ecosystem. Also found along streams and wetlands, willow is one of the major foods of the moose. Intense grazing by moose and elk can reduce willow shrubs to mere nubbins of their potential selves. Along several routes, exclosures or fenced areas have been set up to keep moose and elk out so biologists can measure the effects of browsing on these shrubs.

Narrow-leaf cottonwood.

Succession

The vegetation types in the ecosystem today are really just snapshots, revealing what grows under present conditions and for the moment, but not necessarily reflecting the species and communities that have existed or will exist in the future. The changes from one forest type or vegetation type to another over time is called succession, a concept that has received much debate and clarification over the years.

Lifetimes of forests are generally longer than the lifetimes of the people observing them. But present-day sites can give ample clues to what is going on. Ecologists look particularly at the understory of a forest, at the young trees coming up in the shade of older trees, for one major clue.

A major disturbance or event such as a volcanic eruption or landslide can leave completely bare rock or soil. The first organisms to set up shop on the bare surface are probably lichens and mosses, initiating primary succession. They help break up the rock and also trap blowing soil, building up a seed bed that can be used by grasses or flowers or tree seeds blowing around. Eventually, what started as bare rock supports soil and a full-blown plant community.

In the traditional explanation of succession, plants living in the soil change conditions as they grow there. They live, die, and decompose, giving organic matter and plant chemicals to the soil, and eventually they cast enough shade to inhibit or encourage other plants. Over time, the

First steps in plant succession and soil formation. Moss and lichen help break down rock so larger plants can become established.

original plants make so much shade or create such different conditions that their own seeds cannot germinate and grow in the same place. But more shade-tolerant plants are quite able to grow under the canopy of the sun-tolerant pioneers that paved the way. As the older plants die, shade-tolerant species replace them. Their seedlings are generally able to grow in the shade of their parents, so they replace themselves to form a stable community that does not progressively change—a climax forest.

An older community of climax species doesn't grow as fast as the early community. Old forest communities rarely remain intact for long; fire, logging, wind storms, insect infestations, landslides, disease, and other disturbances make openings in some or all of the old community. Then pioneer plants start a new sequence of forest communities, which may or may not be the same as the earlier succession. Resetting the successional clock to earlier stages but not to the bare rock stage is called secondary succession.

You can explain the exact mechanisms and processes of succession in other ways. Regardless of the theory, distinct changes in vegetation, and consequent changes in animals that inhabit the vegetation, happen all the time. They are integrally responsible for the patchwork mosaic of vegetation and wildlife communities that characterize our ecosystem.

Weeds

Many of the pretty flowers you see along the roads in spring, summer, and fall are considered to be noxious weeds. Spotted knapweed, Russian knapweed, Canada thistle, and musk thistle—all members of the same family as dandelions, daisies, and sagebrush—and common mullein are examples of weeds that provide colorful displays but are of concern to humans. Some weeds, or exotics, originated outside the ecosystem or even outside the continent. They were introduced deliberately or accidentally into areas where a lack of natural enemies and other factors help them to outcompete and crowd out native plants. Other weeds may be native but are not considered good food for domestic grazing animals or otherwise conflict with human goals in a particular area. Weeds are of particular concern in national parks, where the maintenance of native plant species is a goal.

The slender trees on the left are subalpine fir; the fuller, more convex in the center is a spruce; lodgepole pine is at the right with tufts of long needles.

WILDLIFE

One of the major attractions of the Yellowstone region is the abundance of wildlife, frequently visible along the roadsides. This ecosystem is intact enough that many animals still have appropriate habitat at the moment, even though the space in many cases may be cramped or broken up.

One of the unique features of the animal life is that, with the exception of the wolf, every major vertebrate wildlife species thought to have been present in historic times still lives here. Many of these are rare, threatened, or endangered, or of special concern to biologists for one reason or another. These will need careful watching for any changes in or threats to their populations if the system is to remain as relatively intact as it is.

Most visitors expect to see elk, bison, and moose; bears have also been a great drawing card, though they are now more difficult to see. Here you will find the largest herds of elk in North America, the largest free-roaming herd of bison in the lower 48 states, and one of two significant populations of grizzly bears in the lower 48 states.

But numerous other, perhaps less dramatic, species of wildlife play various roles in the ecosystem. Some are primary consumers or herbivores, grazing and browsing on the vegetation. Others are secondary or sometimes third-level consumers, feeding on the herbivores and other animals. A few, like the bears, are omnivores and eat just about anything.

We'll consider briefly the status and population characteristics of some of the mammals, birds, and fish in this section, and provide more details on various wildlife species throughout the roadside routes.

When to Observe Wildlife

Seeing wild animals depends on the time of year, time of day, and on sheer luck. Summer, the height of the tourist season, is actually one of the worst times for observing great numbers of wildlife, because many head for the unpopulated backcountry. Early morning, early evening, early spring, late autumn, and winter are the best times to see relatively large numbers of deer, moose, elk, bison, mountain sheep, and waterfowl. Bears come out of their dens in March and April, and return to them in late October and November.

So, What Will We See?

Seven species of ungulates or hoofed mammals, two species of bears, three of wild cats, coyotes, wolverine, pine marten, and about 70 smaller mammals live in the region. More than 300 species of birds have been seen here, along with 128 species of butterflies, a couple of dozen reptiles and amphibians, about 22 fishes, and uncounted invertebrates and microorganisms. Few of these smaller animals are ever seen from roadsides, and many are rare.

The numbers of each species can only be estimated. It's impossible to count many animals since they move, hide, die, and otherwise elude researchers. Populations fluctuate from year to year depending on the harshness of the winter—the major population regulator—and on available food supply.

Grazing and Browsing Herbivores

Four of the native hoofed animals are members of the deer family: white-tailed deer, mule deer, Rocky Mountain elk, and Shira's moose. They are ruminants, with the typical four-chambered stomach and habit of cud chewing. Rocky Mountain sheep and bison are bovines, members of the cow family; they have horns, not antlers like the deer. Horns are worn by both sexes and are permanent; antlers are sported by males only and are shed and regrown each year. The pronghorn antelope, the other native ungulate, is in its own family. Mountain goats, also bovines, also live in the region, but are not native to the area; they were introduced, as were domesticated cattle and sheep.

Bull elk

Elk (*Cervus elaphus nelsoni*)

The number of elk in the region is currently estimated at around 63,000. Some 40 percent of these live inside Yellowstone Park at least part of the time. The rest are scattered throughout the ecosystem, with about 8,000 spending the winter at the National Elk Refuge in Jackson Hole, Wyoming.

Elk live in herds or populations, and the herds don't mix with each other very much. Bulls have a majestic set of antlers that they shed in early winter and grow back each spring; it's rather impressive to watch them maneuver the huge racks through a dog-hair stand of pines. Bull elk gather a harem of females and breed in the autumn. The sound of a bull elk bugling his high-pitched mating call is a sure sign of fall. Calves are born in late May or early June.

Elk eat grasses and sedges, forbs or wildflowers, willows and some other shrubs, and juniper; other conifers like pine may also be eaten when the alternative is starvation. Young aspens are a favorite food, and part of the decline in aspens may be due to elk appetites.

Elk out-compete most other grazing animals, especially mountain sheep, because of their broad eating habits and ability to use a variety of habitats. Elk can also be a problem for ranchers because they graze the same fields as do cattle and sheep, and browse on young trees and shrubs. But these 700-pound herbivores are also prized game animals that provide many western families with meat for most of the year.

Elk readily cross road and boundary signs. The area that encompasses their seasonal wanderings is one way to delineate the whole ecosystem. Before this area was settled, elk streamed out of the high plateaus and mountains in the fall to winter in the valleys now occupied by ranches and towns; many of their former winter grounds and migration paths have been altered by settlement and roads. They now winter upon national forest lands and areas purchased to serve as winter elk ranges that lie outside of the parks. They also use private land, which has sometimes caused heated discussion among area residents, ranchers, park officials, and state fish and game officials on how best to manage elk winter needs.

Mule deer, left, and white-tailed deer.

White-tailed *(Odocoileus virginianus)*
and mule *(O. heminonus)* **deer**

Most white-tailed deer live along the river valleys in the lower elevations. They abound in some places but are absent from others, and are rare in Yellowstone Park. The region may contain a total of 2,000. Whitetails are browsers that feed mostly on young twigs and shrubs; they prefer heavy brush to open grasslands or higher forests. Often the first hint you may have of a whitetail is the flash of its tail, raised as the deer runs away.

You are much more likely to see mule deer. They are widely distributed, and may be more abundant now than in former times. Habitat changes like forest clearing for logging and agriculture can benefit them. As many as 120,000 might be living in the ecosystem. Mule deer live near forest boundaries with grass and sagebrush, and are not as shy as white-tailed deer, waving their huge ears as they stare at you before bounding away. It is a mistake to call them black-tailed deer; the true black-tailed deer is a distinct though closely related West Coast subspecies.

Both white-tailed and mule deer mate in November, and fawns are born in late spring, up to June. Their only sound usually is the male's gutteral grunts in the autumn mating season, but if you surprise them they will snort. Deer are considerably smaller than elk, with males reaching 200 to 240 pounds, and the females closer to 140 to 175 pounds; mule deer are a bit larger than whitetails. Both species are game animals throughout their ranges, except within national park borders.

Pronghorn antelope

Pronghorn Antelope
(*Antelocapra americana*)

Pronghorn antelope are small, rather delicate ungulates that rank among North America's swiftest land mammals, capable of speeds up to 60 mph in short bursts and a sustained pace of half that. Speed is their main defense mechanism on the open plains, their prime habitat. Pronghorns are not true antelope, but a unique North American species. Pronghorns of both sexes have horns, permanent bony structures with outer coverings that they shed and regrow annually.

Pronghorn young, usually twins, are born in May and June. The grayish-brown kids are left hidden in the grass for a few days, protected mostly by their lack of a distinct odor. The mother often separates the two kids just in case a predator should stumble across one or the other; she may wander away from them a short distance, probably to distract predators.

Like deer, pronghorns are fussy about what they eat. Their small stomachs require them to choose foods with high nutritional value. They mostly browse, though they will also eat grasses and weeds. Pronghorns are fond of sagebrush, the shrub with the volatile oils that many other animals find unpalatable.

Shira's Moose (*Alces alces shirasi*)

These huge, dark beasts are almost always seen near wet spots — streams, soggy meadows, bogs — where willow, their favorite food, grows. The moose is the largest member of the deer family, with males reaching around 750 pounds; the Shira's moose is the smallest subspecies, and darker in color than many others. About 2,000 to 4,000 moose live in the ecosystem. Watch for them in early morning or late evening among the willows.

Moose look somewhat passive and docile, but during the autumn rut season males can get ornery and dangerous; and females will defend their young, charging people who appear threatening. Some people who know both say they would rather meet a bear than a bull moose in rut; indeed, there are more encounters between moose and people than there are between bears and people. Some of us would rather not come too close to

Bull moose

either one. Moose mate in the fall, when both males and females make a deep, grunting call. Calves are born in May-June. Grizzly bears occasionally eat the young calves; but, without the wolf, the adult moose in this region has no major predator, except man.

Bison (*Bison bison*)

The plains bison was originally native to this area, but by about 1900 was nearly extinct. In 1907 bison were brought in from several other bison ranges and interbred with the remaining wild Yellowstone herd. The present bison populations are all descendants of these. Some 3,000 to 4,000 bison now live in five herds within the ecosystem: Lamar Valley, Pelican Valley, Bechler River area, the Mary Mountain herd near the Firehole-Yellowstone rivers in Yellowstone Park, and Teton National Park.

Bison are most visible along the Lamar Valley Road in the winter, and in the warm thermal areas along the Firehole, Gibbon, and Yellowstone

20

rivers, feeding mainly on the grasses and sedges. They mate in late summer, and their reddish calves are born in May. Soon after the young are born, many of the cows and calves head for back country, although cow and calf herds are common along the Hayden Valley road in summer. Occasional lone bulls can be seen during summer along the roads. Bison may look appealing, but they are strong, wild animals that can charge quickly and have injured or killed a number of people.

Bison have caused heated controversy in the region in recent years because they can carry

Bison

brucellosis, a bacterial infection that causes abortions in cattle and undulant fever in humans. Bison regularly migrate out of park boundaries into neighboring cattle ranches and public lands where cattle are grazed, causing great concern to the ranchers who have eliminated brucellosis from their herds at great expense and difficulty.

Bighorn Sheep
(*Ovis canadensis*)

Bighorn sheep, or Rocky Mountain sheep, are rarely seen except in winter. They spend most of the year in high alpine meadows feeding on the grass, sedges, and wildflowers. Most of the sheep are in Wyoming, in the Absaroka Mountains; their numbers are estimated to be about 6,000, typically in small herds of 15 to 60. The magnificent coiled horns can weigh 8 to 12 percent of a ram's total 300-pound weight. Bighorns mate in late autumn, and lambs are born around the first of June.

Bighorn sheep

Bighorn sheep have health problems, among them lungworm; which makes them susceptible to pneumonia, especially during years when dry summers or harsh winters make food scarce. Sheep also have bouts with mange, and pinkeye, a bacterial infection that causes blindness — not a wholesome condition for a cliff-dwelling animal. Bighorn sheep need rocky outcrops and small cliffs with grassy slopes; elk can also use this habitat and outcompete the sheep for food.

Mountain goat

Mountain goat
(*Oreamnos americanus*)

Mountain goats are the rarest of the large grazing animals in the ecosystem. They were introduced in the Beartooth Mountains in 1942, later in the Madison Range in Montana and the Snake River drainage in Idaho. Counting these animals usually involves flying over their range. The Beartooth population has been as high as around 300 animals. Goats have rarely been spotted in Yellowstone Park, although one was seen in 1989. The possibility that they might be extending their range poses a problem for the national parks, which discourage the introduction of exotic species into the fauna.

Mountain goats live in habitat even more harsh than bighorn sheep, preferring higher, rockier, steeper slopes. They usually winter on the high windswept, south-facing ridges, where wind blows the snow off the grasses, although some come lower to more protected areas. Avalanches and accidents are major causes of death.

Well, Not All Herbivores are Hoofed

The large grazing and browsing mammals are most conspicuous from a roadside vantage point, but other animals also eat plants.

Rodents. Nearly half of all the mammals in the ecosystem are rodents. Some 40 species occupy a wide variety of niches from underwater to underground, from treetops to mountaintops. Most of these little gnawing animals are herbivores, feasting on grasses, seeds, buds, bark, branches, and flowers, and having enormous influence on the vegetation and thus the wildlife habitats of the ecosystem. Rodents play many varied roles in the ecology of the region: from the 40-pound beaver, whose habits can modify streams and create wetlands, to the industrious pocket gopher, whose

Ground squirrel

underground burrowing can move several tons of soil in a year, to the voles and mice that provide the main source of food for most of the predators. There are nine members of the squirrel family in this group, including the yellow-bellied marmot, two ground squirrels, the prairie dog, three chipmunks, the red squirrel, and the flying squirrel. Others include deer mice, the bushytail woodrat, seven voles, and the muskrat, along with the western jumping mouse.

Other vegetarians. In addition to rodents, other small herbivorous mammals include a couple of species of cottontail rabbits, the snowshoe hare, and the tiny rock-dwelling pika. Some birds also graze. Watch for gaggles of Canada geese or small flocks of sandhill cranes plucking up grass and other vegetation in fields and wet meadows. And never underestimate the power of the puny: hungry grasshoppers and other insects can mow down vegetation as thoroughly as a herd of elk.

Omnivores

Two species of bear range the region, the black bear (*Ursus americanus*) and the grizzly (*Ursus arctos horribilis*). The familiar raccoon (*Procyon lotor*) is a smaller bear relative, uncommon here.

The black bear lives in many parts of North America. It ranges in color from black to brown to cinnamon. Years ago, black bears lined the roads of Yellowstone Park begging for food, creating the famous bear jams. During the late 1960s, policies were changed to allow bears to feed only on natural food, not human junk food. Strictly enforced regulations and garbage control have succeeded to the point where bears are now rarely seen along roadsides. Biologists suspect this situation may change if bear populations start to reach the carrying capacity of the park, which may cause the bears to move into marginal habitats, including roads and developed areas.

Black bears now wander through forests and adjacent meadows, munching on green grass and herbs, berries, ants, and carrion. Carcasses of animals that died during the winter are very important in the nutrition of both black and grizzly bears. About 5,000 to 6,000 black bears may now live in the region, perhaps some 500 to 600 of them within Yellowstone Park.

Black bear

Black bears living in Yellowstone Park grow slower and the populations have fewer females and cubs than those at lower elevations outside the park. Lower areas have milder temperatures, longer growing seasons, and lush vegetation, so they support larger bear populations. The high and cold Yellowstone Plateau grows less food, so bears mature and reproduce slowly. Female bears must reach about 16 to 20 percent body fat composition to reproduce.

Black bears mate in June or July, although implantation of the fertilized egg doesn't occur until November. When cubs are born in early February, they are very small and dependent. Young bears stay with, and learn from, their mothers for their entire first and second years of life, so cubs are born only every other year. If food conditions are bad, the mother may skip an extra year before giving birth again.

The grizzly bear, also called the brown bear, is the same species found in Alaska and Canada, although the Yellowstone population is now isolated from all others. Some 1,000 to 1,200 grizzlies altogether may live in the lower 48 states, most of them in the Northern Continental Divide and the Yellowstone ecosystems. Lewis and Clark encountered the grizzly bear all along the Missouri River in Montana in 1803 to 1805, but its range is now restricted to more isolated high country. Grizzly numbers were reduced to about 200 in the Greater Yellowstone ecosystem, though they are probably now increasing.

The Interagency Grizzly Bear Study Team, a group of scientists and managers from various federal and state management agencies, was started in 1974 to monitor and conduct research on the grizzly, and to coordinate its management. The grizzly is listed as a threatened species in the lower 48

Grizzly bear

states, although it is possible to hunt them in parts of northern Montana during a tightly controlled season.

Grizzly bears are larger, more aggressive, and more unpredictable than black bears. Many of the stringent rules about hiking, food storage, and camping are intended to minimize bear encounters. Before 1972, it was considered great sport to dump garbage at accessible sites near lodges and restaurants both inside and outside Yellowstone Park, and watch grizzlies feed. This policy made the bears familiar with people and their food supplies, and led to the deaths of many bears and some people.

The policy that allowed such bear feeding was changed in 1972, creating controversy, and for a while contributing to confrontations as bears continued to seek food among the people it had come to rely on. Today grizzly bears feed naturally on grasses and herbs, yampa and biscuitroot roots, pine seeds, berries, and other vegetation for 90 percent of their diet. In spring bears feed heavily on carcasses, elk calves, leftover pine nuts, and spawning cutthroat trout for a high protein boost after their long winter's nap. They also sometimes prey upon adult elk, moose, cattle, and domestic sheep.

The number of breeding female grizzly bears is considered a key to the success of the population. Grizzly bear sows don't reproduce until they're about five years old, and then, like black bears, have cubs only every other year. When food supplies are excellent, a sow may have three or four cubs, but one or two is more usual. In drought years, the number of surviving cubs decreases further, probably because male grizzlies eat them.

The biology of small populations of animals with low reproductive rates and limited habitat is the current focus of much bear research. In 1989, about 30 breeding female grizzly bears were observed in the ecosystem, and the number of breeding females and numbers of cubs has been above break-even for most of the 1980s. But the number could quickly decline if confrontations continue, if bear habitat continues to be fragmented and disturbed, if the climate continues to be warmer and drier, and so forth.

Black bears head for their dens in October; and grizzlies, in November as the winter snowpack accumulation gets serious. Grizzlies den at a wide range of elevations, but usually slightly higher than black bears. Males emerge from dens in March, and the females with cubs come out in April.

Black and grizzly bears compete with each other; dominance is based upon body size, which gives an advantage to grizzlies. Black bears can live in populated areas with somewhat less trouble than grizzlies, probably because they're smaller and less aggressive. The activities of grizzly bears are closely monitored around the ecosystem, but relatively little information is collected about the black bear.

Grizzlies tend to be more active when they are young, when it's not too hot or too cold, when it's foggy, during breeding season, when the moon is not full, and when food is scarce and they have to be out and about more often searching for a meal. Perhaps fortunately for all concerned, they seem to be least active when visitors are trying to see them.

Carnivores: Predators par excellence

Ecosystems are rarely complete unless they have predators at the top of the food chain. Predators mostly prey on smaller animals like rodents and rabbits that have incredibly high reproductive rates, but they also help cull sick and weakened larger animals like elk and deer. Other roles played by predators are complex and hotly debated among ecologists: in some cases predators may not limit the numbers of their prey animals, but they may influence where they move and how they behave. Predators certainly help to recycle nutrients and energy by eating dead animals. Predators are tightly woven into the fabric of the ecosystem and are extremely important to its functioning.

Predators come in all shapes and sizes — from the 600-pound grizzly, which eats both plants and animals, to the .08-ounce pygmy shrew, which eats insects; from aquatic animals like trout, to airborne ones like bald eagles, owls, and hawks, even tiny parasitic wasps.

Coyote (*Canis latrans*)

Coyotes are the large predators you are most likely to see. They are active hunters all year long, feeding mainly on grasshoppers, small rodents, mice, voles, rabbits, and ground squirrels. They will attack and eat a deer in the right circumstances, or a sick or dying elk, and they will scavenge just about anything. Coyotes rarely attack large and vigorous animals. Coyotes also prey on domesticated sheep and calves, and are legally controlled outside of the parks.

Coyote

Coyotes easily become familiar with people. It is not too unusual to see them along roads or picnic areas, hunting among the sage and other bushes. An unusual incident during the winter of 1990 illustrated a problem with animals that become too habituated to humans: a cross-country skier was attacked by a coyote near Old Faithful. When people feed coyotes and other wild animals, the animals become somewhat dependent and may get aggressive when hungry. The result of such encounters is almost always what it was at Old Faithful: the animal loses its life.

Coyotes are widespread throughout North America. They probably mate for life, and den as individual family groups, not in packs like wolves; five to ten pups are born per litter in April and May. The very young pups are sometimes preyed on by great horned owls, golden eagles, cougars, and grizzly bears. Coyotes may hunt singly or in small groups, often along established routes. If you're travelling at night, stop the car occasionally and listen for the high pitched yowls and yips of this interesting and controversial predator.

Mountain Lion or Cougar (*Felis concolor*)

The cougar was once one of the most widespread mammals in North and South America, inhabiting forests, swamps, grasslands, deserts, and mountain highlands. Heavy predator control in the early 1900s reduced their numbers drastically. Montana paid bounties on cougar until 1962. It is now a game and trophy animal in all three ecosystem states and is considered abundant and increasing. Exact numbers are not known, but fluctuate with the populations of deer, its major prey. Most sightings of lions in Yellowstone Park are in the northeast corner. This population is now the subject of a research project.

Cougars mostly eat mule deer, but they occasionally feed on elk and livestock. They move widely from summer range to winter range in search of prey. A single lion covers up to 100 square miles in its home range.

Gray Wolf (*Canis lupus*): the missing link

Wolves were present in the Yellowstone Ecosystem until the late 1920s, when the last ones were systematically trapped and shot by ranchers and

Wolf

government predator control agents. According to many animal ecologists, the absence of the wolf is a serious flaw in the functioning of this system; it's the only vertebrate species thought to have been present in the Yellowstone area at the time of European settlement that is missing today. It is a federally listed endangered species in the Northern Rocky Mountains, and reintroduction of the wolf into Yellowstone Park is now under debate.

Wolves prey on the hoofed animals throughout the year. They are efficient predators, which could contribute to population control and herd health of prey species. Wolves might also influence where and when ungulate herds move, and would probably make their prey animals more wary. Wolves also eat rodents, rabbits, beaver, and other smaller animals.

Wolf reintroduction is a deeply divisive issue in the states surrounding the national parks. Some ranchers and sportsmen are concerned that wolves will reduce elk and deer herds, and attack domestic sheep, horses, and cattle. Since wolves don't read boundary signs and need to follow their prey source to stay alive, animals introduced inside Yellowstone Park most likely would wander out of the park, particularly in winter. Possible changes in land-use patterns on public lands around the parks, and compensation to ranchers for wolf kills, are among the ideas that are being explored to make wolf reintroduction acceptable. Should things be worked out, or should a natural recolonization occur, you may someday spot or hear a wolf in Yellowstone.

Raptors: Predators on the Wing

Large predatory birds are known as raptors, and include eagles, hawks, ospreys, falcons, and owls. Two eagles live in the ecosystem, the bald and the golden; three falcons, the peregrine, the prairie, and the merlin; and 27 species of hawks and owls, along with the osprey. The status of many of these birds is unknown, but the peregrine falcon and the bald eagle are federally listed endangered species; the ferruginous hawk and the burrowing, great gray, and boreal owls are of special concern for a variety of reasons.

Raptors share a shaky throne at the top of the food chain with the large mammal predators. They need large habitats to find sufficient food, and suffer from the effects of poisons and pollutants introduced farther down the food chain. Like other predators, raptors have historically been persecuted and destroyed in great numbers.

Bald Eagle (*Haliaeetus leucocephalus*)

The Greater Yellowstone ecosystem boasts one of the largest populations of bald eagles in the continental United States. Some 80 nesting territories have been found, and more than 200 eagles spend the summer along the region's rivers and lakes. Three separate populations of eagles have been identified in the ecosystem: those that nest on the Yellowstone Plateau, those along the Snake River and its tributaries, and those in the headwaters of the Madison and Red Rock rivers and the upper Henry's Fork River in eastern Idaho.

Osprey, top; golden eagle, left; and bald eagle, right.

The bald eagle requires riversides and other wetland areas year round. Almost all nests are within two miles of a body of water, in tall trees with easy access and a good view of the water. Eagles prey on fishes, waterfowl and other birds, and small mammals, and they aren't beneath scavenging on carcasses or even stealing a fish from an osprey. Standing three feet tall, with a seven-to eight-foot wingspan, this enormous bird requires a significant amount of food and a large territory.

The bald eagle is classified as an endangered species in the lower 48 states, and although their populations have increased in recent years, they are still on the critical list. More than 70 percent of the most productive and critical habitat for bald eagles is threatened with development, including subdivisions, logging, energy development, urbanization, impoundments of water for irrigation, and increasing recreational activity.

Burrowing Owl (*Athene cunicularia*)

As tiny as the eagle is huge, the burrowing owl is an example of a raptor whose existence hinges on many complex ecological factors. It lives in open tall-grass and sagebrush prairie habitats, nesting regularly on the western, eastern, and southeastern fringes of the ecosystem. Every few years some burrowing owls are found nesting in the open high plateau regions of Yellowstone Park and the eastern portions of Jackson Hole. This nine-inch tall predator depends on small rodents and insects for food, and it also depends for nest sites on finding holes in the ground that some other animal has made. Skunks, badgers, prairie dogs, and ground squirrels are the usual excavators of the burrows these owls call home. But skunks, badgers, prairie dogs, and ground squirrels are decidedly unpopular among humans because of those very same holes; what's good for a burrowing owl is not so good for a cow or a horse or a person. In prime habitat in summertime, these owls consume tremendous quantities of small voles and deer mice, as well as grasshoppers, carrion and scarab beetles, and Jerusalem crickets.

Fishes

Many fish are predators, too, particularly the stars of Greater Yellowstone waters, the various species of trout. A trout can consume about five percent of its own weight every day in summer, preying on a whole range of smaller organisms from plankton to aquatic insects to smaller fish. Fish are also prey, of course — for grizzly bears, pelicans, eagles, ospreys, and people.

Perhaps even more than other wildlife species, fish are highly influenced by their physical environment. They are affected by water temperature and velocity, oxygen levels and pH, sediment levels, heavy metals and toxic substances, especially during spawning and winter. Certain native fishes — the cutthroat trout, the mountain whitefish, and the Montana grayling in particular — have been affected by the introduction of closely related exotic

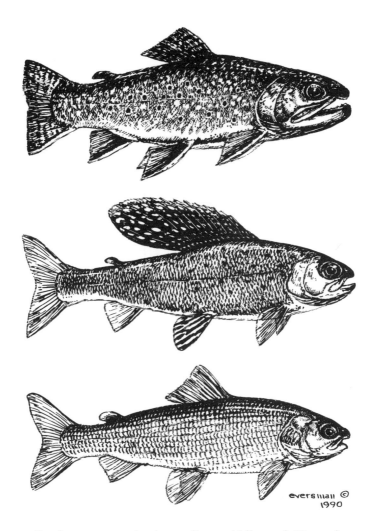

Brook trout, top; Arctic grayling, middle; and Mountain whitefish, bottom.

trout, the brook, rainbow, lake, and brown trout, which hybridize and compete with the native species.

Some of Greater Yellowstone's other fishes include three suckers, two sculpins, the redside shiner, four chubs, two dace, and a carp.

Reptiles and Amphibians

Relatively few reptiles and amphibians live in the ecosystem, presumably because of the cool, dry conditions. Amphibians and reptiles are cold-blooded. At most about 24 species are known or suspected to live in the

FOOD WEB OF THE
GREATER YELLOWSTONE ECOSYSTEM

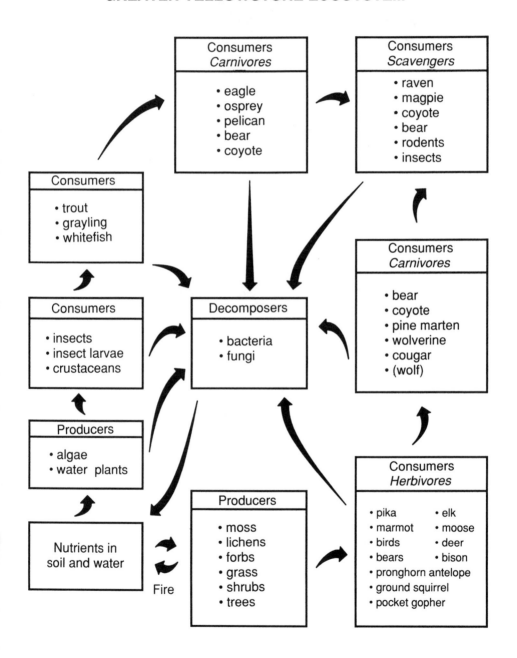

Consumers
Carnivores

- eagle
- osprey
- pelican
- bear
- coyote

Consumers
Scavengers

- raven
- magpie
- coyote
- bear
- rodents
- insects

Consumers

- trout
- grayling
- whitefish

Consumers
Carnivores

- bear
- coyote
- pine marten
- wolverine
- cougar
- (wolf)

Consumers

- insects
- insect larvae
- crustaceans

Decomposers

- bacteria
- fungi

Producers

- algae
- water plants

Nutrients in
soil and water

Fire

Producers

- moss
- lichens
- forbs
- grass
- shrubs
- trees

Consumers
Herbivores

- pika
- marmot
- birds
- bears
- pronghorn antelope
- ground squirrel
- pocket gopher
- elk
- moose
- deer
- bison

region, though about half of these are rare or introduced. Some 12 snake species can occur, but the rubber boa, two garter snakes, the bull snake, the prairie rattler, and the racer are the most familiar. Only one salamander, the tiger salamander, lives here, often in abandoned rodent burrows. The western chorus, spotted, and leopard frogs inhabit locales below 8,000 feet. And four toads can be present: the western and the Great Basin spadefoot, the plains spadefoot toad (at the eastern boundary), and the Rocky Mountain. Two lizards, the short-horned lizard and the sagebrush lizard, prefer thermal areas. Painted turtles can live in the far northern portion of the ecosystem; and snapping and spiny softshell turtles can live in the Beartooth region, at low elevations.

Relatively little is known about any of these species or their ecological role. The short-horned lizard is rare and others might be at the edges of their ranges. Frogs, toads, and salamanders might be declining throughout North America, including this region, perhaps because acid pollution and sedimentation are damaging their eggs and larvae.

Insects and Other Invertebrates

A complete census of invertebrate species doesn't yet exist, but some 12,000 species of insects are thought to live in the ecosystem, including beetles, flies, ants,wasps, bees, butterflies, moths, and mayflies. Other invertebrates include crustaceans such as copepods, freshwater shrimp, and pillbugs; millipedes and centipedes; and scorpions, ticks, pseudoscorpions, mites, and spiders. A few dozen species each of segmented worms and mollusks also live here, along with sponges, flatworms, ribbon worms, roundworms, horsehair worms, rotifers, and other species.

Is this stuff wildlife? Well, they're wild and they're alive, and they form the very foundation of life throughout the ecosystem. Bees, flies, butter-flies, moths, and beetles are the primary pollinators of flowering plants. Invertebrates serve as critical food items in every aquatic and terrestrial food web, and help break down dead plant and animals remains to help in the decomposition process. Certain insects help aerate the soil by burrowing through it, and invertebrate grazers such as grasshoppers can have as much influence on grassland vegetation as elk.

Bark beetles and budworms affect lodgepole, fir, and spruce forests. When the infected trees die and decay, they provide life for: insect predators such as woodpeckers; cavity nesters such as bluebirds; populations of fungi and fungi-eating insects; and deer and elk, which feed on the vegetation that comes up in forest openings after trees die and fall.

Elk feel at home everywhere in the Mammoth Hot Springs area.

Miscellaneous Birds

More than 300 species of birds live within the ecosystem; slightly over half are known or suspected to nest here. Only about a quarter are year-round residents; most use the region either as breeding, molting, or winter grounds, or as a through-way during spring and fall migrations along the Snake River-Missouri River corridor. Migrating birds find critical resting and feeding areas in meadows and marshes. Some, like the semipalmated sandpiper, use specific mud flats from year to year.

Birds live in every kind of habitat. Along rivers and lakes you can see dippers, bald eagles, ospreys, trumpeter swans, pelicans, whooping and sandhill cranes, flycatchers, and more than 30 species of ducks and other waterfowl. Sage thrashers, sage grouse, and vesper sparrows prefer the sagebrush flats and hayfields, while the forests are home to many species including owls, woodpeckers, warblers, chickadees, hawks, grosbeaks, jays, nutcrackers, sparrows, tanagers, and many others. Even the sparse alpine regions support bird life, from the nesting water pipit and rosy finch, to tree swallows, ravens, and golden eagles.

With such diversity, birds play a variety of roles. Some, like eagles and hawks, eat small animals; other, like woodpeckers, eat insects. Some, like trumpeter swans and Clark's nutcrackers, are primarily vegetarians; and many, especially their chicks and eggs, serve as prey themselves. The five species of hummingbirds are important plant pollinators, and fruit and seed eaters like the Bohemian and cedar waxwings and the Clark's nutcracker are vital dispersers of seeds. Turkey vultures, bald eagles, and ravens are important as scavengers, helping to decompose and recycle the remains of dead organisms.

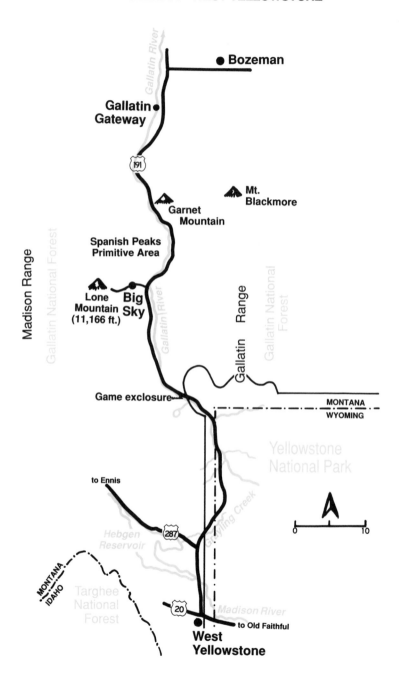

MAP 1
U.S. 191
BOZEMAN—WEST YELLOWSTONE

● Bozeman

Gallatin ●
Gateway

191

Mt.
Blackmore

Garnet
Mountain

Spanish Peaks
Primitive Area

Madison Range

Gallatin National Forest

Lone **Big**
Mountain **Sky**
(11,166 ft.)

Gallatin River

Gallatin Range

Gallatin National Forest

Game exclosure

MONTANA
WYOMING

Yellowstone
National Park

to Ennis

Grayling Creek

287

Hebgen
Reservoir

MONTANA
IDAHO

Targhee
National
Forest

0   10

20

Madison River

to Old Faithful

● **West**
Yellowstone

U.S. 191
Bozeman—West Yellowstone
91 miles/146 km.

Bozeman is at the southeast end of the Gallatin Valley, which stretches about 35 miles from Three Forks to Bozeman. Bozeman was the site of a number of meetings among several early explorers, meetings that led to the formation of the world's first national park, Yellowstone, in 1872. Highway 191 heads west from Bozeman for eight miles to Four Corners, the intersection with Highways 84 and 85; then proceeds south through the scenic Gallatin Canyon. The road climbs from 4,800 feet at Four Corners to 6,667 feet at West Yellowstone. It passes through a steep-sided canyon the Gallatin River eroded between the Gallatin and Madison ranges running north from the Yellowstone Plateau.

Valley of the Flowers

The broad Gallatin Valley was excellent bison hunting grounds for the Crow, Sioux, Blackfeet, and Shoshone Indians. Tall grasses and profuse flowers led them to call this the Valley of the Flowers. Several spring creeks flow through the valley, with excellent but difficult fly fishing, though much of the valley has been drained for agriculture. Still, the rich soil is some of the best in the state, supporting dairy herds as well as wheat and barley fields.

Three Forks and a Buffalo Jump

At Four Corners you might take a side trip 40 miles west on Highway 84 to Three Forks. This will take you to Headwaters State Park, where Lewis and Clark named the three forks of the Missouri River: the Madison, Jefferson, and Gallatin rivers. Guided by the Indian woman Sacajawea, they followed the Jefferson to the Continental Divide and the forks of the Columbia River, then on to the Pacific Ocean. At Logan, three miles west of Three Forks, a turnoff leads to a buffalo jump used by Indian tribes before they acquired horses. The jump was used to trick bison over the cliff for butchering. An interpretive display at the site describes this dangerous but effective early hunting technique.

From Three Forks you can take Highway 287 south to Ennis, or return to Bozeman's Four Corners and continue with on.

A Changing Landscape

South of Four Corners, you will pass through what is now predominantly agricultural land. Bozeman Hot Springs, less than a mile south of Four Corners, is typical of hot springs common in mountainous areas. A warm pool here uses the heated, mineral-rich water.

To the west, the Gallatin River flows beside the strand of water-loving cottonwood trees threading across the otherwise open valley. The Gallatin Range is on the east and the Madison Range picks up a little farther south on the west.

Cottonwoods and willows line river banks, marking water courses through drier valley grasslands. This is good habitat for whitetail deer, some moose and beaver, and many voles and birds.

The mouth of the Gallatin Canyon illustrates how grassland in valleys gives way to forests as elevation and precipitation increase.

The open lower portions of the Gallatin Range are important winter range for the Gallatin Face elk herd. The grassy slopes provide winter forage, and the nearby forest provides essential shelter from weather and predators.

Straight ahead you see the narrow mouth of Gallatin Canyon. The high mountains that dominate the skyline in the Madison Range are the Spanish Peaks.

At the mouth of Gallatin Canyon, about 12 miles south of Four Corners, you see a sudden change in the landscape with increasing elevation and precipitation: from the native grassland of Idaho fescue and bluebunch wheatgrass, to Rocky Mountain juniper and limber pine, finally to Douglas fir. Douglas fir dominates the densest forests on the hillsides from the mouth of the canyon to above the Big Sky recreational development 30 miles south. Spruce is common along the Gallatin River and on the banks of the many tributary creeks. Human land use changes from ranching and agriculture in the valley to mostly forestry, fishing, and recreation farther into the canyon.

The trees at the lowest elevations are juniper and limber pine. Douglas firs form dense stands on slopes above these. Chokecherries in late summer provide food for birds.

To Spray or Not to Spray. . .

The Douglas fir and spruce here were hit very hard by the western budworm, and you can see skeletons of dead trees standing among the survivors. The major budworm infestation during the late 1970s and early 1980s provoked many demands that the Forest Service "do something": spray the moths and their larvae. But spraying would have killed other insects as well, including those that are food for the trout in the river. There was no spraying and the serious infestation spiraled down on its own. The decision not to spray on a wide scale led to healthier trees that are more resistant to budworms, and to the protection of other organisms.

Canyon Wildlife

The canyon abounds with large mammals: deer, elk, moose, bighorn sheep, grizzly bears, and black bears. Deer tend to live at the lower elevations and along the road, making it prudent to drive alertly at dusk. Elk and moose can best be seen at the southern end of the canyon, closer to the stretch of road that goes into the northwest corner of Yellowstone Park, about 47 miles south of Four Corners.

Black bears live throughout this area, and grizzlies seem to be expanding their range in the Madisons. Bighorn sheep are sometimes visible from the road in winter, when they come to a privately maintained salt lick near Big

Sky; watch for sheep on the western rocky slopes beginning several miles north of Big Sky. In the summer, sheep prefer the privacy of the back country.

The most common mammal in the Gallatin River is the human, fly-fishing for the blue-ribbon river's brown and rainbow trout.

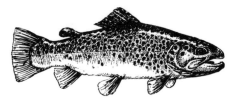

Rainbow trout

Brown trout

This Land is Your Land, That Land is My Land. . .

All along this route and others, you will notice small brown signs announcing "Forest Access" or "Fishing Access." These signs help illustrate the pattern of land ownership: federal lands interspersed with private lands. Along this route, the bulk of the mountain ranges are part of the U.S. Forest Service national forest system. Parts of the Madison Range fall within the Beaverhead National Forest, other parts of the Madison and most of the Gallatin Range are in the jurisdiction of the Gallatin National Forest, and the Lee Metcalf Wilderness Area is scattered in four separated units throughout the Madison Range. Much of the forest is a checkerboard of public and private ownership. Alternating blocks of land belong to the U.S. Forest Service and to private timber companies and other landowners, a legacy of frontier days when the government granted blocks of land to the railroads to encourage settlement. Land in the lower elevations, along the road, and along the river is mostly privately owned, and access to the public lands must be granted by private landowners.

Private lands make up only about 10 percent of the ecosystem, depending on where you place the boundaries. But they tend to be in ecologically important spots, such as these riparian and critical low-elevation winter ranges and migration routes. Many conservation issues in the region currently focus on the challenges of public versus private land use. A good example exists just down the road at Big Sky.

Big Sky

The Big Sky Resort is in the Madison Range on the west side of the canyon, about 35 miles south of Four Corners and abutting part of the Lee Metcalf Wilderness. This spot gets heavy snow in winter, and the excellent downhill and cross-country skiing was one of the prime reasons for

Lone Mountain at Big Sky, a major recreational and residential development.

developing the resort; the cold temperatures make for very light, powdery snow with a minimum of the ice and slush encountered in warmer and wetter climates.

The development has generated controversy since its inception in the early 1980s, in part because of the danger that such a large development might damage watersheds, air quality, wildlife habitat, and vegetation. As in any steep mountainous area, avalanches and landslides pose a potential hazard to humans and their property.

Between Two Ranges

Although you see little difference in the vegetation and animal life between the two ranges, they differ geologically. The Gallatin Range on the east has had more volcanic activity, with some spectacular lava flows and old volcanoes within Yellowstone Park. The Madison Range is mostly faulted and folded sedimentary rock.

The valley broadens as you leave Big Sky. This was a major lettuce producing area in the early 1900s, and before that the valley produced oats and hay for Yellowstone National Park horses. Now the major business is tourism, both from the Big Sky resort and from numerous guest ranches and outfitters. The canyon narrows again in about 10 miles, where the rock is more resistant.

The Porcupine Game Range near Big Sky is a state-owned parcel of land managed primarily as elk habitat.

Moose on the Loose!

Watch for the pull-off on the west side of the road about 51 miles south of Four Corners, just north of the Yellowstone Park boundary, where the Snowflake Springs game exclosure is visible near the river. The exclosure prevents elk and moose from grazing and browsing inside the fence. It was set up in 1948 to monitor the effects of their munching. Do you notice a difference in the vegetation inside and outside the exclosure?

Open grasslands and bare areas in the valley reveal clay soils, while conifers are growing in patches of sandy soil. Along the river, rich moist areas support extensive growth of willows, one of the favorite foods of the moose. Watch all along this stretch on both sides of the road for several miles for a glimpse of these large, dark animals; they can be seen year-round, most easily in early morning or early evening.

This mix of grassland and forest also provides an ideal area for elk from Yellowstone Park, the Firehole-Madison-Gibbon herd, and the resident Gallatin herd to congregate during the fall rut. From this staging area, some elk migrate to wintering grounds in the Madison Range; many others winter here along the river floodplain.

The Head of the River

About 52 miles south of Four Corners and 28 miles north of West Yellowstone, you cross the northwest corner of Yellowstone National Park. This is the headwaters of the Gallatin River, fed by streams beginning high in the mountains to the southeast, and by Snowflake Springs on the west side. The Gallatin River was named after Albert Gallatin, secretary of the treasury when Lewis and Clark explored the Missouri and Columbia rivers.

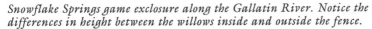

Snowflake Springs game exclosure along the Gallatin River. Notice the differences in height between the willows inside and outside the fence.

Specimen Creek

Specimen Creek, four miles inside the park boundary, is the head for a trail that leads to a small segment of petrified forest similar to that of Specimen Ridge in the Lamar Valley in Yellowstone Park (map 8: page 92). This is national park land, even if you have not gone through a formal entrance: no collecting.

The Fan and the North Fork fires combined forces in 1988 along this stretch. The Fan fire, about 16,000 acres, was apparently started by lightning inside the park. The enormous North Fork fire, over 400,000 acres, was started by humans in the adjacent national forest and was fought with a certain amount of futility as soon as it was discovered. The North Fork fire was one of the most publicized ones, shown in the videos and books as the one leaping across Old Faithful. Most of the burned forest was lodgepole pine, the dominant tree in the park and in this part of the Gallatin Canyon.

Approaching the Yellowstone Plateau

About 76 miles south of Four Corners and 15 miles north of West Yellowstone, you go up and over the ridge that separates the Gallatin from the Madison river drainages, and follow Grayling Creek toward West Yellowstone. The high point of the road, about 12 miles north of West Yellowstone, offers a panoramic view of the flat Yellowstone Plateau to the east and the Madison River and Hebgen Lake on the west.

The Fan fire in 1988 left many skeletons of lodgepoles against April snow. Lodgepole pine, at the right, can get large and bushy when it is growing alone without close competition.

Hebgen and Quake lakes

U.S. 287 veers west from U.S. 191 about eight miles north of West Yellowstone, taking you past Hebgen Lake, actually a reservoir, and Earthquake Lake, more popularly known as 'Quake Lake, to the Madison River Valley and Ennis, Montana (map 18: page 164). U.S. 191 continues south to West Yellowstone.

Grizzly Country

The road into West Yellowstone goes past several turnouts, one of which is the Bakers Hole Campground, three miles north of town. You are in good grizzly bear country now, dangerous for tent camping.

Grizzlies cover huge amounts of territory foraging for food and finding shelter and safety for themselves and their cubs, some 70 to 100 square miles in a single season. A heavily used route runs from the mountains near Hebgen, east into the park and through this campground.

Roads, campgrounds, businesses, and homes in the middle of this important grizzly path have contributed in the past to confrontations between grizzlies and people, which almost always result in the death of the bears. Recent efforts, including restrictions on camping with hard-sided vehicles only and installation of bear-proof trash containers in the town of West Yellowstone, have helped to reduce these events, though a disturbing number of grizzlies still are lost nearly every year.

Winter in West Yellowstone

No matter where you live, you probably have heard on your local weather report that "the heaviest snowfall and coldest temperature in the country today was at West Yellowstone, Montana. . . ." This area averages over 120 inches of snow per year, making it a lively place for snowmobilers and the Olympic Nordic ski teams.

Increasing winter activity throughout the Yellowstone region is provoking discussion and controversy as park and forest managers and people with recreational interests struggle with issues of winter solitude and wildlife survival. Winter can be the most critical period in the life cycle of wild animals that don't migrate to warmer areas, and even slight disturbances can cause them to expend energy they need to get through these extremely heavy snows and long cold periods. Elk have been known to move away even from a quiet cross-country skier, whose upright posture may look too much like a grizzly bear for any sensible prey animal to take a chance on.

At West Yellowstone, you may proceed west on Highway 20 toward Idaho Falls, Idaho (map 19: page 170), or east into Yellowstone National Park (map 3: page 54).

MAP 2
U.S. 89
LIVINGSTON—MAMMOTH HOT SPRINGS

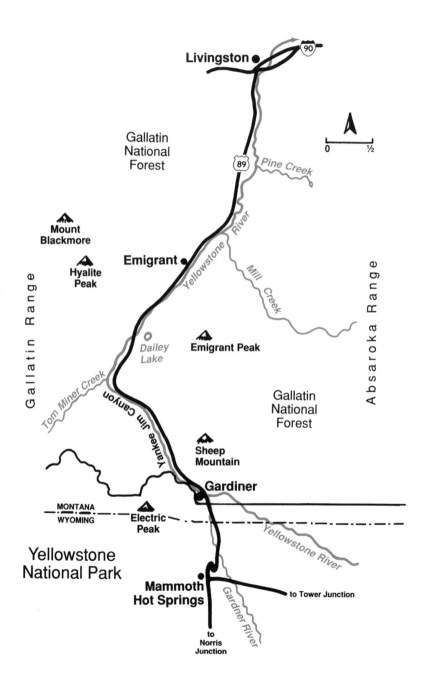

U.S. 89
Livingston—Mammoth
60 miles/96 km.

The Windy City (Not Chicago!)

East and west of Livingston along Interstate 90, watch for windmills, evidence of the incessant winds characteristic of this area. Built to harvest the energy of the tremendous winds here, most have not succeeded in producing dependable amounts of power, in part because these winds are gusty, unpredictable, and frequently too strong for the machines to handle; political decisions about storing and selling the energy also complicate the picture.

The winds here are due primarily to the proximity of the higher Yellowstone Plateau. The lower elevations in the valleys and plains to the east heat up more during the day than do the higher elevations of the plateau. The warm air in the valleys and plains rises, and the cooler air rushes down to replace it. This same phenomenon is generally responsible for strong winds along the entire eastern front of the Rocky Mountains.

Paradise Valley

As you head south on U.S. 89, it will be apparent that the valley of the Yellowstone River, Paradise Valley, is today primarily agricultural land, with irrigated hay and grain fields and much cattle grazing. The Yellowstone Valley in its non-agricultural condition is basically grassland and sagebrush. These native vegetation types are visible around the perimeters of cattle fences and in various undeveloped spots along the road.

The Yellowstone River is the longest undammed river in the United States and one of the few in North America that flows northward. It begins high in the wilderness areas of the Shoshone National Forest southeast of Yellowstone Park, empties into Yellowstone Lake, then flows out of the lake and north through this valley. Eventually, the Yellowstone River joins the Missouri River at the border between North Dakota and Montana.

Several species of fish inhabit this world-class fishing stream, including whitefish, mottled sculpins, two suckers, four species of trout, and the long-

47

Grass grows on the south and west exposures; trees on the north and east slopes of Paradise Valley.

nose dace. Elk, deer, and moose find extensive summer habitat in the adjacent Absaroka Mountains on the east side and the Gallatin Range on the west side. In winter, several herds use the low open areas of Paradise Valley for critical winter range.

The Absaroka and Beartooth ranges on the east side of the river stretch 170 miles from Livingston, along the spectacular alpine area of the Beartooth Plateau, to Dubois, Wyoming. Part of the range has been designated the Absaroka-Beartooth Wilderness, the largest single expanse of undisturbed land above 10,000 feet in the United States.

The River's Edge: Riparian Ribbons

Cottonwood trees line the banks of the river, and willows grow in the wetter low areas, making excellent habitat for whitetail and mule deer. Whitetails tend to stick most closely to the cottonwood, while the mule deer usually prefer the sagebrush. This division of the food and resources, or resource partitioning, helps enable two such similar animals to occupy the same general habitat. White-tailed and mule deer crossing in early morning and evening make it important to drive carefully.

Shrubs also grow along the route, following the little stream cuts that come down from the higher mountain peaks. Look for these ribbons of green, which indicate the presence of water at least sometimes during the

Sand bar in the Yellowstone River with typical island plant succession: willows grow first; cottonwoods follow.

year; many of these streams have water in them only when the snow is melting during early spring.

Golden and bald eagles frequent the big old cottonwoods along the river; some bald eagle nests are visible in winter when leaves are off the trees. Kestrels, sparrow hawks, seem to prefer fenceposts and overhead wires, where they sit in watch for the small rodents that are their primary prey. Canada geese nest along the river and are often visible in the meadows where they graze on the grasses.

Pine Creek

About ten miles south of Livingston, Pine Creek enters the Yellowstone River. The road east across the Yellowstone takes you to the U.S. Forest Service Pine Creek Campground on the west slopes of the Absarokas. This is a cold-air drainage spot. Cold moist air flows down like cold water from the mountain, where Douglas firs, the largest trees in this area, grow. The black lichen draped on the branches is *Bryoria,* or old man's beard. A fairly rugged trail with good views of Paradise Valley leads from here to Pine Lake, a lovely mountain lake.

Microclimates on the Slopes

At many locations along this route you will notice a pattern common throughout this part of the West: more trees on east and north sides of ridges than on west and south sides. South and west sides receive more hot sun than east and north sides do; this creates warmer, drier air on south and west sides, which dries the soil. Grasses and sagebrush tolerate dry conditions, so they predominate on south and west sides of a slope, while the thirsty trees grow on north and east sides.

From Floodplain to Forest: Going Up

Forests on the mountain sides are dominated by Douglas fir, with juniper and sagebrush growing slightly below. You will encounter Douglas fir by the road around Yankee Jim Canyon, about 46 miles south of Livingston, where the elevation has risen to some 6,000 feet, appropriate for Douglas fir. The Yankee Jim Canyon Picnic Area, at the base of a talus slope, provides a chance to get acquainted with Douglas fir and lichen-covered boulders. A small pull-off on the west looks out at the Yellowstone River, big sagebrush, and cottonwood trees.

The Trees are Coming! The Trees are Coming!

Just north of Corwin Springs, about 54 miles south of Livingston, junipers and Douglas fir are invading grasslands at the base of the mountains. A similar invasion is occurring in other areas of the West, for unknown reasons. One theory is that perhaps fires once kept the grassy areas open, and fire suppression in recent years may have allowed trees to begin growing. Another idea is that it may take hundreds or thousands of years for soil fungi necessary for tree growth to build up and allow the trees to move in. Yet another possibility is that at least in some areas sheep grazing in the 1800s perhaps have disturbed soil enough to allow trees to grow where they previously had not. Researchers are now exploring this curious phenomenon, sorting out the combination of factors.

Neighbors

Near Corwin Springs, on the west side of the road, a major development has been under way for several years. The Church Universal and Triumphant (CUT) purchased the Royal Teton Ranch in the early 1980s and moved its headquarters here. Church members have been moving in great numbers into the valley and are working the land — grazing, farming, and developing it for residences, underground shelters, and industry, including the tapping of geothermal resources — all with minimal environmental restrictions.

The borders of CUT property touch those of both a national park and a national forest. The ranch occupies what was once prime grizzly bear habitat, and encompasses critical winter range for migrating elk and bison, as well as some bighorn sheep and pronghorn antelope. A major spawning stream for the Yellowstone cutthroat trout runs through the property as well. This development thus has the potential to affect many key elements of the ecosystem, and has created great local controversy.

The activities of human neighbors of protected areas like Yellowstone Park can be critical to the long-term success of the park or reserve. Wildlife, water, air, and ecological processes don't follow our political boundaries, and they may depend on much larger areas to continue functioning. A major fuel spill early in 1990 on CUT property heightened concerns that major unmonitored activities in such productive and ecologically sensitive areas might do far-reaching damage.

Gardiner and the Cold Desert

Gardiner, Montana, is at the confluence of the Gardner (spelled without the 'i') and Yellowstone rivers. This is an extremely dry area with fewer than 12 inches of precipitation per year, similar to Tucson, Arizona. But because this is at 45 degree north latitude and 5,310 feet elevation rather than the 32 degree latitude and 2,390 feet elevation of Tucson, it is an example of a cold desert. The vegetation is mostly grass, sagebrush, and even cacti. It provides a warm, dry refuge for many forms of wildlife in winter; pronghorn antelope often congregate here year round. And this is one of only a few areas in the ecosystem where rattlesnakes are common in summer.

The North Entrance to Yellowstone Park is in Gardiner. Beyond the toll booth the road rapidly climbs from 5,314 feet at the entrance, along the Gardner River, to 6,329 feet at Mammoth, the park headquarters.

A Sheepish Situation

At one of the first turnouts inside the park you can look up at Sheep Mountain, an important winter range for bighorn sheep. During the summer, the sheep are elusive, spending most of their time in the remote back country toward the Lamar Valley to the southeast. They start coming down here when snow builds in the higher region, and go back as soon as the snow melts. They may be nearly impossible to see along these roads between early April and early winter, but provide a great treat for winter tourists.

About 325 bighorn sheep live in this area. They range from Cinnabar Mountain near Corwin Springs north of Gardiner, across Sheep Mountain and Mt. Everts near Mammoth Hot Springs, and over to the road in the Lamar Valley.

According to archeological evidence, bighorn sheep have inhabited this area for 8,000 years. Many mining interests worked here from about 1870 to 1910. At that time, commercial hunters also moved in and killed thousands of deer, elk, and bighorn sheep for their hides. The populations of elk and deer rebounded well after hunting ended in the 1890s, but bighorn sheep are still recovering.

Sheep are still scarce perhaps because of competition with other ungulates for a limited food supply. Elk and bighorns use essentially the same food — grass, sagebrush, and other shrubs. Elk seem to compete with sheep for food, especially in severe weather, so sheep populations are relatively low. Lambs are particularly susceptible to competition.

The sheep are also mildly infected with a lungworm (*Protostrongylus*), and in the early 1980s an eye infection caused blindness in many animals. These afflictions probably diminished their vitality.

Why is nothing done to cure sheep eye infections or otherwise improve their situation? Within national parks, managers try to allow all ecological processes to proceed on their own. Disease and competition both act to control wildlife populations everywhere, and so are important elements in maintaining as natural a sheep population as possible.

Where the Deer and the Antelope. . .
and the Elk and the Bison . . . Play

Other wildlife also winter here, where the snow is not as deep as elsewhere in the park. In addition to sheep, it is common to see elk, deer, and coyotes along this stretch in winter, and bison and antelope year-round. Bald eagles frequently perch in trees along the river. Wild animals are not aware of political boundaries and they frequently pay winter visits to Gardiner backyards and historical wintering grounds that are now ranch lands.

People in Gardiner sometimes feed the elk during harsh winters. But bison wandering out of the park are less welcome because they may carry the disease brucellosis, which can be fatal to cattle. A researcher has recently shown that brucellosis can be spread in the lab from bison to cattle, though the passing of the disease in the wild is as yet undocumented. Since Montana ranchers certify their cattle to be brucellosis-free, this is economically important to area ranchers. Elk also carry brucellosis, and the feeding of elk in winter crowds animals together, a situation ripe for the spread of such diseases.

Along the Gardner River

The road between the North Entrance of the park and Mammoth Hot Springs follows the Gardner River. It is a rocky stream that begins at about 9,000 feet in the Gallatin Range southwest of Mammoth, and flows into the Yellowstone River near Gardiner.

Hot springs make Boiling River a popular place to soak in a natural hot tub. When the river is high, during spring runoff in June, the hot pots are closed because the high water obscures the rock division between them and the river, creating a dangerous situation.

The Gardner River has abundant brook, brown, and rainbow trout. All were introduced about 1890 and have mostly replaced the native cutthroat trout and graylings. The trout population is now sustaining itself without further stocking, as are several other native fish that still call the Gardner home, including the long-nose dace, the long-nose sucker, and the

Browsed juniper near Mammoth Hot Springs. As animals graze on hillsides, they wear small terraces, horizontal lines among the grass and sagebrush.

mountain whitefish. The relatively small, cool, fast-flowing Gardner River, with its gravelly bottom and abundant vegetation and insect life, provides excellent habitat for these fishes.

Lollipop Trees

Between the north entrance and Mammoth you probably noticed the unusual shape of many of the junipers — bare trunks instead of branches all the way to the ground. These lollipop trees illustrate the heavy grazing and browsing pressure this area gets during most of the year, especially in winter. Elk are generalists in their dietary preferences; they will munch on almost any plant, including the pungent juniper. Look for lollipop trees especially around the Mammoth Campground.

The campground at Mammoth is used for a longer period than others in the park because of the relatively mild weather. In winter elk wander around the campground, and through the lawns of the park employees.

The visitor center at Mammoth includes museums with historical exhibits recounting the time of the park's first administrators, the U.S. Army, which built the town of Mammoth in the 1880s as its park headquarters. Biological and geological exhibits offer an overview of park natural history features. Inquire here for fishing and hiking regulations.

At Mammoth, proceed east toward Tower Junction (map 7: page 84), or south toward Norris (map 6: page 76).

MAP 3
WEST YELLOWSTONE—MADISON JUNCTION

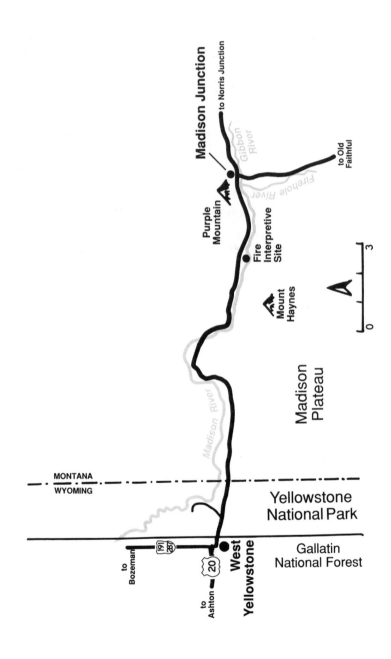

West Yellowstone—Madison Junction
14 miles/23 km.

This route passes through a maturing lodgepole pine forest that has recently experienced insect infestation and fire. You follow the Madison River, a historic world-class trout stream with a complex community of plants and animals, and pass through a steep mountain canyon with rock slides on both sides of the road. You can see bison and elk along the route; it is an important wintering area for large park mammals. Pull-offs are on both sides of the road. Be sure to stop and look closely at the features we can only briefly introduce here.

Lodgepole Pine Forest

The forest near the west entrance to Yellowstone National Park is a lodgepole pine stand characteristic of much of the high central portion of the ecosystem. Notice the dense growth of thin, pole-like trees with relatively bare grassy ground beneath them; these are the lodgepole pines, so-called because their slender trunks made excellent tepee poles for Indians. Some 80 percent of the forest in the Yellowstone Park is lodgepole pine.

Lodgepoles are tall and pole-like only when they grow in dense stands like these, where crowding and darkness shade the lower branches. Lodgepoles that grow alone in good light have a full complement of branches to the ground. Their species name, *contorta*, comes from the West Coast where mountain and oceanside stands grow contorted and twisted.

One shrub that grows occasionally under the pines is called antelope bitter-brush, a member of the rose family. The bitter leaves and twigs provide a major source of food for elk and deer in winter and spring, and the fruit is an important food for ground squirrels and chipmunks later in the summer. Along with bitterbrush you can see grayish-green sagebrush, an important shrub throughout the region.

Sparse undergrowth in dense lodgepole pine forests.

Agents of Change: Insects and Fire

Many of the lodgepoles along the first few miles are being killed by the mountain pine beetle (*Dendroctonus ponderosae*). Female beetles burrow through the outer bark of live trees, into the tender inner bark where they lay their eggs. Pine chemicals combine with beetle chemicals to make airborne signals, pheromones, that attract other female and male beetles. An epidemic of beetles can erupt in a very short time if conditions are right. Another pheromone signals that "this tree is full—try another." Infestations are cyclic, occurring every 25 to 40 years and lasting 9 to 15 years, typically until 70 to 80 percent of the trees larger than five inches in diameter have been killed.

Young beetle larvae hatch and spend the winter in the wood of the tree, then eat their way out through the nourishing inner bark or phloem. This interrupts transportation of sugars from the leaves to other parts of the tree. The beetles also spread a blue-stain fungus that blocks water conduction in xylem tissue up the tree. These activities kill the tree.

Insect attack weakens trees and also makes them more vulnerable to fire, wind, and other agents of change. Just east of the area of insect-killed trees, is another area of dead trees, black and obviously burned. The North Fork Fire of 1988 roared through this area, burning insect-damaged trees as well as healthy trees, sagebrush, and other vegetation. This stand of lodgepoles

56

was older than the one near the entrance, with a lot of fallen trees and dry branches on the ground to fuel a hot fire.

Notice the characteristic patchy mosaic created by the fires. Completely incinerated areas are next to scorched brown areas, or untouched green trees. In a system where fires burn naturally, this patchy pattern helps prevent extensive insect and disease infestations, because large expanses of old trees ripe for attack are rare. The exclusion of fire for many years in the park and other places may have altered the natural role of forest pests such as the mountain pine beetle.

Insects and fire are two important agents of change in the ecosystem. They help to continually reset the successional clock in patches of the forest, maintaining a diversity of habitats and species. In both cases, when the larger trees fall, they create sunny spaces for new forest floor vegetation, which provides more food for deer, elk, and other animals. The dead and dying trees also provide food and homes for insects, as well as for birds such as woodpeckers, which feed on the insects, and bluebirds, which nest in holes in the trees.

The River Community

The Madison River starts at Madison Junction, where the Firehole and Gibbon rivers come together; it flows west out of the park toward Hebgen Lake. A clear, clean mountain river like the Madison provides a rich habitat for fish and other kinds of animals and plants.

Growth after 1988 fires: grasses, heartleaf arnica, and fireweed flourish in newly available sunlight.

Something Fishy is Going on Here

The Madison River is a world famous trout fishing stream, one of the few in Yellowstone Park that historically had native trout in abundance. Other rivers on the Yellowstone Plateau had waterfalls and other natural barriers that kept fish from reaching them. Almost half of Yellowstone Park's rivers and most of the lakes were empty of fish life before the late 1800s, when active stocking began.

The stocking programs introduced rainbow, brown, lake, and brook trout. These exotic species generally replaced the native fish. Today the Madison River is almost exclusively filled with rainbow and brown trout and mountain whitefish; of these, only the whitefish is native. Two other species of native fish, the cutthroat trout and the Montana grayling, no longer live here.

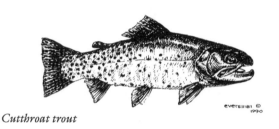

Cutthroat trout

Introduction of species of plants and animals from some other region creates problems in many national parks and natural areas. Exotic species often outcompete native species for resources, and they frequently increase dramatically because they no longer have their own predators or parasites to limit their numbers. Sometimes they eat native species, or infect them with diseases to which they have no immunity. Sometimes the natives hybridize with the exotics and lose their unique genetic makeup; other times they simply vanish.

Exotic trout are no longer planted in the rivers within park boundaries, but their earlier introduction changed the composition of the region's fish communities. Brown, rainbow, and brook trout have generally replaced or hybridized with cutthroats.

Fish Food

Fish in the Madison River feed mostly on aquatic and terrestrial insects and invertebrates. Depending on the season, the timing of insect hatches, and weather conditions — as well as on the age and species of the fish — trout feed on mayflies, stoneflies, dragonflies, beetles, moths, worms, snails, clams, crayfish, fairy shrimp, and even other fish. Many of these prey animals feed on the river's vegetation, algae, and plankton. Watch for signs of fish feeding—splashes and dimples in the water's surface, especially at dawn and dusk. At Seven-Mile Bridge, halfway along this route, you can watch for fish year-round. Run-off from thermal areas keeps water at about 50 degrees all year — a great temperature, if you're a trout.

Trumpeter Swans

Trumpeter swans also feed on the river's submerged vegetation and insects. One or two mating pairs of these large, graceful swans can be seen year-round at Seven-Mile Bridge but, particularly in June and July. The swans build floating vegetation nests, six to seven feet in diameter, by uprooting plants in a large ring and piling them into the center. Eggs are laid in late May, about the same time bison calves are born. Look across the meadow for these brilliant white birds; the female typically huddled over her nest while the male guards it from the middle of the river.

Trumpeter swan families are a rare treat to watch. Both parents swim alongside as the chicks swim and feed in shallow water. The young eat mostly aquatic insects, crustaceans, and some aquatic plants; as they get older, their diet turns to plants.

The chicks weigh only seven or eight ounces when they hatch, but grow to almost 20 pounds in just eight to ten weeks. Fully feathered with the gray juvenile plummage by nine to ten weeks, trumpeter chicks can fly usually by mid-October — about when they learn to trumpet.

Other River Residents

Along the river's banks and surrounding flood plain, small mammals like ground squirrels and meadow voles find shelter and food. Red-tailed hawks soar along seeking those small mammals for their own meals; ospreys or fish hawks come to fish along the river throughout the summer. At dusk in summer, also watch for common nighthawks, small, insect-eating birds with long, pointed wings that zip around like bats catching dinner on the wing. The nighthawk's call sounds like a nasal "peent."

Look Out Below!

On the other side of the river, and along the road on both sides for a few miles, a huge pile of rocks lies at the base of steep cliffs. In mountain canyons, pieces of rock weathered and broken from higher mountain sides collect in these piles or talus slopes. You might think a slope like this would be unstable and dangerous, but the color of the rocks tells you that the rock hasn't moved much for many years.

Notice that the rock is dark. Some of the color is caused by weathering, but most is due to lichens. Lichens are part fungus and part algae. The growth of some kinds is so slow that a colony expands less than one sixteenth of an inch a year. By knowing the growth rates of various lichen species and the size of the colonies, scientists can date glacial or prehistoric activities. "A rolling stone gathers no moss," or lichens. If you see abundant lichen cover you know the rocks have moved very slowly, or not at all, for a long time.

Notice also the large boulders in the Madison River, which were shaken loose from the adjacent mountain slopes. Those with extensive lichen cover, and even small trees growing out of them, have been there for many years; others with little or no lichen cover were jarred loose during the 1959 earthquake and have not yet developed much of a flora.

Meadow Mammals

The canyon widens as you approach Madison Junction, where the Gibbon River flowing from the north, and the Firehole River flowing from the south, join to form the headwaters of the Madison River. In this wide

Talus slope. Black and yellow-green lichen growing on the rock indicate little or no rock movement.

Bison graze in unburned meadows along the Madison River, surrounded by trees burned by the 1988 North Fork fire.

moist meadow surrounded by warm thermal areas, herds of elk and bison spend the entire year.

The Madison headwaters provides one of the three general wintering areas for bison within Yellowstone Park, in part because the nearby thermal areas provide open water and warmer ground with less snow than elsewhere in the region. Many of the bison that winter here disperse in late May and early June to summer ranges throughout the park, and might not be visible from the road through July and August.

Elk in this area are part of a large population living in the Firehole, Madison, and Gibbon River valleys all year. Other herds migrate to winter feeding grounds, but the warmer thermal areas help this herd in winter, so they have less need to migrate.

Both elk and bison graze on herbaceous vegetation: grasses, sedges, and forbs that don't ever become woody like a tree or shrub. Elk also browse on woody shrubs like junipers and sometimes conifers, which can have their bottom branches totally removed or highlined. Because elk and bison don't eat exactly the same things all the time, these two large beasts can occupy the same landscape without competing too much with each other.

Approaching Madison Junction, turn north to Norris Junction and the Norris Geyser Basin (map 4: page 62), or south to Old Faithful and West Thumb (map 13: page 126).

MAP 4
MADISON JUNCTION—NORRIS JUNCTION

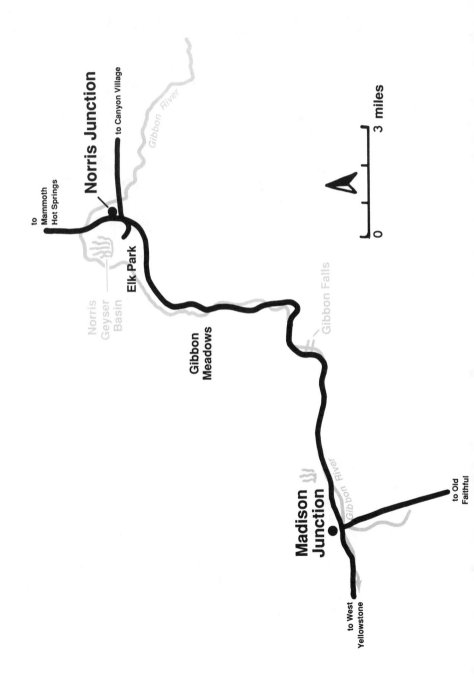

Norris Junction

to Canyon Village

Gibbon River

to Mammoth Hot Springs

Elk Park

Norris Geyser Basin

Gibbon Falls

Gibbon Meadows

Gibbon River

Madison Junction

to Old Faithful

to West Yellowstone

0   3 miles

Burned hillsides and unburned stream banks south of Gibbon Falls on the Gibbon River.

Madison Junction—Norris Junction
14 miles/23 km.

This road mostly follows the Gibbon River, a smaller and shallower stream than the Madison River, between Madison Junction and Norris Junction. Above Gibbon Falls, rainbow trout, cutthroat trout, and grayling were introduced in the late 1800s into the lakes that drain into the Gibbon. Rainbows hybridized with the cutthroats. Now the trout here are considered rainbows, not cutthroats.

The road follows the rim of the Yellowstone Caldera, with spectacular cliffs on the north and west sides, and the Gibbon River on the east and south. The road crosses the river several times. Along this route you see a variety of demonstrations of the ecological effects of different kinds of fire on vegetation and soils.

The boggy area in the lowland east of the Madison River is mostly covered with grasses and sedges, willows, and other forbs or herbaceous plants. The large, moist meadows south of the road provide food, shelter and nest sites for many small mammals and birds, and lush feeding grounds for the larger bison and elk. This area is part of the winter range for the Gibbon-Madison-Firehole elk herd. Bison frequently lounge around the hot springs on the north side of the road. These soggy low spots escaped most of the fire action in 1988.

63

Have You Ever Met a Marmot?

About six miles east of Madison Junction is Gibbon Falls, which historically prevented fish from reaching the upper reaches of the river.

Yellow-bellied marmots live in the rocks by the falls. These large rodents related to the eastern woodchuck have a reddish-brown back, golden belly, and small fur-covered ears. They're larger and much more shy and elusive than the ground squirrels you may also see scurrying about. Marmots live throughout the region, at all elevations; look for them in open, grassy areas, especially near rocks.

Marmot

Fire!

The effects of the 1988 North Fork fire are profound along this route. The canyon near Gibbon Falls and a little farther upstream evidently caught some of the hottest, most intense fires. Many trees burned to a crisp as the fires channeled into this narrow canyon. Dead trees were removed along this road in 1989, as usable lumber when possible, to make the road safe. Ordinarily, dead and fallen trees within national parks are left alone to decompose and return valuable nutrients to the soil.

Slippery Soils

Just above Gibbon Falls on the west side of the road you can see a mudslide. The slopes are steep here and the soil is slippery stuff weathered from the volcanic rhyolite rock; vegetation burned in the 1988 fires, removing root systems that had previously helped to stabilize the soil. The summer after the fires was unusually wet, with lots of rain after heavy snows during the winter of 1988-89. After one particularly heavy rain shower in August, a small part of the hillside came loose and oozed across the road, pushing a camper and family of three into the Gibbon River. Trained rangers and park employees were right behind. They pulled the people to safety, but not the camper.

This illustrates one of the potential effects of intense forest fires that denude a steep hillside. The plants' binding roots no longer stabilize the soil, and moisture can lead to slumping and other downslope movement.

Serious erosion problems on steep slope where fire burned the plants whose roots helped bind the soil.

But fires are not the only cause of slumping. Any unstable slope can slide if it receives lots of moisture on a slippery base and has little to hold it back. Many natural landslides exist in the region, especially along the Lamar River Valley (map 8: page 92), on the Beartooth Plateau (map 15: page 142); there is also a really spectacular one near Jackson, Wyoming (map 25: page 198). Slumping can dump silt and dirt into clear streams, impairing fish spawning.

Who Grows There?

In some places along this route during the summer of 1989, lush green vegetation sprouted in the blackened soil; in other places it was pretty bare and black. What comes back after a fire, and how quickly, depends somewhat on what was there before. In some drier parts of the forest floor, the vegetation was sparse to begin with—lots of pine needles, a few lichens and mosses with no root systems, and some pussytoes and other hardy flowers. In other wetter places, wild strawberries, lupines, heart-leafed arnica, and grasses and sedges were prominent. These wetter places, richer from the start, were lush and beautiful during the first post-fire springs and summers; in the drier spots, the ground was still barren.

Bulbs, underground stems and roots, and some seeds can survive fire rather well; indeed, they are adapted to survive surface fires. But intense fires that burn deep into the soil can destroy these plant parts and make rapid regrowth difficult. In areas of intense fire, ecologists predicted that the burned soil may become hot enough to destroy essential soil fungi and

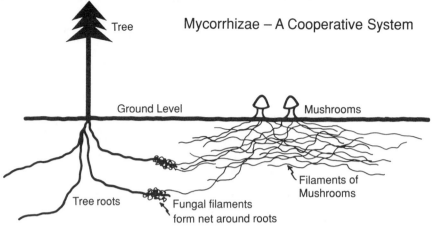

Mycorrhizae – A Cooperative System

Tree

Ground Level

Mushrooms

Filaments of Mushrooms

Tree roots

Fungal filaments form net around roots

Fungus + Roots = Mycorrhizae

Trees and most other green plants are associated with fungi, frequently mushrooms. Filaments of fungi form nets in and around roots. The fungus transports nutrients, especially phosphorus, nitrogen, and potassium, from soil to the plant. The plant transports sugars from photosynthesis to the fungus. Since both organisms benefit from the association, it is termed a mutualistic symbiosis.

bacteria. This can be a critical detail, for bacteria are necessary for nitrogen fixation and decomposition. Mushrooms and other fungi make associations with herb and tree roots, and are essential for good growth.

After the 1988 fires, when biologists scraped even the blackest of the burned areas with a knife, they often found that the blackened part went down usually no more than one inch; much of that was burned vegetation from the top of the soil. Temperatures in only a few burned locations were hot enough to destroy the soil microflora; both plants and microflora were

Mushrooms, visible the first year after the 1988 fire, indicate that most important microorganisms survived the heat.

A Yellowstone black hole. Tree root systems sometimes smolder enough to remove the roots and leave a black hole in the ground. Burned tree roots left holes in the ground, colonized by moss, liverworts, and other plants.

toasted in certain spots where tree roots burned right down into the soil, leaving deep holes. Look for these as you drive along, or when you stop at various pull-offs.

Trees

How is it that some trees survive fires? Part of the answer lies in the type of fire that sweeps through an area. If the fire is a fast and low ground fire, the bark of many trees protects the delicate conducting and growing tissue of the inner bark and outer wood. Adult trees usually survive, sometimes with scars; seedlings and saplings, though, often burn. Relatively frequent ground fires thin a forest stand, and prevent dead material from piling up and fueling hotter fires. Ground fires burned in many places along this road. Look for black marks at the bases of otherwise healthy-looking lodgepole pine trees, with luxuriant grass and flower growth in the lower levels.

If the fire is a hotter, higher crown fire and burns the needles, tree survival depends on how many needles did not burn, and on whether the growing tips of branches burned. Trees can survive some needle loss. They can also survive if the active conducting tissue—xylem in the outermost wood and phloem in the innermost bark—and the cambium, which makes new xylem and phloem, are not damaged. Obviously along some spots on this route, the fire was both low and high, and hot; many trees totally became charcoal. But others were only partially burned, and might survive.

Take a Closer Look: Tiny Seeds Sealed in Fire Capsules

Along with regular cones, lodgepole pines can also have special serotinous cones that are sealed with a sticky resin and require high heat from a fire or intense sunlight to open. These cones may stay tightly attached to the tree branches for years, until conditions are right for them to burst open. When the tiny seeds are released during a fire, they naturally and quickly revegetate the burned area. Stop at a roadside pull-off and look for tiny pine seedlings coming up in areas that Were heavily burned. Away from heavily burned areas, see if you can locate tightly closed serotinous cones on some older branches of unburned trees; they might be mixed with regular cones that open without heat.

Sagebrush lizard, an elusive resident of Norris Geyser Basin.

New Views

Those who knew the area before the fires of 1988 notice a phenomenon that first-time visitors can miss: in most burned areas, visibility increased by yards or miles, depending on the spot; and some hills and ridges of the plateau are now visible for the first time since the last big fires hundreds of years ago. Many of the roads in the park were lined to the edge with lodgepole pine trees, and visibility in most spots, especially in narrow canyons like this one, was limited to the roadside trees, not the whole forest. The overall topography was a mystery until now.

Norris Geyser Basin

About 12 to 13 miles from Madison Junction your nose will tell you you're approaching the Norris Geyser Basin, the largest and hottest in Yellowstone Park. It has the most spectacular geyser, Steamboat, which is so irregular and unpredictable that few people have seen it erupt.

Hot springs and geyser runoff waters support some unique biological systems. They have been extensively studied in this basin and throughout Yellowstone Park. An excellent display at Norris illustrates this fascinating thermal community. See map 13 on page 126 along the Firehole River for a more detailed roadside view.

The warm streams that flow out of Norris Geyser Basin feed into the Gibbon River. Since the water stays warm and open, the Gibbon can support elk and bison during the winter.

At Norris Junction, turn west to go to the visitors' center and museum; then go north toward Mammoth Hot Springs (map 6: page 76), or head east toward Canyon Junction and the east side of the park (map 5: page 70).

Norris Geyser Basin, the hottest and most active thermal area in the park.

MAP 5
NORRIS JUNCTION—CANYON JUNCTION

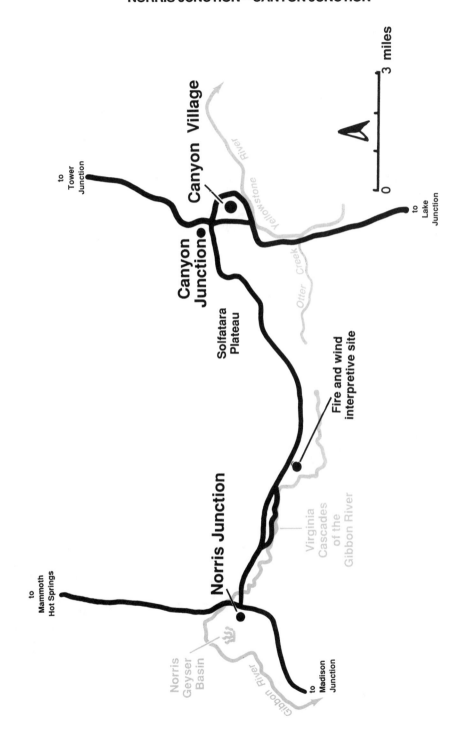

Norris Junction—Canyon Junction
12 miles/19 km.

This high short stretch of road goes through lodgepole pine forest, where you can see dramatic effects of wind and fire.

Virginia Cascades and the Dapper Dipper

A one-way, two-and-a-half mile loop side trip along the Virginia Cascades Road leaves the main road about two miles east of Norris Junction. This diversion takes you through an area of windblown and heavily burned trees, and along the Virginia Cascades of the Gibbon River. The rushing mountain stream provides ideal habitat for the American dipper or water ouzel, a plump dark gray bird. A little smaller than a robin, it bobs up and down as it stands on rocks and logs, and will actually take a dip and walk along the bottom of the stream looking for a snack of aquatic insects or small fish. Look for dippers along all the small, fast creeks throughout the ecosystem during summer; during winter many move to lower elevations in search of open water and food.

Wind and Fire

A fierce wind blew down millions of lodgepole pine trees in a swath along this road and along the West Yellowstone-to-Ashton Road (map 19: page 170) in 1984. You can identify these trees because they were uprooted; the shallow root systems, coated with light-colored soil, are visible all along this road. The tangle of downed trees was nearly impossible to walk through; then young trees began to grow up through the jumble. The North Fork fire then burned through here in 1988, creating one of the desolate pictures so frequently seen in the media that summer. An interpretive walk has been built four miles east of Norris Junction. Less regrowth of vegetation here than in other burned sites is possibly due to more extreme heat reaching the soil when the horizontal tree remains just !ay there burning.

Double trouble: trees blown down in 1984, burned in 1988. Notice the light colored volcanic soil clinging to the shallow root systems.

An earlier fire had made a path through older trees on the north side of the road. A sign pointed out the regeneration of the burned patch and compared the newer growth with the old. The sign burned during the 1988 fire, and now there are two burned areas to follow.

Solfatara Plateau: Living at the Extremes

Some maps identify the area north of this road as the Solfatara Plateau, solfatara being an Italian word for sulfur mine. This is a fascinating area for soil microbiology. The rhyolitic rock contains hydrogen sulfide, that foul-smelling sulfur compound characteristic of rotten eggs and thermal areas.

Chloroflexus, a type of photosynthetic bacteria, uses hydrogen sulfide in its photosynthetic pathway, and deposits pure, or elemental, sulfur outside its cells. Other bacteria such as *Sulfolobus* combine sulfur with oxygen to make sulfate. Sulfate dissolves in water to make sulfuric acid; the sulfuric acid weakens rock and makes it crumbly and bleached. In 1990, other types of sulfur bacteria were discovered in the hot gas and rock vents at the bottom of Yellowstone Lake.

Names such as *Thiobacillus thiooidans* and *Sulfolobus acidocaldarius* reflect the habitat: "thio" and "sulfo" refer to sulfur, "acido" indicates acid,

Life in Hot Water

 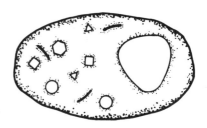

Prokaryote Cells

Small—about 1/25,000 inch in diameter
Cell components not separated
by membranes

Organisms	Hottest water in which they can live*
Heterotrophic bacteria	192°F
Photosynthetic bacteria	162°F
Cyanobacteria	162°F

* Actual hottest water depends on individual species and water chemistry.

Eukaryote Cell

Larger—more than1/25,000 inch in diameter
With a nucleus. Cell components separated
by membranes

Organisms	Hottest water in which they can live*
Fungi	143°F°
Algae	140°F
Protozoa	133°F
Crustaceans	122°F
Moss	122°F
Insects	122°F
Plants	112°F
Fish, aquatic vertebrates	100°F

Adapted from Brock, T.D. 1978. Thermophilic microorganisms and life at high temperatures.
Springer-Verlag, New York

and "caldarius" refers to heat. Drop these names at your next cocktail party to really make an impression!

An unusual green eukaryotic alga, *Cyanidium caldarium*, also inhabits aquatic habitats; this tough organism can stand a pH as acid as .05 — similar to the pH of the sulfuric acid in chemistry labs. *Cyanidium* also thrives in very hot acid springs and streams in the Norris Geyser Basin.

Extreme heat, high mineral or metal concentrations, very acid or very basic conditions are all extreme habitats that most living organisms avoid; their cells are just not adapted to living in such hostile environments. So how is it that some organisms—particularly single-celled prokaryotes like bacteria but also a few simple eukaryotes—can exist in such habitats? The answer isn't exactly known, but somehow the cells of these organisms must be able to exclude the offending substance, or detoxify it within the cells, or otherwise live with it. Understanding the metabolic or detoxification

Dense stands of lodgepole pines are called doghair stands. Lower branches fall off because of the shading by adjacent trees.

mechanisms of such important bacteria as *Sulfolobus* or *Chloroflexus*, or algae like *Cyanidium*, might someday help us detoxify harmful pollutants in our own environment.

Forest Succession at Work

A mile or two west of the junction at Canyon Village, the lodgepole pines are being replaced in a cooler, wetter spot by spruce and subalpine fir, a good example of forest succession. With a variety of successional stages providing different vegetation and moisture conditions, a diverse array of wildlife can be spotted in this vicinity fairly regularly, including elk, mule deer, moose, and coyotes. Even an occasional grizzly bear puts in an appearance.

At Canyon Junction, continue east into Canyon Village and the north rim of the Grand Canyon of the Yellowstone River, then south on the main road to Fishing Bridge, Lake, and points south and east (map 10: page 106); or go north over Mt. Washburn to Tower Falls (map 9: page 100). You can also head directly south at Canyon Junction, skipping the canyon rim loop and joining Route 10 about 4.5 miles south on the main road to Yellowstone Lake.

MAP 6
NORRIS JUNCTION—MAMMOTH HOT SPRINGS

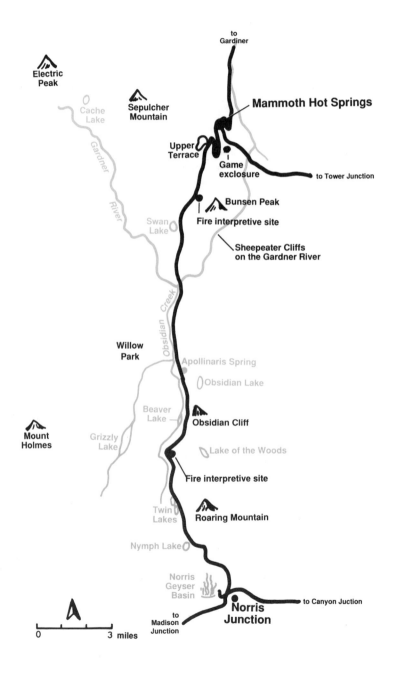

to
Gardiner

Electric
Peak

Cache
Lake

Sepulcher
Mountain

Mammoth Hot Springs

Upper
Terrace

Game
exclosure

to Tower Junction

Gardiner River

Bunsen Peak

Swan
Lake

Fire interpretive site

Sheepeater Cliffs
on the Gardner River

Obsidian Creek

Willow
Park

Apollinaris Spring

Obsidian Lake

Beaver
Lake

Mount
Holmes

Grizzly
Lake

Obsidian Cliff

Lake of the Woods

Fire interpretive site

Twin
Lakes

Roaring Mountain

Nymph Lake

Norris
Geyser
Basin

to Canyon Juction

**Norris
Junction**

to
Madison
Junction

0   3 miles

Norris Junction—Mammoth Hot Springs
21 miles/34 km.

Norris Geyser Basin is one of the most active in the park because the heat source for brewing the water is closer to the surface than in the others. The rock deposited is geyserite, composed mostly of silica.

The springs in Norris Geyser Basin are on the acid side, with a pH that ranges from 1.9, about that of stomach acid, to 4.6, like coffee or tomatoes, to a fairly neutral pH of about 6.8.

Land of Lakes

North of Norris Geyser Basin the road crosses the Gibbon River; a cabin across the river contains a history exhibit open during summer. About two miles north of Norris, the road passes Nymph Lake, and Frying Pan Spring, which empties into the lake. Nymph Lake is too warm and too acidic to support fish; its water drains into the Gibbon.

Twin Lakes are about a mile farther north. South Twin Lake is cooler and less acidic than North Twin Lake. Both are fed by underground springs and thermal runoff, and both had trout populations introduced into them in the early 1900s. But every fish disappeared, in part because the lakes have no inlet or outlet streams for spawning.

Slightly north of the Twin Lakes is Roaring Mountain, which once roared, it's said. Today it hisses more than roars, at least on the side by the road. The taming of this mountain illustrates that underground changes, associated with faulting or ground movements, can change the patterns of water circulation.

Grizzly Lake, not visible from the road, is about a two-mile hike from the trailhead six miles north of Norris Junction. It is full of brook trout that apparently entered from nearby Obsidian and Straight creeks; inlet and outlet streams for spawning enable the trout populations to sustain themselves.

At Beaver Lake, almost eight miles north of Norris Junction, you pass into the Yellowstone River drainage. Obsidian Creek flows into Beaver Lake, then empties into the Gardner River near the Indian Creek Campground. Brook trout live here, apparently having come upstream after being introduced in Obsidian Creek.

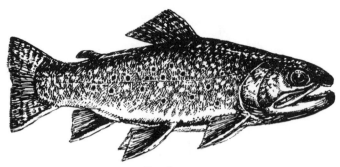

Brook trout

Beaver Lake is quite shallow and was originally dammed by beavers; look for the dam at the far northwestern corner of the lake. Beavers are still active in the streams along this route. They prefer deciduous species such as aspen and willow for eating and making their dams, which block stream flow and form shallow ponds. When the beavers have used all the preferred tree types, or when trees disappear for other reasons, the beavers abandon the valley and look for different sites, leaving ponds and wide boggy meadows as souvenirs of their occupancy. Beaver populations in the ecosystem were decimated by excessive trapping. Some drainages are now protected, and beavers are being reintroduced or are coming back on their own.

Obsidian Cliff

Obsidian Cliff is on the east side of the road, with a parking lot on the west side of the road, just north of Beaver Lake. The cliff once had much more of the shiny black obsidian rock than it does now; too many people over the years have assumed that one little piece would not be missed. Yellowstone obsidian was traded by Indian tribes in a trading network that extended throughout the Missouri and Ohio river drainages. Pieces of the rock were found among Indian relics in the Ohio River Valley. Obsidian breaks into sharp points, with an interesting conchoidal pattern. It is so hard and so smooth that lichens and mosses are usually found growing not on the obsidian itself but on the rougher, less resistant impurities.

Willow Park

Willow Park, with its exhibit about moose life appropriate to such a large expanse of prime moose habitat, is about 11 miles north of Norris. Moose are most likely to be seen early in the morning or at dusk during spring, summer, and early fall, feeding on the willow leaves, gooseberry, sedges, herbs, and aquatic plants that grow in the soggy areas. In winter, snow can limit access to certain foods, and some moose move up into higher country where they can feed on woody browse that sticks up above the snow. A stop here to scan the wet meadow can be thrilling. The largest member of the

Pair of moose at Willow Park. The young male on the right still has small antlers.

deer family and one of North America's largest land mammals can often be seen at fairly close range. Mature bull moose produce some of the world's most impressive antlers, with broad palm-shaped tines arching above huge dark bodies that could rarely be mistaken for anything else. Four subspecies of moose inhabit the boreal forests of North America, with Shira's moose here in the northern Rocky Mountains.

Reminders of the North Fork Fire

The heavily burned area near Willow Park is a remnant of the 1988 North Fork fire, the one that threatened Old Faithful and West Yellowstone. Most of the burned trees in the park were lodgepole pine, but many in this part were spruce and subalpine fir. At a roadside pulloff, stop to check for young pine seedlings and wildflowers in season. Notice that many trees were partially singed, with needles and branches on one side affected but other parts still green; this uneven burning on even a single tree mimics on a small scale the uneven, patchy way a fire usually sweeps around a landscape. The survival rate of partially burned trees is not exactly known; the tree will probably survive if most of the photosynthesizing needles and buds for new growth survived the flames.

Sheepeater Cliffs and Swan Lake Flats

As the road climbs and the forest begins to thin out about 11 miles north of Norris, Sheepeater Cliffs appear east of the road. The cliffs are named after a tribe of peaceful Shoshone Indians, the only people to live permanently in Yellowstone before it was set aside as a park.

The broad, flat expanse between Indian Creek Campground and Bunsen Peak is called Gardner's Hole, or Swan Lake Flats, a summer home for a few of Yellowstone's famous trumpeter swans. This natural sagebrush grassland is soggy in spring from melting snow. Listen then for choruses of frogs peeping. The Western chorus frog will probably be what you hear; common throughout Yellowstone Park, it is one of only three native frogs in the largely high and dry ecosystem. These tiny frogs, less than two inches long, attach small masses of eggs to leaves and stems in the water. By late summer, when the shallow puddles and lakes have dried, the tadpoles have grown legs. The adult frogs can then disperse into the woods and grasslands.

Western chorus frog

Mountains looming west of the road — Quadrant, Little Quadrant, Sepulcher, and Electric Peak — are the southeastern end of the Gallatin Range that extends north about 90 miles to Bozeman, Montana.

A Real-life Bunsen Burner

Bunsen Peak, the large cone-shaped old volcano on the east side of the road, was named for the inventor of that old laboratory stand-by, the Bunsen burner. Bunsen also figured out how geysers work. Bunsen Peak has burned repeatedly in its history, including 1988. Close examination from all sides, including the Mammoth-to-Tower road, map 7, page 84, will show tree stands of various ages. A foot path leads to the top; it winds, or did, through lodgepole pine that gives way to whitebark pine more typical of higher elevations. The north and east sides of the peak are cooler and wetter and support Douglas fir stands of various ages. The patchwork of burned areas on Bunsen Peak is a fine example of the vegetative mosaic fire creates. Look for the Bunsen Peak Road on the east side for a one-way trip around the other side of the mountain.

The Golden Gate

Rustic Falls on Glen Creek marks the top of Golden Gate, where the road begins its descent into Mammoth Hot Springs. Lichens on the canyon walls provide splashes of color on the volcanic rock, a pale welded ash called rhyolite. The various colors of the lichens are formed by acids, and not by pigments like those responsible for color in flowers and leaves of higher plants.

The Hoodoos, or Silver Gate, are a mass of white thermal deposit and volcanic tuff that slid off Terrace Mountain, the flat-topped cliffs high on the west side of the road. The dense tree growth indicates that the hoodoos are now pretty stable.

The major forest tree type changes along here from lodgepole pine to Douglas fir, probably because of the change in soil types from sterile rhyolite to slightly more fertile Absaroka volcanic soils. The open spots also support some aspen stands. The North Fork Fire, which burned at West Yellowstone, Old Faithful, and east to Tower Junction, roared through this area, capriciously taking some trees and leaving others.

Upper Terrace Drive

The loop road leading to the Upper Terrace area of Mammoth Hot Springs is west of the road about, 1.5 miles above Mammoth. Drive through to see the changing thermal landscape. Active springs allow the orange, yellow, green, and brown bacteria and cyanobacteria, or blue-green algae, to live in the runoff water. When the water stops running, as happens when thermal plumbing shifts around, these organisms die and the colors dull.

Junipers, limber pine, and Douglas fir on the Upper Terrace Loop. The thin, delicate crust supports a sparse array of hardy grasses and flowers.

Activation of a spring, the New Highland Spring, brings minerals and hot water to a spot that is occupied by trees and shrubs. The minerals and heat kill the roots of the plants so that only their woody skeletons are left; the white deposit is called travertine, one of the few calcium carbonate substrates in this park. The water contains dissolved calcium carbonate, unlike the silica minerals of the geyser basins at Norris or Old Faithful. Calcium carbonate makes the water weakly alkaline. Its temperature is well below boiling, about 170 degrees, cooler than the water of Norris Hot Springs and most geysers.

The gates at the entrance to Upper Terrace indicate how far the road is kept open during the winter. Beyond the gate, you can ski from December to March, along the road trail that winds through the junipers, limber pine, and Douglas fir; the sky can be blindingly blue in winter, and the steam from the springs adds action and mystery. In all seasons, drivers, walkers, and skiers must stay on the road or boardwalks to avoid breaking through the thin crust.

You can walk on the boardwalks from Upper Terrace down to Lower Terrace, coming out nearly at the Visitor Center. You can also drive around the loop and back to the main road, which winds around and downward giving you fine views of Bunsen Peak and Mount Everts, the long flat-topped mountain across the Gardner River from Mammoth.

White terraces indicate no present activity; dead trees indicate a pattern of activity, then no activity (allowing trees to grow), then renewed activity (which kills trees).

"Exclosure" or "Enclosure": Looking In or Looking Out?

A stop at a subtle pull-out on the east side of the road between the Upper and Lower terraces looks down over an exclosure. . . or enclosure, depending on your perspective. Either way, it's a fenced area that deer, elk, and moose cannot enter. Notice that the meadows here have grass, sagebrush, and some young Douglas fir and juniper; inside the exclosure, there are tall shrubs—willow, Rocky Mountain maple, and others—safe from the appetite of anything larger than a mouse. Biologists use exclosures to estimate the impact of grazing and browsing mammals.

Mammoth

Mammoth is the park headquarters, where the park's first administrators, the U.S. Army, constructed the 19th-century buildings. The administrative and research offices are open all year round. Elk make themselves at home here, keeping the grass clipped and illustrating that for a wild animal, town boundaries are invisible. It's also possible to spot coyotes on occasion as they trail the voles and other small rodents that live among the sagebrush. The Visitor Center has historical and biological exhibits, as well as occasional art exhibits depicting aspects of the park; downstairs in the Visitor Center is a research library open to the public during certain hours.

At Mammoth, proceed east to Tower Junction and points east and southeast (map 7: page 84), or north toward the North Entrance and the towns of Gardiner and Livingston, Montana (map 2: page 46).

A game exclosure northeast of the switchbacks from Mammoth Hot Springs. The fence separating the grazed grassland on the left from fairly lush willows and other shrubs on the right is concealed by a Douglas fir.

MAP 7
MAMMOTH HOT SPRINGS—TOWER JUNCTION

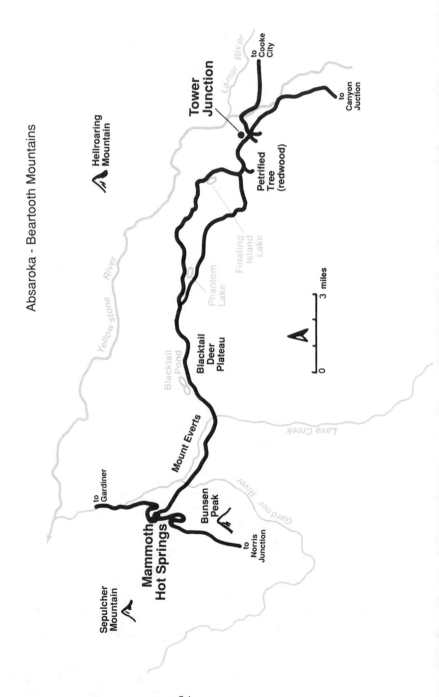

Mammoth Hot Springs terraces along the road from Tower Junction. Thermal features like the hot springs were major factors in the establishment of the world's first national park.

Mammoth Hot Springs—Tower Junction
18 miles/29 km.

This route takes you across the northern part of the park's Grand Loop road, rising up and over the Blacktail Deer Plateau, past phantom lakes, floating islands, and fossil trees. Wildlife abounds along the Yellowstone Valley, which, with the nearby Lamar Valley forms one of the largest open expanses in the ecosystem, commonly referred to as the Northern Range.

Into the Douglas Fir Forest

The road east from Mammoth to Tower Junction crosses the Gardner River, then follows Lava Creek. It passes two pleasant waterfalls: Undine Falls north of the road and Wraith Falls on the south side, about a half mile farther east. Both require a short hike through cool spruce stands that are distinctly different from the hot, dry grass and sagebrush along the road. The Yellowstone River is visible along most of the rest of the road, flowing northwest out of the park.

The dry grassland-juniper vegetation type of the Mammoth Hot Springs area changes gradually to Douglas fir on the moister slopes, with spruce mostly along the stream bottoms. Pockets of aspens indicate occasional

85

sunny, exposed sites with readily available groundwater. Most of the trees growing out of apparently bare rock cliffs on the north side of the river are lodgepole pine.

This route crosses one of the few parts of the park where Douglas fir is prominent, as well as one of the few places where Rocky Mountain maple and other deciduous shrubs like ninebark are common. Watch for a large thistle commonly known as Everts or elk thistle; an early explorer named Truman Everts, for whom Mt. Everts is named, was said to have survived for over a month by eating the roots and stalk of this thistle.

Douglas fir forms the lowest forest zone in Yellowstone Park, though limber pine occasionally forms a lower elevation forest in some portions of the ecosystem. Elsewhere in the West, ponderosa pine inhabits this zone, but for some unknown reason no native ponderosa pine grows in most of the Yellowstone region.

One of the reasons Douglas fir can live in this part of Yellowstone Park is that the soil is richer than in most other parts of the park. In the valleys and lower hillsides, for example, the soil is a thick glacial till with calcium from the thermal deposits. The soil on the hills was weathered from a volcanic rock type called andesite; it contains more iron and magnesium minerals than the lighter-colored rhyolite soil south of here. It also holds water better so that more plants can establish themselves before the dry weather of summer.

Patches of the Douglas fir forests along this road were heavily hit by the 1988 fires. Large Douglas firs resist all but the hottest fires because of their thick bark, but many young and adult trees, and other understory plants, burned in the intense fires that came through here.

Tree Barks Are Different From Each Other

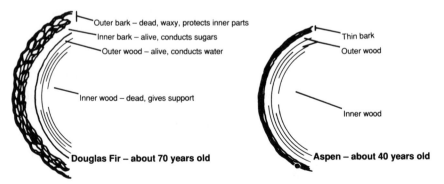

Fire history in parts of Yellowstone National Park is studied by looking at fire scars on old Douglas firs. Their thick waxy bark protects living parts of tree trunks from some fire. Douglas fir survives many ground fires that kill pines and aspens.

Regeneration during the spring and summer of 1989 was spectacular — grasses, sedges, and wildflowers like fireweed and lupine formed brilliant, colorful carpets under the stark black snags. Douglas fir tree seedlings, shaded among tree skeletons and taller plants, were visible two years after the 1988 fires.

The Budworm Blues

The Douglas firs in this area were very hard hit for several years by an insect, the Western budworm, *Choristoneura occidentalis*. The female moths hatch in early August, already containing many eggs. Pheromones, aerial chemical signals, attract the males to fertilize the eggs. Mating and egg-laying occur immediately on the needles of the trees. New larvae hatch in about ten days, but hibernate almost immediately because by mid-August the leaves are pretty tough; the trees have stopped growing and are starting their preparation for winter.

The caterpillars emerge the following May and head for the youngest growing tips of the branches. The new leaves are also emerging and are young, tender, and nutritious, though the previous year's needles will do in a pinch. By mid-July the caterpillars have grown to about one inch in length; they pupate in a cocoon made by webbing needles together. In 10 to 12 days, the adult moths emerge, find each other, and the cycle starts over.

If the trees are attacked by too many moth caterpillars for too many years, they lose too much photosynthetic leaf tissue and eventually die. The lack of adequate photosynthesis can be a direct cause of tree death, or they can become so weak that they can't fend off other diseases or effects of severe winters. Even trees have their problems!

Blacktail Pond and Blacktail Plateau

Blacktail Pond with its brook and cutthroat trout is north of the road six miles east of Mammoth. The low valley where Blacktail Pond is located was evidently once a fairly good-sized stream valley; notice the old stream beds running through here on the north side of the road. Presumably, this was a stream bed when glaciers were melting.

The road climbs up to a large dry area, the Blacktail Deer Plateau. Apparently the landmarks of this area were mistakenly named for mule deer. Their black-tipped tails are characteristic, but the Rocky Mountain mule deer is a different subspecies than the true blacktail deer, which lives on the West Coast. Many mule deer live along this stretch of the road, but they're usually visible only in early morning or late evening, especially along the edges between forest and meadow. They browse on shrubs and coniferous trees; grazers, such as pronghorn antelope, prefer grasses.

The Blacktail Deer Plateau is dry, and had a large stand of big sagebrush before the fires of 1988. Some sprigs still stand, but much of the sagebrush

Blacktail Pond, a popular fishing stop on the north side of the road.

burned. Buttercups, lupines, fireweed, and grasses were the first to return after the fires. Big sagebrush began to grow again the first year after the fire, from seeds blown in.

Don't Add This Sage to Your Stew

This sagebrush, by the way, is one of several species in this region; the largest is big sagebrush, which can reach at least six feet tall, as it does on the southeast slope of Mt. Everts. None is used as the spice known as sage; that comes from the genus *Salvia* in the mint family. These sagebrushes are in the aster or daisy family, Asteraceae or Compositae. They bear tiny yellowish stalks of flowers in late August and September. You can see remnants of these through the next growing season, as little tan brushes sticking up on the top of the shrub. Many game animals and birds browse on sagebrush in the winter; it's not usually a preferred food because of its volatile oils, but is frequently the only available food in winter.

Elk of the Northern Herd

From here and across the Lamar Valley (map 8: page 92) is the range of the famous and controversial Northern Yellowstone elk herd, which was estimated to number over 20,000 animals before the harsh winter of 1988-89 reduced it by about 20 percent.

Notice on a map that to the north the Gallatin National Forest is adjacent to the park boundaries; this allows relatively free movement of elk in and out of the park in summer. Quite a lot of back country south and southeast of this road provides summer range.

In winter, when higher areas receive much more snow, the elk move down to this valley and graze on what they can find on south- and west-facing slopes, or slopes where wind blows away most of the snow. Thousands of elk of the northern herd congregate here after dispersing throughout this part of the ecosystem during the summer.

Elk are both browsers and grazers. They graze on a wide range of vegetation, including sedges, grasses, and other herbs. In winter, this kind of vegetation is less available, and the elk browse on woody plants like willows, aspen, junipers, and needles of Douglas fir, and subalpine fir as a supplement to the lower-growing plants.

Winter Range

Winter range like that found here is critical to the survival of elk and other hoofed animals. Although Rocky Mountain mule deer and elk are metabolically adapted to survive winters, they coast precariously through the season on what they could store up in the fall. Males usually have used up much of their stores earlier, since winter hits right after the energetically intensive fall mating season. Females are carrying next spring's fawns and calves, and young animals born the previous spring are going into winter not quite grown up and not fat. So access to mild winter range is essential.

Alternating sagebrush grassland, lodgepole pine, and Douglas fir typify the winter range for thousands of elk, bison, and other animals.

If one spot gets too covered with snow or too crowded, the herd needs to move to another range with less than two feet of snow.

When alternate winter ranges are occupied by people or otherwise inaccessible, animal movements are curtailed; winter range can get over-used, and crowded animals can get sick and die. The population size that can maintain itself is limited in part by the available winter range.

Since 1985, private organizations, the state of Montana, and the federal government have purchased a large amount of land north of Yellowstone Park as winter range for elk. Hunters have been primary contributors of money for the purchases.

Elk are important to the ecosystem both as consumers of vegetation, and as prey for predators such as coyotes and cougars, particularly when the elk are young or in a weakened condition. The corpses of individuals that don't survive winters are extremely important to carrion-eaters: grizzly bears, black bears, coyotes, ravens, and bald and golden eagles. Bones and antlers are important sources of calcium, magnesium, and other minerals for insects and rodents.

Bison

Bison abound in the Yellowstone River Valley and along the Lamar Valley (map 8: page 92); together these valleys form one of the three wintering units for bison in Yellowstone Park. In summer this herd sometimes moves higher onto the Mirror Plateau south of the Lamar River, and are not usually visible in great numbers along this road during July and August. They generally return to wintering areas in late fall.

Severe winters with heavy snow provide the main natural population control for bison, since they apparently have no predators, and suffer few diseases. Before traditional migration routes were fenced off, bison would migrate great distances from areas of heavy snow to more suitable winter feeding grounds. It was not uncommon to find bison and elk from the Northern Yellowstone herds as far north as Emigrant, Montana.

Today the wild animals are not welcome grazers in hay fields and haystacks because they compete with cattle for sometimes scarce food. Bison and elk can carry brucellosis, a disease that causes calf abortion in cattle as well as undulant fever in humans. It is important to ranchers to keep bison completely separated from cattle and their grazing areas.

Because of the abundance of animals here and their tendency to roam beyond protected park borders, the area just north of the park boundaries is a very popular, active hunting area.

Pronghorns: When is an Antelope not an Antelope?

Pronghorn antelope also appear along this road in spring, summer, and fall, especially along the Blacktail Plateau. Not really a member of the true antelope family, which is found only in Africa, pronghorns are small, swift plains animals that apparently evolved in North America along with the grasslands. They are limited to open, dry, grassy areas, where they usually browse on sage and other low-growing shrubs. In summer they become grazers when more succulent foods are available.

Because of their small size and the restrictions of a small stomach, pronghorns are more fussy about what they eat than larger ungulates like elk or bison. This is one reason you will find them only where the vegetation is rich in nutrients and easily obtained.

Unlike many of the hoofed animals, which are more easily seen at dawn and dusk, pronghorns are often visible during the day, usually in groups. They depend on their excellent eyesight and fleet-footedness to avoid predators. Pronghorns may be the swiftest mammal in North America, with a cruising speed of some 30 mph, which they can maintain for three to four miles. By the time it is five days old, a pronghorn fawn can out-run a human adult.

Phantom Lakes and Fossil Trees

Small lakes along the road—Phantom Lake about nine miles from Mammoth, and Floating Island Lake about four miles farther east—usually have abundant ducks, coots, and yellow-headed blackbirds during spring. By late summer, Phantom Lake normally dries up and fewer birds are visible, but these spring stopping-off points are important to the survival of many migratory birds. The lakes are shallow and have no good inlet or outlet streams, so they don't support fish populations, but they do provide some of the few places where frogs and salamanders can lay their eggs in spring.

About 16 miles east of Mammoth, two miles west of the Tower Junction Ranger Station, a short road leads to one easily accessible fossil tree. This is a remnant of the extensive fossil forests on Specimen Ridge in the Lamar Valley (map 8: page 92). Successive volcanic mudflows covered forests that managed to grow well between eruptions. The wood in the buried trees was replaced with silica, petrified. An excellent discussion of these forests and petrification processes is in William Fritz's book, *Roadside Geology of the Yellowstone Country*. It's hard to imagine magnolia, avocado, and hickory trees growing here, but that's what the fossil evidence shows. Obviously the climate has altered a bit in the past 50 million years!

At Tower-Roosevelt Junction, turn northeast to Cooke City, the Beartooth Mountains, and points east (map 8: page 92). Or turn into the driveway of Roosevelt Lodge, where you can observe an old fire scar in a huge Douglas fir tree. Continue straight ahead for Canyon Junction (map 9: page 100), Fishing Bridge/Lake, and the southern part of the ecosystem.

MAP 8
TOWER JUNCTION—COOKE CITY

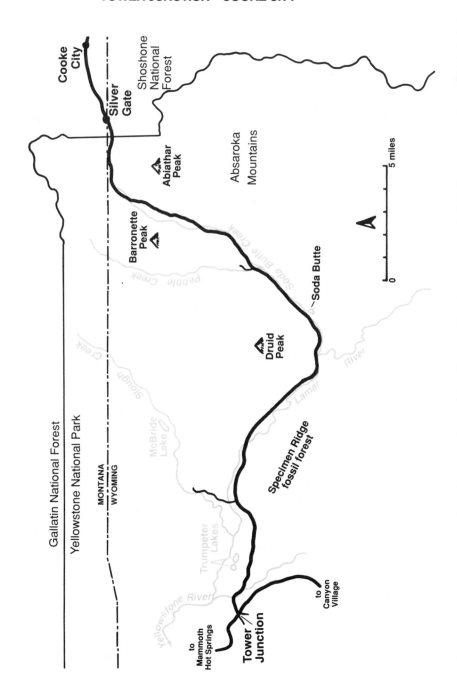

Tower Junction—Cooke City
33 miles/53 km.
(open year-round)

Rivers Along the Road

Where the road first crosses the Yellowstone River, watch for belted kingfishers swooping down to the river. This excellent fisher-bird is readily recognized by its huge pointed beak and rattling call. Common along the waterways throughout the region, kingfishers nest in holes dug in exposed banks, where they lay five to eight pure white eggs.

The first river that parallels the road is the Lamar River, which created the spectacular Lamar Valley. The Lamar River originates in the high country in the remote eastern part of the park and flows mostly northwest to join the Yellowstone about one-half mile north of Tower Junction.

Female Belted kingfisher.

The Lamar Valley supports abundant wildlife populations in late autumn, winter, and early spring. The valley is some fifteen miles long and three to five miles broad. It runs east from Tower Junction to Soda Butte, an old geyser cone on Soda Butte Creek. The Lamar was called the "secluded valley" by explorer Osborne Russell on his journey through this area in the 1830s, and is still one of the least travelled routes in the park. Today it's more commonly referred to as the Northern Range of Yellowstone Park's ungulate herds.

American Coot

Wide Open Spaces

Specimen Ridge south of the road is the major site of Yellowstone's petrified forests. Repeated mudflows in the Absaroka volcanic pile of about 50 million years ago buried many layers of tropical or sub-tropical forests— magnolias, breadfruit, avocado, redwood, sycamores, walnuts, oaks, and others.

Most of the vegetation along the valley bottom consists of grasses and sedges, with sagebrush in drier places. Near the geology exhibit about 2.5 miles east of Tower Junction watch for two shallow ponds on the north side of the road, the Trumpeter Lakes. They hold water only in early spring, when the snow is melting. These spring ponds host swans, geese, ducks, red-winged blackbirds, yellow-headed blackbirds, American coots, and shorebirds such as avocets, killdeers, and phalaropes at a critical time of year. The ponds then dry up. In summer and fall, particularly north of the road, you can still spot their low, green depressions, more lush than the surrounding grasslands because of remaining soil moisture. No fish live in the Trumpeter Lakes.

Tiger salamander that lives near the ponds.

Another good indication of abundant water near the surface is the presence of aspen trees in scattered spots at the foot of the mountains. In summer these members of the willow family make a bright green highlight against the darker conifers; in autumn, a golden glow. Many aspens in the West produce prolific suckers from their roots, especially after a fire kills the adult tree. All the trees in a grove of aspens most likely came from the same parent, so they are genetically very similar. You can see evidence of this in the fall, when every tree in a grove turns color at precisely the same time. Patches of aspens that cloned from other parents turn at different times.

Slippery Slopes

Sometimes, so much water soaks into these slopes that soil tends to creep downhill, deforming the trunks of the aspens. The tree tries to grow straight up, but pressure against the base of the tree curves it downhill, making the trunk a bit J-shaped. Curved tree trunks due to downward creep of soil, snow, and rock are rather common in mountainous country, where the downward movements help keep the face of the landscape in a continual state of change.

Cottonwoods

In the picnic area about eight miles from Tower Junction, notice another deciduous tree along the river, the cottonwood, a close relative of the aspen. The cottonwood is a much larger tree, with thick, deeply furrowed gray bark. Like the aspen, it uses and stores a lot of water. You will see cottonwoods throughout the ecosystem growing along rich river banks, streamsides, and lakeshores; their strings of green winding across even the most parched plain flag a river, stream, or other dependably wet area. As you drive around the region, see how many times you notice the name Cottonwood Creek.

Living on a Rock and Lichen It

Conspicuous boulders between Tower and Soda Butte Creek Canyon are glacial erratics, so-called because they differ from the bedrock beneath them and must have been moved into place. Glaciers, originating in the high country of the Beartooth Plateau region to the northeast, left these odd chunks of granite from the higher valleys resting on glacial outwash and till.

These granitic rocks are very hospitable to lichens. This is a particularly good stretch of road to observe many kinds of lichens and think about their contribution to soil formation. The black crust on the granite boulders contains a number of different kinds of lichen. Other lichens are orange, green, white, or grey. Watch for the vivid crust of yellow and green lichens on the outcrop of volcanic rock near the bridge across the Yellowstone River near Tower Junction.

Lichens are unusual organisms, part fungus and part algae. They hug the surface of the rock by extending tiny root-like growths into nooks and crannies between mineral grains, prying them apart. They also produce carbon dioxide that combines with water to make carbonic acid—the same acid that makes soda pop fizz. The acid dissolves carbonate minerals, and helps erode limestones. Lichens swell when they're wet and shrink when

Glacial erratic, colonized by many lichens, near Trumpeter Lakes.

they dry; the continual cycle of expanding and contracting plucks tiny pieces of rock, further contributing to rock weathering.

Lichens often grow with mosses, tiny plants that sometimes are confused with them. Together they build up a soil layer in their little domain on the rock. Eventually, enough soil accumulates that seeds can sprout. Some of those seeds grow into trees standing on a bare rock.

In these ways, lichens and mosses help speed the process of converting these large boulders on soil surfaces into the very soil of the valley. A recent study estimated that some lava flows weather 10 to 100 times faster when lichens are growing on them. Be sure to stop at one of the pulloffs to see how many lichens you can find.

Welcome to the Bison Ranch

The Lamar Ranger Station, about 12 miles east of Tower Junction, is the site of an old bison ranch. In the early 1900s it was feared that the bison was becoming extinct; by 1898 fewer than 50 were known to survive. Park officials brought in bison from plains herds in Montana and Texas, and interbred them with the subspecies of plains bison remaining in Yellowstone Park. The resulting herds were raised here much as cattle are on ranches today: released to wander the high meadows in summer, and rounded up for wintering, feeding, and culling at the Lamar Bison Ranch.

By the 1950s the bison were doing well enough to be weaned from ranch life and returned to the wild, a decision that was in keeping with the mission of a national park to maintain plants and animals in a natural state. Today all the bison in the park are descended from this blended Lamar Valley herd, and many of these animals winter in the Lamar Valley. Bison closer to Mammoth sometimes wander out of the park at Gardiner, Montana, creating great controversy in neighboring towns and ranches.

Predators and Prey

In addition to the bison, the Yellowstone and Lamar river valleys host the famous Northern Yellowstone elk herd. Mule deer also live here, and bighorn sheep are fairly common in the high back country in summer. With such abundant herbivore populations in this area, it's understandable that this is also where the greatest populations of predatory animals live. Mountain lions or cougars, coyotes, black and grizzly bears, and smaller predators like the wolverine and the pine marten, are all important parts of the picture.

There has long been scientific debate on the exact nature of the predator-prey relationship. A long-held idea holds that the number of predators controls the size of the prey populations, but much research suggests that the relationship may be far more complex. In some cases prey population numbers depend more on other factors such as food availability or adequate winter range. In this scenario, even though predators do not actually control the numbers of prey animals, they can play a vital role in keeping the prey population healthier and more alert.

Predators also influence where prey animals go and how they behave. In many situations, the tables are turned: the amount of available prey in sufficiently weak or vulnerable condition to be caught, dead or alive, sometimes determines how many predators can survive. Clearly, the predator-prey relationship is complex and interdependent, an integral aspect of the ecosystem.

Lions and Coyotes and Bears, Oh My. . . .

Cougars are scarce within the park, having never recovered fully from heavy persecution in the past. Reports of cougar sightings from May through October are scattered throughout the park, but winter reports are generally along this portion of the Lamar River and a few other places. Most observations, tracks, or other signs of cougars have been from the Douglas fir forests, canyons, and rugged terrain at lower elevations along the Gardner, Yellowstone, and Lamar rivers.

Whether all the cougars reported actually live within the park or have home ranges that extend beyond park boundaries, is still unknown. The cougar is designated a game animal in the surrounding states, and numbers killed in the Yellowstone River drainage north of the park have increased in the past 15 years. Biologists think this population is the one most likely to recolonize Yellowstone Park, in part because it's the largest nearby cougar population and in part because the Yellowstone River drainage is the only major corridor for them to enter the park in winter. Young cougars dispersing away from their parents' territories will probably establish new territories within the park. These big cats are thought to feed mainly on mule deer, but they also eat smaller animals. Years ago, cougars may have eaten more elk than they now do.

Coyotes and bears catch small animals, like ground squirrels and pocket gophers; while with larger mammals, like deer and elk, they tend more to be scavengers. In spring they might make easy kills, but coyotes and especially grizzlies depend heavily on corpses uncovered by melting snows for an abundance of meat from early May until mid-June. Grizzlies also eat spawning trout in spring.

The Big Bad Wolf?

If and when wolves are reintroduced to Yellowstone Park, the Lamar Valley will probably be one of their prime habitats. Wolves were native to this region, as to much of North America, but they were systematically exterminated, even within park boundaries, during the early years of predator control. The last live wolf was seen around 1927, though unconfirmed reports from around the region have been trickling in over the past few years. Their restoration to Yellowstone Park, though controversial, would complete the cast of predatory characters of earlier times.

One concern about wolf reintroduction is the prospect of their wandering out of the park to prey on livestock; wildlife will generally cross the artificial boundaries drawn within the ecosystem. Part of the negotiations between wildlife agencies and local ranchers focuses on some kind of compensation for livestock damage from wandering wolves. The boundary dilemma also affects bison, elk, and other wildlife whose natural ranges do not correspond to political jurisdictions. Nearly all national parks and protected areas throughout the world share that problem. It is important to consider an entire ecosystem when managing wide-ranging wildlife.

Predators on the Wing

Raptors are predatory birds, commonly visible along this route and elsewhere, especially in open areas with good visibility for hunting. Small kestrels, sparrow hawks, are often seen on wires and fenceposts, scouting for small rodents; prairie falcons and golden eagles soar or dive into the sagebrush and grassy hillsides after small prey. Ospreys and bald eagles soar along the rivers and lakes in search of fish.

Soda Butte: Going Up

An old, inactive thermal feature, Soda Butte, is about four miles east of the Lamar Ranger Station. From this point on up to Cooke City the road follows Soda Butte Creek, a tributary of the Lamar River. The creek bottom is fairly wide, underlain by sedimentary rock and soils. Grasses, sedges, and sagebrush are the dominant plants in the valley, intermixed with rabbit-brush and many colorful spring wildflowers. Birds such as sage thrashers and sage grouse use this habitat, along with small mammals like pocket gophers and deer mice.

About 20 miles from Tower Junction, Pebble Creek Campground marks the junction of Pebble Creek coming in from the northeast and Soda Butte Creek. At this point, you climb from an elevation of 6,264 feet to 7,351 feet at the Northeast Entrance and Cooke City. You are now entering the Absaroka Mountains, an impressive chain that reaches from Livingston, Montana, to Dubois, Wyoming, about 170 miles. The Absaroka Mountains (pronounced ab-sorka or ab-sorkee, a Crow word for black bird) are primarily volcanic, with spectacular peaks and wilderness areas.

Soda Butte Creek flows through Ice Box Canyon, so called because ice can last all year round on the moist shaded rocks. The road is no longer in a broad valley but in a mountain canyon with spruce-subalpine fir forests on both sides.

The spectacular peaks—Baronnette at 10,404 feet on the west and Abiathar at 10,928 feet on the east—are primarily Absaroka volcanic rock. Note that the trees grow up on the mountain sides until the slopes become too steep to hold soil. This kind of edaphic timberline, defined by soil conditions, differs from timberlines like the ones on the Beartooth Plateau (map 16: page 156) or the Grand Tetons (map 26: page 202); there, a combination of elevation, wind, temperature, and soil conditions deter-mine where trees can and cannot grow.

Many mountains also have avalanche chutes, bare stripes between trees where snow slides regularly crash down. Avalanches are common in high mountain region and pose an increasing hazard as people try to develop the mountains for recreation and industry. These massive snow slides tend to run in miniature valleys and gulches, rather than on ridges. They are especially likely where the slope steepens, and when wind, melting snow, or sudden large accumulations create strong layering within the snow.

As one climbs, the temperature drops about 3.5 degrees for each 1,000 feet of increase in elevation. While daytime temperatures can be quite warm, you can see that this is overall a colder, wetter climate than lower in the park and in the adjacent valleys in Wyoming and Montana.

From roughly early June through October you can proceed east from Cooke City across the magnificent Beartooth Highway, US 212, to Red Lodge, Montana (map 15: page 142). Or, about 12 miles ahead you can turn south on Wyoming 296 and travel along the Clarks Fork of the Yellowstone River to Cody, Wyoming (map 17: page 160).

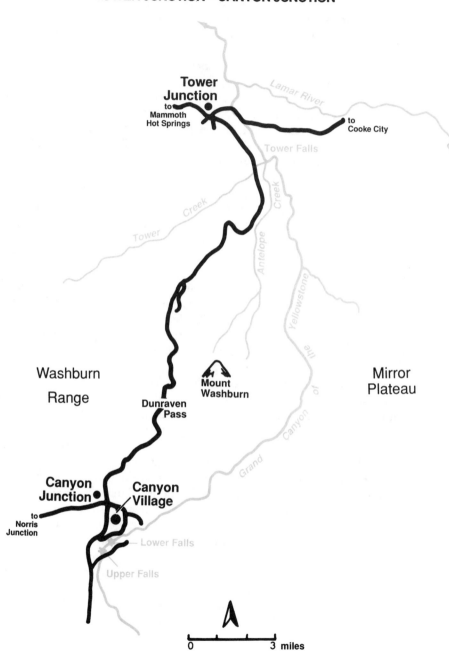

MAP 9
TOWER JUNCTION—CANYON JUNCTION

Tower Junction
to Mammoth Hot Springs

Lamar River

to Cooke City

Tower Falls

Tower Creek

Antelope Creek

Yellowstone

Mount Washburn

Washburn Range

Dunraven Pass

Mirror Plateau

Canyon of

Grand

Canyon Junction

Canyon Village

to Norris Junction

Lower Falls

Upper Falls

0   3 miles

Tower Junction—Canyon Junction
19 miles/31 km.

The road from Tower Junction and Roosevelt Lodge follows the Yellowstone River through Douglas fir stands. Fingers of fires licked around here during 1988, demolishing some stands and skipping others. Moose, deer, and elk can sometimes be spotted among the trees.

Tower Falls, about a mile from Tower Junction, is where Tower Creek falls from more resistant volcanic rock to the softer rock along the Yellowstone River. The road above Tower Falls parallels Antelope Creek, with beautiful stands of wildlflowers in the spring. Many vistas of broad meadows and forested hills open up as the road climbs out of the Douglas fir.

Mt. Washburn

The road climbs the north and west flanks of Mount Washburn, an ancient volcano and one of the sources of volcanic flows that buried trees to make the petrified forests on Specimen Ridge. Pull-offs along this stretch provide excellent opportunities to watch for grizzly bears in the meadows, primarily in early morning and evening. Binoculars are usually necessary to pick out the dark, bulky shapes that can look deceptively like large rocks; in fact, the bears are perhaps patiently grazing, or digging around for plant roots, gopher caches of roots and rhizomes, or ant colonies.

Toward the top of Mt. Washburn, about seven miles south of Tower Falls, Chittenden Road on the east side leads to a parking lot. From there, you can walk to the top of the 10,243 foot peak, above timberline. The fire lookout at the summit gives a magnificent view. You can also reach the summit from the picnic area at Dunraven Pass; from there the path, an old motoring road, is a more gradual three-mile walk. The vegetation at the summit has many characteristics of alpine flora: flowering plants, for example, are low, hugging the ground out of the wind. Moss and lichen cover here includes species that are characteristic of alpine or arctic tundra. For more examples of alpine vegetation, see the Beartooth Plateau, (map 15: page 142).

On either hike, or along the road along Dunraven Pass as you drive over Mt. Washburn, be on the lookout in summer for bighorn sheep; this is one of the few places you are likely to encounter sheep on their summer range.

101

Good grizzly habitat: broad meadows and forest patches on the flanks of Mount Washburn.

A Tangled Tale: Seeds and Squirrels, Bears and Birds. . . and More

Some of the burned trees in this area were lodgepole pine, but many were whitebark pine, which has a complex and interesting relationship with the Clark's nutcracker, the red squirrel, and the grizzly bear.

Whitebark pine, like other pines, prefers to germinate and grow in sunny spots. The Clark's nutcracker in late summer picks the pea-sized seeds out of the soft whitebark cones, then stores the seeds in caches in sunny mountain meadows. Nutcrackers have been seen marking their caches with pebbles and sticks, but still they often forget where they stored the seeds, returning to only about half of the sites. Many of the seeds finally germinate and contribute to the growth of the whitebark pine forest.

This diligent work on the part of the nutcracker is important for the pines, since their seeds don't have wings; they need animals to help disperse them away from the home tree. Clark's nutcrackers oblige by taking some 32,000 whitebark pine seeds per bird per year when the cones are prolific; even after eating half of these, the birds leave thousands of seeds neatly planted with a chance to grow.

Red squirrels also feed efficiently on the seeds of the whitebark cones, and are actually responsible for taking most of the whitebark pine seeds in a forest. They take the whole cone, and stash their supply in huge piles or middens—as many as 3,000 cones per stash—farther inside the forest. This doesn't contribute as much to the spread of the whitebark pine, since the seeds are in shady spots and in deep piles, poor conditions for germination and growth. But it does provide a convenient central food supply of these large, high-fat seeds, not only for the squirrel, but also for grizzly bears.

Grizzly bears use meadow-forest places like those found up here, especially when they can find and feed on the seeds in squirrel and nutcracker caches. In fact, these seeds provide a prime fall food for grizzly and black bears when cone crops are large, about every five to seven years. Some biologists have suggested that nearly half of a typical grizzly bear's fat supply averaged over its lifetime comes from whitebark pine seeds, most of which are snatched from the squirrel's hard-earned stash. The bears thus compete with the squirrels for their food supply—and sometimes the bears even eat the proverbial goose that laid the golden egg—the squirrel that stashed the seeds.

Other characters play this rather complex game, too. Once Clark's nutcrackers have begun to break open cone scales, seeds become available to other birds and small rodents: Steller's jays, ravens, pine grosbeaks, chickadees, golden-mantled ground squirrels, and chipmunks all take advantage of the services of the nutcracker. Many of them drop seeds,

The whitebark pine, squirrel, Clark's nutcracker, grizzly bear connection.

103

which can germinate far from the original source. The pine marten, a relative of the weasel, takes advantage of the squirrel middens, too, not so much to eat the seeds as to find shelter from winter weather. Occasionally the marten, like the bear, will also dine on both seeds and squirrels.

The tangled web woven around the whitebark pine seed is just one example of the thousands of intricate relationships that weave through any ecosystem. As you drive around the Greater Yellowstone region, think about how the threads you can see might be connected to other less visible strands.

Fire in the Whitebark Pine Community

The North Fork Fire of 1988 swept through the whitebark pine stands on Mt. Washburn. Mild to moderate fire is considered essential in whitebark pine communities. When trees get old and fall, they provide ground-level fuel for mild fires to sweep through; the resulting open areas provide the sunny conditions needed by the pine seedlings to grow well. If fire doesn't intervene, other more shade-tolerant seedlings, like subalpine fir, may have the advantage and take over the community. On the other hand, intense fires like those that hit some areas here can, in fact, lead to the succession of other species in certain areas, if there are too few whitebark pines close by to provide enough new seeds.

Backcountry

Midway between Tower Junction and Canyon Junction, Dunraven Pass takes you across the highest point on this road, 8,859 feet. Snow accumulates to great depths in winter. The road usually opens in June.

Burned whitebark pine along the road on Mount Washburn spells decreased food source for birds, squirrels, and grizzly bears.

View east from Dunraven Pass, looking past thermal areas along the Yellowstone River to remote backcountry.

Many views along the road between the pass and Canyon were opened by the fires of 1988, which removed dense stands of pines. If you look carefully to the east, you can see a dark gorge with occasional glimpses of yellow in the forest; this is a generally inaccessible part of the Grand Canyon of the Yellowstone River. You are gazing toward the Mirror Plateau, between the Yellowstone and Lamar rivers, and the Absaroka Mountains farther east.

The park map shows no roads to the east and southeast for at least 30 miles. This is an example of backcountry—by definition at least 250 yards from pavement and at least a half mile from park facilities. Backcountry here can be dangerous, because it is part of the range of the grizzlies that roam the Washburn area, apparently extending their range toward the southeast. Extensive backcountry like this, with no roads and little human intrusion, is critical to the survival of grizzlies and other large mammals, which must cover vast amounts of territory in a season to find sufficient food and shelter.

Into Canyon

The road drops fairly abruptly to Canyon Village (7,744 ft.) through lodgepole pine forest. A visitor center at Canyon Village offers excellent exhibits explaining the Upper and Lower Falls of the Yellowstone. The many animal and bird displays introduce the native wildlife.

At Canyon Junction, turn east into Canyon Village and the road to the north rim of the canyon, and then south toward Fishing Bridge and Lake Village (map 10: page 106); or go west toward Norris (map 5: page 70) or you can also head south, skipping the canyon loop.

105

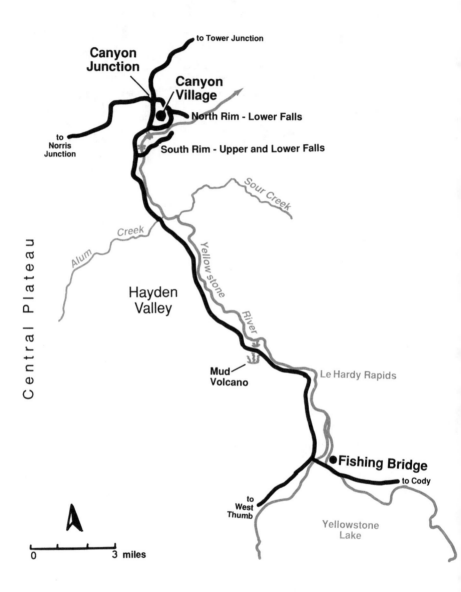

MAP 10
CANYON JUNCTION—FISHING BRIDGE/LAKE

to Tower Junction

Canyon
Junction

Canyon
Village

North Rim - Lower Falls

to
Norris
Junction

South Rim - Upper and Lower Falls

Sour Creek

Creek

Alum

Yellowstone

Hayden
Valley

River

Mud
Volcano

Le Hardy Rapids

Central Plateau

Fishing Bridge

to Cody

to
West
Thumb

Yellowstone
Lake

0   3 miles

Canyon Junction—Fishing Bridge/Lake
16 miles/26 km.

This route takes you through the serene Hayden Valley of the Yellowstone River, with its rolling hills, sagebrush meadows, marshes and ponds. The variety of habitat types and open vistas make this one of the best areas to observe birds and large mammals, especially during early spring and late fall and during the early morning and evening hours.

First, the Canyon

At Canyon Junction, head toward Canyon Village and follow the signs for the north rim loop road. Turnoffs from the first mile or two of this road take you to the rim of the magnificent Lower Falls of the Yellowstone River. The yellow color of the rock on the canyon walls is that of the volcanic rocks; the black color is weathered rock or lichens growing on the rocks.

These overlooks impressively convey the delicateness of this system: the soil obviously is very thin and the trees—mostly lodgepole, subalpine fir, and whitebark pines—cling precariously. The request that you stay on the paths is not made lightly.

After rejoining the main road, you will see a turnoff to Upper Falls, a delightful stop where a short walk brings you to the brink of the falls. Look in the rushing waters for the little gray dipper, a bouncy bird that can walk under water. A half-mile farther south, a road takes you across the Yellowstone to the south rim of the canyon and more breathtaking views of both Upper and Lower falls.

107

Hayden Valley, along the Yellowstone River, ideal wildlife habitat.

Then the Valley

At about 4.5 miles from Canyon Junction you drop down to the Hayden Valley, a broad, treeless expanse. It was a big glacial lake until the Yellowstone River drained it. The silty base of the river holds water, which explains the marshes—extremely productive and fertile places for all sorts of wildlife.

Wildlife Watch

Stop at various pull-outs in the Hayden Valley to watch the wildlife. Early in the spring while the snow is melting, the air rings with the peeping of Western chorus frogs, one of only three kinds of frog in this generally cold and dry ecosystem. On various parts of the river you can see gulls, trumpeter swans, Canada geese, snow geese, ospreys, pelicans, great blue herons, bald eagles, northern harriers, and several species of ducks including mallards, goldeneyes, and mergansers.

The boundary between meadow and forest on the other side of the river is a great place to see grizzlies wandering about in the sagebrush during early morning and evening, scavenging carcasses or searching for edible ant mounds or plants. Coyotes also hunt along here, and bison graze. At Buffalo Ford, the pull-out closest to the Mud Volcano, the river is shallow enough for bison to cross when they decide the grass is greener on the other side.

Buffalo Ford on the Yellowstone River.

West of the Hayden Valley the landscape rises to the Central Plateau, which separates this valley from the Firehole River Valley. During the summer, bison and elk from both valleys sometimes mingle on the plateau, but in winter the snows isolate the populations on either side of the ridge.

What's That Smell?

Mud Volcano and Sulphur Caldron, about ten miles north of Lake Junction, have relatively little water and are so full of sulfur, acids, and clay particles that they can be detected some distance away by their odor and sound. This rather hostile thermal area lacks the lovely colors of some of the hot ponds, such as those at Norris and Upper Geyser basins, because the acid and sulfur inhibit the growth of the most colorful algae. The water here contains five times more sulfur than at Norris. When thermal activity diminishes, which it does occasionally as underground water systems shift gears, tough grasses return to colonize the less active spots.

A Popular Fishing Stretch

Between the Mud Volcanoes and Lake Junction, catch-and-release fishing is allowed for native cutthroat trout after spawning season is over. The fish spend most of the time in Yellowstone Lake, but move into the river to spawn. Trout are visible at LeHardy Rapids during spring spawning migrations.

Forest Succession

Pines in the vicinity of Yellowstone Lake are larger and older than in many other parts of the park; they apparently have burned less often than in other places. The overstory, or largest trees, is lodgepole pine, and coming in underneath in sunnier spots are other lodgepoles, or spruce and subalpine fir in shadier spots. The pine-spruce-fir series illustrates forest succession: the pines, which need sun, grew and shaded the soil beneath them; the spruce and subalpine fir need less sun and grow under the pines. If no fires burn this forest, spruce and fir might keep succeeding themselves indefinitely. A severe fire would reset the successional clock back to sun and lodgepole pine.

At Fishing Bridge Junction, the main loop road continues south to Lake Village and around Yellowstone Lake to West Thumb (map 12: page 120). Take the east branch of the road for Fishing Bridge, the East Entrance of the park, and Cody, Wyoming (map 11: page 112).

U.S. 14-10-16
Fishing Bridge—Cody
80 miles/128 km.

This route skirts the north shore of Yellowstone Lake, taking you along the edge of productive grizzly country, up over the Sylvan Pass high in the Absaroka Range, and down the eastern edge of the Yellowstone Plateau to the grasslands of Cody, Wyoming.

A New American Spectator Sport: Fish-watching

Almost immediately, the road crosses the outlet of Yellowstone Lake. This is the Yellowstone River, which originated as a mountain stream high in the Teton Wilderness to the southeast, and emerges here as a full grown river. This at one time was a prime fishing spot, especially when the cutthroat trout were spawning. But in 1973 the bridge was closed to fishing to protect spawning runs from being overfished. It has now become a popular spot for fish-watching, particularly during the spring spawning season of May and June, when river trout are moving upstream and lake trout are moving downstream to deposit millions of eggs in the gravel near the bridge. Resident fish that don't migrate can be observed here at other times of the year, too.

Seriously, Though. . . .

The Fishing Bridge Campground is one of the most likely spots in the park to meet a grizzly; that's why only hard-sided camping units are allowed. Cutthroat trout are one of the bear's most nutritious spring and summer diet items, very high in protein and more digestible than many other foods. With all the fish in the lakes and streams here, and the convergence of so many fish at the same time at the Fishing Bridge spawning area, this is a busy spot for bears. For the bears, though, this is not sport but survival.

Bears use spawning streams not only for fish, but also for good grazing in the riparian or riverside habitat. Some 90 percent of a grizzly bear's diet is plants, and the bears eat the lush vegetation that grows along some of the streams and rivers even if the fishing isn't great.

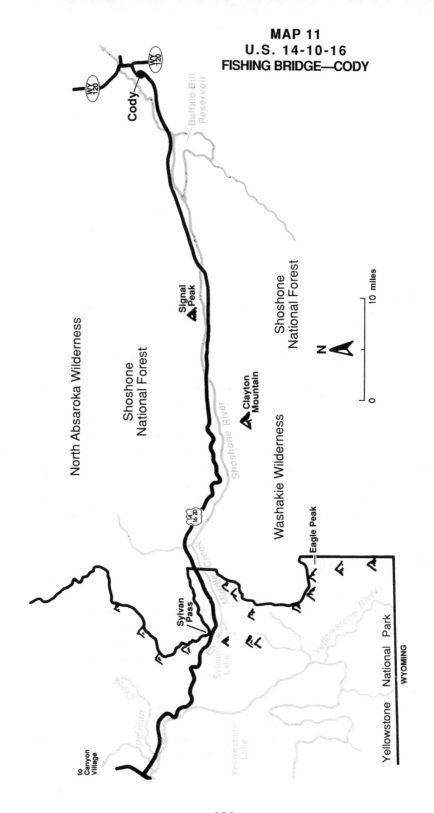

MAP 11
U.S. 14-10-16
FISHING BRIDGE—CODY

WY 120

Cody

Buffalo Bill Reservoir

North Absaroka Wilderness

Shoshone National Forest

Signal Peak

Shoshone National Forest

Clayton Mountain

Shoshone River

Washakie Wilderness

N

10 miles

0

14 to 20

Middle Creek

Eagle Peak

Yellowstone River

Sylvan Pass

Sylvan Lake

Pelican Creek

Yellowstone Lake

Yellowstone National Park

WYOMING

to Canyon Village

Grizzly bears are using Yellowstone's streams and rivers much more than they did back in the days when they were artificially fed at human garbage dumps. Since the dumps closed in 1974-75, bears have begun to relearn traditional feeding patterns, roaming huge tracts of land, sometimes 70 to 100 square miles in a single season, searching for vegetation and safety. In spring they heavily use some of these streams for fish. Bears now use some 93 percent of the Yellowstone Lake tributaries that support cutthroat trout. This is primarily because of the high density of fish during spawning, but also because of physical characteristics of the streams and streamside vegetation that make them stable and secure habitats.

Unfortunately for the bears, the Fishing Bridge-Lake area is also a prime human hangout, creating a situation ripe for conflicts, which the bears rarely win. To have wild bears fishing from trout streams rather than scavenging in human garbage dumps was just what managers hoped to achieve when the dumps were closed, but it has led to unanticipated dilemmas and controversy. In spring the entire area is heavily posted for people to avoid the streams and woods, but different management techniques are being discussed to make this critical habitat more secure for bears.

About a mile east of Fishing Bridge the road crosses Pelican Creek, a major stream flowing into Yellowstone Lake from the northeast. White Lakes, with cutthroat trout, and Wapiti Lake, with no fish, are accessible to the north from trails that begin near Pelican Creek. The riparian areas of the Pelican Valley just north of the road are used by some 14 to 20 grizzlies each summer, for fishing, feeding on carcasses of animals that didn't make it through the winter, and preying on young elk and bison during the month-long calving season in May.

Tilt! The Lake is Tipping!

About three and a half miles east of Fishing Bridge, Indian Pond fills a little volcanic crater between the road and Yellowstone Lake. The cutthroat trout in Indian Pond have no good spawning streams since the pond is mostly spring fed. Biologists think that the population is maintained by mixing of water with Yellowstone Lake during periods of especially high water.

The center of the Yellowstone Caldera seems to be rising about half an inch a year, as it has done during several previous episodes, tilting the lake slightly toward the southwest. The results of episodic lifting of the caldera can be seen in several places along the edge of Yellowstone Lake where layers of mud deposited under the water are now high and dry, forming massive terraces.

113

Indian Pond along the north shore of Yellowstone Lake.

Along the North Shore

This drive along the north edge of the lake follows grass and sagebrush, soggy meadows with sedges, lodgepole pine forests, and spruce and Douglas fir as the road ascends above lake level. There are also a few thermal features. This varied terrestrial landscape and its aquatic component of cutthroat trout provide habitat and food for a wide variety of birds and mammals: gulls, pelicans, ducks, geese, ospreys, eagles, bison, elk, moose, black and grizzly bears, and many others.

About seven miles east of Fishing Bridge, the road crosses a tributary stream coming down from Turbid Lake to the northeast. Turbid Lake, which has no fish, is accessible by trail; hot springs around its edges and at its bottom keep the water churned up and murky.

Climbing the Caldera Wall

In another mile, the road up to Lake Butte climbs the rim of the caldera or sunken pit created in the eruption about 600,000 years ago. From the height of 8,348 feet, you can see for miles across the northern part of Yellowstone Lake; on a clear day you can see the jagged peaks of the Grand Tetons over 50 miles away as the crow flies, and other peaks, bays, and landmarks. This is a mixed forest — lodgepole pine, whitebark pine, Douglas fir, spruce, and subalpine fir, with a comparatively lush undergrowth.

114

Sylvan Pass

The main road climbs from lake level at 7,744 feet, and goes past two lakes: Sylvan, about 13 miles from Fishing Bridge, and Eleanor, a few miles farther along the road. Both lakes have cutthroat trout, with catch-and-release fishing.

The highest point of this road is Sylvan Pass, 8,530 feet. "Sylvan" means "of or pertaining to woods," but the pass itself is not very sylvan—it's composed of a variety of volcanic rocks, none of which look very stable. The minimal amount of moss or lichen growth on the rock gives a clue that it tends to shift continually downhill.

Many spectacular avalanche tracks scar the mountains on both sides of the road. Avalanches tend to run in little gullies or chutes, where no trees or shrubs can grow. Vegetation in avalanche tracks is usually fast-growing, low-lying grasses and forbs; so the avalanches here probably run close to ground level. You can tell where avalanches do not run by the presence of trees; notice that this is most commonly on the convex or bulging slopes and ridges.

Avalanche track or chute, typically in a little gully between trees on more concave slopes.

Leaving the Plateau

From Sylvan Pass the road follows the canyon of Middle Creek down a bit to the East Entrance of Yellowstone Park, at 6,951 feet. Beyond the park, you begin to travel through Shoshone National Forest, the nation's first, created by President Benjamin Harrison in 1891.

The road leaving the Yellowstone Plateau here is like the others descending from the plateau: a drop from forested hills with spruce and subalpine fir trees, through predominantly Douglas fir forests, then to juniper and the grasslands.

This is a good road on which to watch the interplay between rock and soil types, exposure and slope, and vegetation. Where resistant volcanic gravels cap underlying sediments, the sides of the cliffs are steep and support only hardy trees that cling somewhat precariously. Where the sediments were softer, the river has cut a wider, flatter valley; meadows and shrub stands along the river can develop. Cottonwoods and aspens are in the lower, wetter places along the Shoshone River.

Differences between north and south slopes, and east and west slopes, are also apparent. Even though winds are westerly and bring in precipitation from the west, west and south slopes get much more warm afternoon

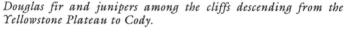

Douglas fir and junipers among the cliffs descending from the Yellowstone Plateau to Cody.

116

Cottonwoods along the Shoshone River, indicating the presence of ground water.

sun, so are drier. East and north slopes are more shaded, lose snow later in the spring, get less warm afternoon sun, and support trees at a much lower elevation than south and west slopes.

Reservoirs and Lakes

Buffalo Bill Reservoir is about seven miles west of Cody, Wyoming. You have seen many lakes in the Greater Yellowstone Ecosystem. What makes a lake different from a reservoir?

Lakes are natural — their basins were scooped out by glaciers, like on the Beartooth Plateau (map 15: page 142) or built by a natural dam such as a landslide, like Quake Lake near West Yellowstone (map 18: page 170), or made when a volcano blew up and left a crater, like Yellowstone Lake (map 12: page 120). Other kinds of lakes are formed by various activities of rivers, wind, and earth movements, and even by biological forces like beavers.

The sources of water to a lake are inlet streams or groundwater, or both; the longest-lived lakes are generally below the water table, so groundwater continually feeds them. Shallow lakes without good groundwater usually fill in with time as the tributaries bring in silt; they may eventually become bogs, then just wet low places. This is a type of ecological succession.

Reservoirs, on the other hand, are made by humans building dams. This process is similar to that of beavers building dams, and humans have been doing so for thousands of years, creating habitat for fish, waterfowl, and other wildlife as they generate power for themselves. In recent times, this

Sagebrush grassland characteristic of rain-shadow locations around Cody and in other valleys between mountains.

activity has accelerated tremendously in scale and scope, as we build major dams on nearly every available major river for flood control and power generation.

Reservoirs tend to silt up with time and become warmer and shallower over the years. This makes them relatively short-lived compared to large, deep natural lakes. Lake-type communities of fish and other organisms may develop in and around a reservoir, especially with the help of stocking programs, but they often don't get the chance to evolve stable and complex systems. The massive alterations of large drainage systems that accompany the creation of a reservoir can change the topography and regional climate in ways that are not fully understood.

Lakes and reservoirs that formed on loose soil with plant growth have a ready source of soluble minerals that makes the water fertile or eutrophic. Groundwater and inlet streams are also a source of minerals. A typical aquatic food chain in a eutrophic lake or reservoir has attached or floating algae at the base. Algae use the inorganic minerals in the water and their own photosynthesis to make carbohydrates, which are eaten by small floating or swimming invertebrates such as protozoans or freshwater shrimp. Small fish eat these, larger fish eat them, and also thrive on the oxygen produced by the algae and plants in shallow water.

Lakes and reservoirs that were formed on harder, barren rock have fewer dissolved minerals in the water, so less algal growth and simpler food chains; these less productive lakes are called oligotrophic and generally don't have fish. Some lakes in the ecosystem, especially at high altitudes, have no native fish simply because fish couldn't get there.

Cody, Wyoming

Cody, Wyoming, is at an elevation of 4,990 feet, and has an annual precipitation of about 9.5 inches. This is semi-desert country, as you can tell by the native short grasses, sagebrush, and cactus.

At Cody, you may head north along Wyoming 120; in about 20 miles you may veer northwest on Wyoming 296, the Chief Joseph Scenic Highway, to Cooke City and northern parts of the ecosystem (map 17: page 160); or continue on 120 to Red Lodge and Billings (map 16: page 156).

MAP 12
FISHING BRIDGE—LAKE/WEST THUMB

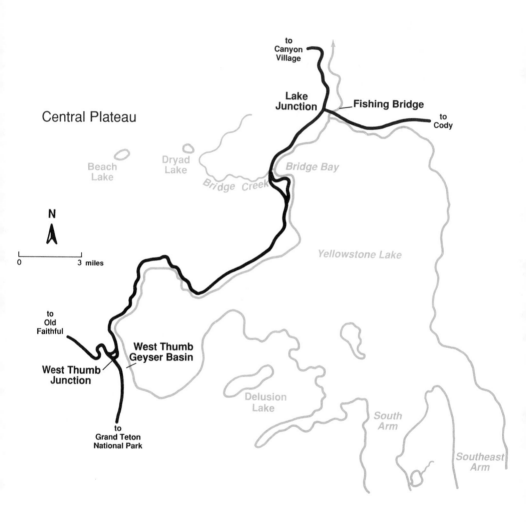

to
Canyon
Village

Lake
Junction

Fishing Bridge

to
Cody

Central Plateau

Beach
Lake

Dryad
Lake

Bridge Bay

Bridge Creek

N

0   3 miles

Yellowstone Lake

to
Old
Faithful

West Thumb
Geyser Basin

West Thumb
Junction

Delusion
Lake

South
Arm

to
Grand Teton
National Park

Southeast
Arm

Fishing Bridge/Lake—West Thumb
21 miles/34 km.

This part of the Grand Loop Road, from Fishing Bridge to Lake and south to West Thumb and Grant Village, closely follows the northwest shore of Yellowstone Lake. The elevation stays fairly stable at about 7,740 feet. On this route we'll examine the mixed conifer forest along the road, see how the lake was formed and is changing, and, mostly, talk trout.

Following the Forest

The road is quite flat; it follows the lake shore inside the caldera. Tree types vary from quite pure lodgepole pine stands to mixed lodgepole pine-spruce-subalpine fir, with younger spruce and fir coming in under the pine.

A roadside stop about eight miles south of Lake Village explains some of this phenomenon, which is often referred to as succession. In this unburned part of the park, lodgepole pine has been growing for probably about 200 years. Lodgepole, like most pines, grows best in the sun, as you can see along the roadsides throughout this region; spruce and fir seedlings grow best in shade, so they usually come in under the pines.

The road is concealed among the trees lining the north shore of Yellowstone Lake. Forests are lodgepole pine, spruce, and subalpine fir.

Young lodgepole pine coming up in a clearing among old lodgepole pine. In this case, lodgepole forest is succeeding itself and is probably the climax type.

Barring disturbances such as fire, wind, or major thermal activity, in about another 200 years the pines will be gone, dead of old age, or beetles, or fungus, or other causes; the largest, oldest trees will be the spruce and fir. Theoretically, since spruce and fir seedlings grow best in shade, they should be able to succeed their parents as the dominant species and keep succeeding themselves. The pine here is called the successional or seral species, the spruce and fir the climax species.

In many other parts of the ecosystem, the lodgepole pine does something unusual: it acts as a climax species, possibly because the volcanic soils in certain places are too poor in nutrients to sustain healthy fir and spruce trees. If you see stands of lodgepole pine that look old but don't have spruce or fir trees coming up in the understory, the lodgepole probably is the climax species for that area.

Some of the trees sport a black hairy growth coming down from the branches; this is a type of lichen of the genus *Bryoria* also known as "old man's beard." Lichens are not parasitic: they have photosynthetic algae within them, so they can make their own food. They do need some sun, and frequently colonize on branches that have lost most of their leaves. Lichens seem to have no obvious negative effect on trees, unless they shade leaves that need sun; but they do add to the flammability of forests since they tend to be very dry. More than 200 species of lichens have been identified from the park and surrounding area.

Yellowstone Lake: From Bang to Basin

The most outstanding feature of this part of the road is, of course, Yellowstone Lake, one of the world's largest lakes higher than 7,000 feet. Its average depth is about 139 feet, but in spots it is 320 feet deep. The lake bottom is made up of rubble and boulders, black obsidian sand, and fine silt and clay mixed with organic matter. Average summer water temperature is 55 degrees, cold enough to cause rapid hypothermia if your boat capsizes.

The lake occupies a basin formed by three awesome explosions of a huge flattish volcano, a resurgent caldera, two million to 600,000 years ago. Pressure from rising hot, molten rock pushed up on the ground above it until the surface could no longer resist, and violent eruptions blew the top off. The volume of lava erupted was many times what Mt. St. Helens produced in 1980.

As the pale rhyolite ash spread all over the countryside, the surface collapsed into the emptying magma chamber below, opening a large basin, the Yellowstone Caldera. The outermost periphery of this basin is marked in orange on the park map given to you at an entrance.

The center of Yellowstone Lake sits smack on the rim of the caldera. This is still an active volcanic area, and part of the caldera floor is now rising about one inch per year, tipping the lake and changing the shoreline. Interpretations of the significance of this vary, but the effect is that trees at the southern end of the lake are now being flooded, while the northern shoreline has risen high and dry.

Yellowstone Lake is fed by more than 124 tributary streams that flow in from all directions. The road crosses several smaller tributaries on this west side of the lake. The major tributaries feed in from the south — the young Yellowstone River from the southeast, and Chipmunk and Grouse creeks, which are the first drainage streams on the east side of the Continental Divide. These streams are in true backcountry, roadless areas with access only by foot or canoe.

These tributary streams constitute part of the lake's watershed. They carry not only water, but also nutrients to the lake, including nutrients released into the soil by fire. Yellowstone Lake and its watershed, with its poor volcanic soils, receives smaller amounts of nutrients than many other lakes.

Lake Residents

Nearly 20 species of plants grow in the lake, including a duckweed and a pondweed. Plants grow in shallow protected areas, three to 30 feet deep, where sunlight penetrates. In and among the plants are small shrimp-like crustaceans, aquatic insects, worms, and tiny clams.

Suspended in the open waters of the lake are tiny plants and animals that form the base of the food chain: different types of algae and photosynthetic bacteria collectively called phytoplankton, and the various categories of small animals collectively called zooplankton, which feed on the phytoplankton.

The major native game fish in Yellowstone Lake waters is the Yellowstone cutthroat trout, a sub-species of cutthroat trout. Cutthroat trout are so-called because they have two red lines beneath their jaw.

The Yellowstone cutthroat trout was native to the upper reaches of the Snake River, which extends into the southern portion of Yellowstone Park. It entered Yellowstone Lake thousands of years ago by crossing from Pacific Creek, a tributary of the Snake River, into Atlantic Creek, a small stream which flows into Yellowstone Lake. The connection between these two creeks still exists, along the Continental Divide south of the lake. Yellowstone cutthroat migrate out of lakes into tributary streams to spawn in the spring and early summer. Smaller streams can be crowded with fish at those migration times, providing an important food source for grizzly bears, bald eagles, pelicans, ospreys, and other wildlife.

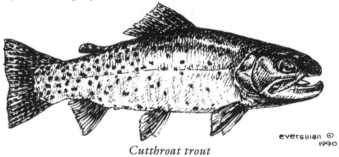

Cutthroat trout

It's a Cutthroat World

The cutthroat trout are vitally important in the food chains of this part of the ecosystem, both as predator and prey. Trout eat freshwater crustaceans and insects, which in turn feed on phytoplankton and zooplankton. The trout also eat other fish, fish eggs, mice, shrews, frogs, and even snakes. The cutthroats themselves provide meals for many carnivores in the lake area, including birds such as eagles, ospreys, pelicans, and mammals such as bears, mink, and otters.

How can so many species feed on these trout without using them all up, or without competing so fiercely that one or more of the predators loses out? The answer perhaps lies in "resource partitioning," where different predators choose different sizes of prey, or different locations to hunt, or different feeding seasons.

In Yellowstone Lake, various fish predators divvy up the food to avoid direct competition. According to park biologists John Varley and Paul Schullery in their book *Freshwater Wilderness*, ospreys take primarily

124

immature cutthroats, while pelicans take adult fish; grizzlies also take adults but tend to stick to those that are spawning in the streams. Humans are allowed to take only fish under 13 inches long; water ouzels or dippers eat only the small-fry; and kingfishers concentrate on fingerlings. In this way the predators only occasionally overlap in their interests, and trout of all sizes and ages have different predators.

Cutthroat Comeback

Fishing regulations were very relaxed until around 1970; fishermen took and often wasted thousands of fish per year, and their discarded bait fish introduced suckers and two species of minnows into the lake. Now there are stringent regulations, including maximum size limits to leave breeding stock, very small creel limits, flies only, no bait, and catch-and-release fishing for cutthroats. Consequently, the populations of cutthroat trout have come back from a few thousand about 15 years ago to many hundreds of thousands in 1989. An average of 50,000 fish were counted in 1989 at Clear Creek alone, on the east side of the lake, where only about 3,500 were counted in 1972. This is good news indeed for the birds and animals that depend on the fish for a large part of their diet.

At West Thumb, turn west to Old Faithful and the west side of the park (map 13: page 126), or go straight south toward Grant Village, Lewis Lake, Jackson Lake, and the Tetons (map 14: page 136).

MAP 13
WEST THUMB—MADISON JUNCTION

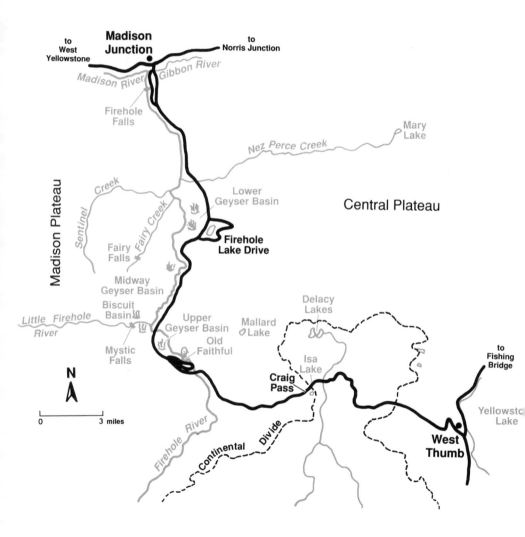

West Thumb—Madison Junction
33 miles/53 km.

Straddling the Divide

The road climbs from West Thumb to the first crossing of the Continental Divide at 8,391 feet; West Thumb is in the Yellowstone or east drainage. At the Continental Divide, you cross into the Pacific drainage. The DeLacy Lakes drain into the DeLacy Creek, which is the low point on this part of the road. As the road climbs again to Craig Pass, another crossing of the Continental Divide at 8,262 feet, you cross back into the east slope drainage. The snowfall at this elevation is probably around 200 inches per year. Snow squalls are common in the early fall and late spring.

Isa Lake with its wonderful water lilies in the early summer straddles the divide. Water from one side of Isa Lake flows from here to Shoshone Lake to Lewis Lake to the Lewis River to the Snake River to the Columbia River to the Pacific Ocean. Water from the other side of Isa Lake flows from here to the Firehole River to the Madison River to the Missouri River to the Mississippi River to the Gulf of Mexico to the Atlantic Ocean. That's the big picture of the Continental Divide.

Isa Lake freezes solidly in the winter so it has no fish; neither do other lakes in this area, DeLacy, Scaup, and Mallard. Trout have been planted in the past, but the lakes have no good inlet streams for trout spawning, so introduced fish populations died out.

After the North Fork Fire

Burned trees along this road and at Old Faithful were part of the 1988 North Fork fire. This fire extended from north of West Yellowstone to this part of the park, affecting most of the northwest corner of the park and some adjacent national forest, about 498,000 acres in all. Most of the trees were lodgepole pine, but in the colder wetter parts along this road many spruce and subalpine firs were also burned.

Where the fires skipped some stands, notice the tall lodgepole pine overstory with young spruce and subalpine fir coming in under them. This is a natural forest succession at this elevation in the northern Rocky

Mountains. The spruce and subalpine fir seeds can germinate and their seedlings can grow in the shade of the older pines. Without fire or windstorms or other natural events creating open sunny areas, the spruce and subalpine fir would replace themselves, making them climax species. The lodgepole pine is here a pioneer or successional species that will eventually be replaced by the climax trees.

Old Faithful: A Gaggle of Geysers

The Upper Geyser Basin, at about 7,365 feet, gives us Old Faithful and many other thermal highlights. The boardwalks up and around this and the other geyser basins take you past springs, geysers, and fumaroles.

Hot springs occur throughout mountainous areas of the world, but in other major geyser locations — Iceland, New Zealand, the U.S.S.R., and isolated spots in Nevada, California, Oregon, and elsewhere — commercial tapping of the thermal systems for power has destroyed the geyser activity. Thermal features depend on the recycling of water from rain and snow through complex underground networks. Until now the use of hot water from this area has been limited, so the features have been protected. But there have been repeated attempts to tap hot water just outside park boundaries, without fully understanding how these areas might connect to Old Faithful and other thermal areas. Recent studies have concluded that at least some water from La Duke Springs north of Gardiner, Montana, is connected to the thermal systems at Mammoth Hot Springs and Norris Geyser Basin; research is continuing on the exact nature and extent of these and other connections.

Fire along the Firehole: Let's Hear It for the 'Weeds'

From Old Faithful, the road continues north along the banks of the Firehole River. The numerous thermal features along this route give dramatic testimony to the accuracy of this famous river's name.

The fires of 1988 provided another good reason for calling this the Firehole River. The massive North Fork Fire picked its way through this region. A most memorable event was the wall of flame that came close to historic Old Faithful Inn, Old Faithful Lodge, and other buildings at the Upper Geyser Basin. In 1988 much of the ground in this area was thoroughly blackened, mostly due to burned needles and above-ground parts of short perennials like pussytoes, heartleaf arnica, lichens, mosses, grasses, and short shrubs like grouse whortleberry and antelope bitter-brush.

Many of the heavily burned sites along here initially looked dead. But in most spots, the blackened soil went down less than one inch, generally closer to half an inch. Below that, the soil was its usual light tan color. As early as the summer of 1989, many hardy green plants were beginning their new life. Lodgepole pine seedlings were already sprouting, reaching a

*One-year-old pine
seedling in 1989.*

height of three to four inches by autumn; grasses resprouted, and brightly colored perennials like lupine, fireweed, heartleaf arnica, glacier lily, wild strawberry, and others grew like. . . well, like weeds!

These plants grew quickly from seeds shed from nearby trees, or blown in from plants that survived on adjacent hills, or from plant parts such as bulbs, underground stems called rhizomes, and rootstocks, that survived deep in the soil. These strategies for surviving fire are well developed in plants subject to periodic fires.

Geyser, Geyser, Who's Got the Geysers?

From Old Faithful to Nez Perce Creek you will pass six major geyser locations: Upper Geyser Basin, Black Sand Basin, Biscuit Basin, Midway Geyser Basin, Fountain Paint Pot, and Lower Geyser Basin. More than 300 geysers and some 10,000 other thermal features are in this ecosystem, more than exist in all the rest of the world combined.

Elk-browsed trees in Biscuit Basin. Hoof prints, droppings, and the browsed or highlined trees like these indicate use of the thermal areas by animals.

Each geyser and thermal system is different because of varying acidities, temperatures, and plumbing systems — the cracks and caverns that hold and recycle hot water. The exact locations of the geysers, hot springs, fumaroles, and other thermal features are constantly changing. Any shift in the underground plumbing system due to slight movements of the rocks changes the flow of water, with serious consequences for plant and animal life in the vicinity. Water from thermal areas can carry minerals that clog up the systems of the trees, and chemicals that are poisonous or alter the acidity of the water. Temperatures might be hot enough to cook the root cells, and the eruptions from geysers might deposit minerals directly on leaves and plug up their pores. The major white mineral in these geyser basins, the one you can see coating the bases of dead trees, is called geyserite. It has a high silica content.

White deposits on the ground are minerals brought up from underground by hot water; continual deposition of new material on top keeps the surface white. Not much can live on the deposits while the area is active. But if the system changes and hot water stops, or if the water cools off enough for plant roots to survive, lodgepole pine can start a new forest. Mosses, lichens, grasses, sedges, and flowering plants will also get a root-hold and form the understory.

Constant changes cause small alterations in the forests, which can be seen throughout Yellowstone Park. New runoff of hot water kills trees, or the absence of hot water in a formerly active area enables trees to come back. As you drive along the Firehole River and elsewhere, can you spot sites that have changed a couple of times?

Mineral deposits form white socks on the bases of dead pines. This indicates that an area formerly inactive became active.

The Thermal Community

One of the first obvious things about the geyser basins, dramatically visible even from the roadside, is their color. Some of the colors may be due to iron or other minerals brought up by the water, but most is due to microorganisms: cyanobacteria, formerly called blue-green algae; true bacteria; and true algae.

Living in Hot Springs

Hot springs in Yellowstone vary in acidity, temperature, and sulfur content. These differences cause variations in the bacterial and algal mats and their colors.

The hottest water in most springs is near boiling, about 198 to 201 degrees Fahrenheit at this elevation. About five different hardy bacteria, visible only with microscopes, can live at this temperature. Water at the edges of springs and flowing in channels away from springs cools. At about 165 degrees, cyanobacteria can live in the water, and colors become visible. Cyanobacteria have the same chlorophyll pigments as green plants; they use water in photosynthesis and release oxygen.

Photosynthetic bacteria live with the cyanobacteria, usually at slightly lower temperatures. Photosynthetic bacteria have some different pigments than cyanobacteria; they can use hydrogen sulfide or other compounds instead of water in their photosynthetic pathway, and they release sulfur, not oxygen. The highest temperature range for any photosynthetic organism is 158 to 163 degrees, much lower if the water is acidic.

Cyanobacteria, photosynthetic bacteria, and more familiar bacteria are prokaryotes. Their cells are extremely tiny and lack a nucleus enclosed within a membrane. Their cell structure seems to permit them to live in hostile environments that other organisms cannot tolerate. Still, the upper temperature limit for any bacteria in alkaline water is about 190 degrees.

Fungi, plants, and animals are eukaryotes. Their cells are 10 to 100 times larger than prokaryotes, and they have true nuclei surrounded by membranes. They generally cannot live in temperatures higher than 100 to 140 degrees. Individual temperatures for living depend on the organism and on chemical characteristics of the environment.

In the Upper to Lower Geyser Basin region, the hot water is alkaline, with pH levels from 8.0, similar to sea water, to 9.3, like baking soda. One spring in the Lower Geyser Basin has a pH of 8.0 and temperature about 125 degrees. Its colored mat has a layer of green sausage-shaped cyanobacteria on top and an orange layer of photosynthetic bacteria underneath. The mat does not get much thicker than one sixteenth of an inch because a third type of bacteria feeds on and thus decomposes old photosynthetic bacteria. The last stages of decomposition can lead to formation of methane, natural gas.

On the other hand, acid water near Norris Junction has a pH of less than 4, almost as acid as vinegar. No cyanobacteria or photosynthetic bacteria can live in water this acid. Its green color is due to a unique eukaryotic green alga, *Cyanidium caldarium*. Some fungi and bacteria might be present as decomposers.

In a third slightly acid spring at Mammoth Hot Springs, green color is due to photosynthetic filamentous bacteria; decomposer bacteria just under the green mat form an orange layer.

The lesson is that it is difficult to generalize about the springs, and to say green is always this species and orange is always that. The important thing to realize is that we are seeing unique communities of microbes.

Killdeer

Other Hot Water Fans

Insects also live among the bacterial mats in hot springs areas. Some tolerate temperatures up to about 112 to 122 degrees, about the same as the tolerance range of mosses and seed plants. Brine flies and their larvae feed on the algae; in turn they are food for larger predators like spiders, dragonflies, tiger beetles, wasps, and mites. These often attract even larger animals like birds and bats.

Hot water from geyser basins empties into the Firehole River, raising the water temperature by about 20 degrees Fahrenheit.

If you stop at any of the geyser basins, you should be able to see abundant brine flies in early summer, and birds such as killdeers and swallows throughout the summer and fall. As the water around a hot spring cools to below 100 degrees, certain fish and amphibians become able to inhabit the water.

Thermal areas attract large mammals, too, especially in winter when other areas are snow and ice bound. Elk and bison often wander in the vicinity of steamy hot springs — sometimes to fall through the thin crust to their deaths.

In early spring along the streams and rivers flowing through thermal areas, look for brilliant yellow monkey flowers, which can grow in water apparently too warm for other flowering plants. They bloom along the warm waterways almost year-round.

As the Firehole River flows past these geyser basins, the water temperature rises by some 20 degrees. Apparently the increased water temperature from the geyser basin runoff has little adverse effect on overall reproductive success of the fish, particularly the very adaptable rainbow trout. However, according to Yellowstone Park biologists, the thermal conditions may have caused interesting shifts in fish behavior to cope with the heat. Some brown trout, for example, move to cooler spots to spawn in winter, and some that stay in the warm areas never mature sexually. Rainbow trout, normally spring spawners, in the Firehole River shift their spawning runs to late fall or early winter.

The hot springs can also bring poisonous elements from deep in the earth up to surface level. Enough mercury and arsenic are in the waters of the Firehole River to make some trout at varying times of the year unfit for human consumption. And these waters are perhaps also responsible for toxic pollutants in the Madison River far from park boundaries: it is possible to have natural pollution even in a well protected national park.

Trails for a Closer Look

The Three Senses Trail on the east side of the road about six or seven miles north of Old Faithful gives you a chance to test your sensory abilities in a geyser basin. All the basins on this route have trail systems that lead to higher points, usually to waterfalls or vistas with a panoramic view of the major geyser basins set like white moonscapes in the forest. These trails generally start along a low point with spruce and deep shade, and go up through lodgepole pine then subalpine fir, and maybe more spruce. See Marschall's guide to the trails of the park for trailhead locations and information.

Meadow Megafauna

Opposite Nez Perce Creek, about ten miles north of Old Faithful, Fountain Flat Drive veers west off the main road through a big flat meadow where bison frequently live year-round; the road dead-ends at the Goose Lake picnic area.

North of Fountain Flat Drive is a large, fairly soggy meadow on both sides, and the Nez Perce Creek, which drains the Central Plateau to the east. This plateau forms a rather rigid seasonal boundary between the Firehole Valley and the Hayden Valley farther east (see map 10: page 106).

The elk that winter along the Firehole are part of the Madison-Firehole-Gibbon herd; they sometimes mingle with elk from the Hayden Valley herd during the summer and early fall. This mingling allows for some genetic mixing during breeding season, but in winter the deep snow on the Central Plateau keeps them apart. The same is true for the bison; many winter here along the river and near the warm water, which keeps the snow depth tolerable. They depart for backcountry by mid-June, and may not be visible from the roadside here during summer. Indeed, the best season to see large animals here, or anywhere in the park, is from late autumn to early June. Snow at higher elevations forces animals to congregate at lower elevations along the rivers.

Take a Closer Look: Signs of Winter Feeding

Signs of the winter feeding are evident on the trees: elk browse pine branches as high as they can reach, so the lower branches are gone. Bison graze grasses and forbs that peek above the snow; their heavy skulls and bony shoulder hump help them plow through deeper snow to reach their food. Bison generally don't browse on trees, though they might rub against the bark and shred it. Look closely as you drive along for signs that elk and bison have wintered along here.

Firehole Canyon Drive

You can follow the main road all the way to Madison Junction, or you can take a short detour along Firehole Canyon Drive, a one-way drive that starts about 12 miles north of Old Faithful, near Madison Junction. This drive follows closer to the river, with numerous waterfalls and rapids, and loops back to the main road.

Waterfalls in Firehole Canyon have historically prevented fish from lower elevations from reaching the upper stretches of the Firehole River. In 1889, brown trout and rainbow trout were planted in this stream above the falls, to improve the fishing experience for tourists. Fish were planted every year until the 1950s, when natural spawning was determined to be successful enough.

Madison Junction

Madison Junction is named for the junction where two rivers, the Gibbon from the north and the Firehole from the south, join to form the Madison River. Named after President Jefferson's secretary of state when Lewis and Clark made their exploratory voyages, the Madison River flows west out of the park (map 3: page 54), then north through the Madison Valley to Three Forks, Montana (map 18: page 164), where it joins the Jefferson and Gallatin rivers to become the Missouri River.

At Madison Junction, continue north to Norris (map 4: page 62) or turn west to the West Entrance of Yellowstone Park and the town of West Yellowstone, Montana (map 3: page 54).

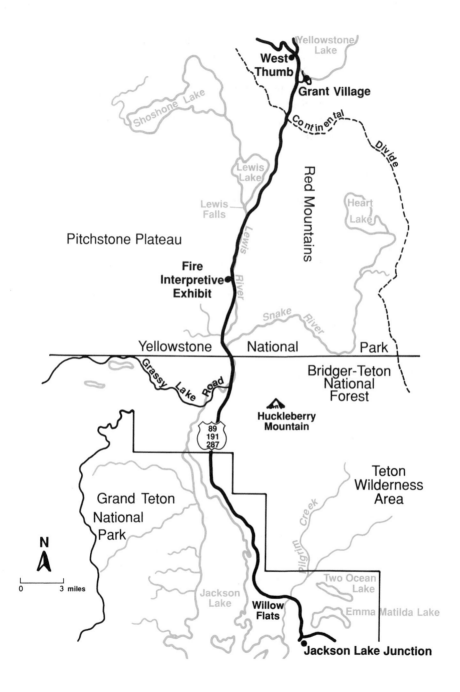

MAP 14
WEST THUMB—JACKSON LAKE JUNCTION

West
Thumb

Yellowstone
Lake

Grant Village

Continental

Divide

Shoshone Lake

Lewis
Lake

Heart
Lake

Lewis
Falls

Red Mountains

Pitchstone Plateau

Lewis River

Fire
Interpretive
Exhibit

Snake River

Yellowstone   National   Park

Grassy Lake Road

Bridger-Teton
National
Forest

Huckleberry
Mountain

89
191
287

Grand Teton
National
Park

Teton
Wilderness
Area

Pilgrim Creek

N

0   3 miles

Jackson
Lake

Two Ocean
Lake

Willow
Flats

Emma Matilda Lake

Jackson Lake Junction

West Thumb—Jackson Lake Junction
44 miles/70 km.

Fire Landscape

The road skirts Yellowstone Lake for about a mile and a half, to the turnoff to Grant Village.

You pass through some stunning fire landscape between here and the South Entrance of Yellowstone Park. The 1988 Snake River Complex fire burned about 142,000 acres in this part of the park and the adjoining Bridger-Teton National Forest, and caused the temporary evacuation of Grant Village. Within the fire acreage, the effects ranged from charred and incinerated, through hardly scorched, to green and apparently untouched. As an example of an unburned area within a burned perimeter, notice the unscathed Lewis Lake Campground on the southwest side of Lewis Lake, about halfway between West Thumb and the South Entrance.

Before the 1988 fires, this road was densely lined with lodgepole pine. Burning the trees along part of this road opened up the views; the Red Mountains to the east are now visible.

The Red Mountains visible through lodgepole skeletons. An example of a vista opened up by the 1988 fires.

Along the Great Divide

The road winds up and over the Continental Divide, at 7,988 feet; it passes between the Yellowstone River drainage, with its water flowing to the Atlantic Ocean, and the Lewis River, a tributary of the Snake River with water flowing to the Pacific Ocean. Shoshone Lake and Lewis Lake on the west side of the road are part of the Snake River drainage, as is Heart Lake on the east side of the road. But Riddle Lake and Delusion Lake, on the east side of the road and not visible from your vehicle, drain into Yellowstone Lake, which supplies the Yellowstone River with some of its water.

A Fishy Story: Every Which Way But UP!

Brown trout from Scotland and lake trout from Lake Michigan were introduced into Lewis Lake in 1890; native brook trout have since moved in from inlet streams. Lewis Falls at the outlet of Lewis Lake to the Lewis River, about 29 feet in height, again illustrates why many higher lakes and rivers had no native trout populations: fish couldn't climb the falls. Heart Lake has cutthroat and lake trout, but access requires some strenuous hiking through bear country. Canoeing from Lewis Lake up the Lewis River to Shoshone Lake is a fairly popular adventure, best done with caution because of the afternoon winds. Lodgepole and whitebark pines, spruce, and subalpine fir ring the hillsides around the lakes in this area.

Moose Meadows

Soggy meadows east of the road near Lewis Lake are prime moose habitat; watch for them among the willows and aquatic plants. Standing up to eight feet high at the shoulders and weighing nearly a ton, the moose is the biggest member of the deer family in the world. Like other deer, moose are vegetarians, and in the spring and summer much moose food grows under water. A moose can usually find all the plants it needs simply by sticking its head under the water, but on occasion a moose will dive completely under.

Somewhat more solitary than other deer, moose aren't usually seen in large herds, but at most in twos and threes. Even then they might not be interacting with each other. In summer you might find one to two per square mile, but in winter when available food may be scarce, as many as 40 or more moose per square mile can live where willow is abundant in the valleys.

Hot Rocks: Pitchstone Plateau

Lewis Falls is at an elevation of about 7,725 feet; the South Entrance to Yellowstone Park at 6,886 feet. The Lewis River Canyon east of the road again exemplifies the characteristics of the rivers descending off the Yellowstone Plateau: a steep canyon cut by water rushing from higher to lower elevations through some fairly resistant volcanic ash flow.

The Lewis River near Lewis Falls. Fishing visitors share space with moose in the willows along the river.

Pitchstone Plateau is west of the road. It is one of the newest volcanically active portions of the Yellowstone Plateau, with fairly large quantities of rock that is three to four times more radioactive than other rock in the region, as well as a crumbly rock called pitchstone, a form of obsidian. A trail leads from the road up to the top of the plateau, where there are no roads. A campground at about 8,715 feet is at one of the few places where water exists on the high, flat, rather barren plateau. Lodgepole pine is common on the lower elevations; it gives way to spruce and whitebark pine alternating with mountain meadows at the higher altitudes.

The southwest corner of Yellowstone Park, where streams drain off the Pitchstone Plateau, is very boggy and soggy. The only way to get there is to walk on one of the trails shown on trail maps, or to drive from Ashton, Idaho. Cave and Bechler Falls are within a mile of each other at the southwest border of the park.

About two miles north of the South Entrance is Moose Falls, one of the coolest, dampest spots in this region, with comparatively lush moss, lichen, and algal growth. Park maps show one road south of the park boundary, the Grassy Lake Road, that starts by the Flagg Ranch and skirts the southern border of the park through the Targhee National Forest. It is slippery when wet, best negotiated carefully and on dry days.

Rockefeller Parkway

The John D. Rockefeller Memorial Parkway connects Grand Teton and Yellowstone national parks. It was dedicated in 1972 in honor of Rockefeller's contributions to the establishment of Grand Teton Park. The parkway stretches from the South Entrance of Yellowstone Park through Teton National Park, nearly to Jackson, Wyoming.

Along this section of the highway, streams feeding into the Snake River create excellent moose habitat. Watch for moose in meadows by the willows, mostly in early morning or early evening.

About five miles south of the Flagg Ranch, you enter Grand Teton National Park.

Wilderness and Wild Places

A map of Grand Teton National Park shows four official Wilderness areas — Winegar Hole, Jedediah Smith, Gros Ventre, and Teton — in the vicinity of Grand Teton National Park. These wilderness areas fall within two national forests, the Targhee and the Bridger-Teton.

These various management areas come under different jurisdictions: the national park is under the umbrella of the National Park Service, Department of the Interior; the national forests are under the U.S. Forest Service, Department of Agriculture. Their management objectives and goals have often conflicted. Generally, in national forests one can camp, hike, ski, hunt and fish, collect firewood, and usually share the space with privately owned cattle and sheep as well as the native wildlife. In national parks it is improper to pick a flower or collect a rock: they are to be left as natural and complete as possible, and vehicles and hikers are allowed only on specified trails.

Moose habitat: soggy meadow with willows along river.

In designated wilderness areas, most of which are within national forests, the goal is to provide a place where, according to the Wilderness Act of 1964, "the earth and community of life are untrammeled by man, where man himself is a visitor who does not remain." So wilderness designation protects an area from most forms of development, from use of motorized vehicles, or from any other use that would damage its pristine nature and ecological values.

Much of the Greater Yellowstone ecosystem, of course, is quite wild and functions somewhat like an official wilderness. The critical difference between wild areas and designated wilderness is that these other remote areas do not enjoy the full protection of law. Many are open for oil and gas leases, mining operations, and other activities incompatible with wilderness values. A strong wilderness system provides a reserve of biological diversity, watersheds, and scientific values that are increasingly hard to find elsewhere.

Fire: Patchwork Patterns

Just north of Colter Bay, about 15 miles south of the Flagg Ranch, a stretch of the 1988 Huck Fire appears along the road. Living trees interspersed with burned ones, and needles still hanging onto dead or dying trees indicate that the fires were not too hot in this area. In some small patches fires did burn intensely, though spottily. This mosaic pattern is typical of fire; centuries of fires are partly responsible for the intricate mosaic of vegetation and wildlife in the region.

More Moose in the Willows

Just north of Jackson Lake Junction, Willow Flats turnout provides another excellent opportunity to watch for moose. Willow shrubs are one of their primary foods; they browse on willow leaves and twigs, and wade into lakes and rivers after succulent water plants. A moose uses its tongue to snip off the vegetation, and its heavy lips to manipulate its food. In spring, summer, and fall these willow flats along the river are prime spots for moose to forage.

Jackson Lake

Jackson Lake, gouged out by glaciers and enlarged by damming the Snake River, is the largest in Jackson Hole, with some 78 miles of shoreline skirting its 25,730 acres. The lake is managed by the U.S. Water and Power Resource Service; it is filled in June and drawn down about 10 feet by September, mostly for irrigation in Idaho and Wyoming. Ice covers the lake from mid-December to about mid-May. The water warms rapidly after it breaks up.

At Jackson Lake, turn east to Moran Junction (map 27: page 206), or southwest to the Jenny Lake Loop (map 26: page 202) and Moose, Wyoming.

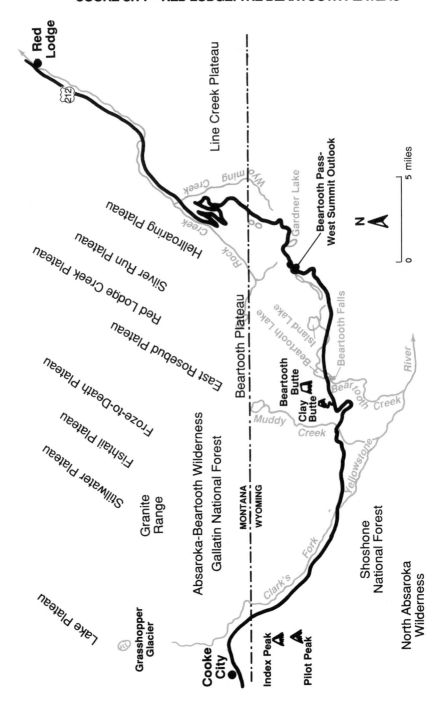

U.S. 212 (The Beartooth Highway)
Cooke City—Red Lodge:
The Beartooth Plateau
65 miles/105 km.

The Beartooth Highway, U.S. 212, runs east and northeast from Cooke City to Red Lodge, Montana, crossing the most spectacular alpine country available to a casual tourist in this country. From Cooke City to a junction about 12 miles east, the highway travels mostly through unburned subalpine forests of spruce, subalpine fir, lodgepole pine, and, at higher elevations, whitebark pine. Wyoming 296, the Chief Joseph Scenic Route, veers south at the intersection through the elegant valley of the Clarks Fork of the Yellowstone River (see map 17: page 160). The Beartooth Highway continues up over the Beartooth Plateau, then descends through pine forests onto the edge of the Great Plains grasslands.

This road travels from the Gallatin National Forest in Montana, through the Shoshone National Forest in Wyoming, and back to Montana, now the Custer National Forest. The road is closed from October through May; exact dates of opening and closing vary with the snowfall.

Cooke City, Montana

Four miles east of Silver Gate, Montana, and the East Entrance to Yellowstone National Park, Cooke City is at an elevation of 7,650 feet, high enough for spectacular snow depths during most of the winter. The only access Cooke City has to the rest of the world from November through May is the road through Yellowstone Park to Gardiner, Montana. It is within the Gallatin National Forest and close to the Shoshone National Forest.

Reminders of the 1988 Storm Creek fire, and the backfire that was set to try to contain it, surround both Silver Gate and Cooke City. This is an area of extensive spruce and subalpine fir forests, which have more undergrowth than do dry pine forests. Forests like these with many old, downed trees, thick underbrush, and bushy lichens draped on the trees burn much more intensely and readily under the right conditions than the younger, relatively barren lodgepole pine forests.

143

*Springtime in the
Rockies: Cooke
City in April.*

Geology of the Plateau

The Beartooth Plateau was raised during Eocene time, approximately 50 million years ago. It is part of the long chain of mountain blocks that rose east of the overthrust belt then, all the way from central Montana to Mexico. The overthrust belt and the mountains west of it rose during Cretaceous time, 70 to 80 million years ago.

Grasshopper Glacier, eight miles north of Cooke City, contains thousands of grasshoppers, frozen into the ice in the late 1890s. Granite Peak, the highest mountain in Montana at 12,799 feet, is 10 miles northeast of Cooke City.

This high, gently rolling country has a remarkably flat upper surface. Actually, this area has several distinct plateaus—Lake, Stillwater, Fishtail, Froze-to-Death, Hellroaring, Line Creek, Beartooth, and others—separated from each other by stream canyons. The only one whose summit is readily accessible by vehicle is the Beartooth Plateau. Most of the sharp peaks visible south of the road are part of the Absaroka Mountains, volcanic rocks erupted about 50 million years ago, which have since deeply eroded.

All the water draining the Beartooth Plateau ends up in the Yellowstone River, one way or another. Streams on the southwest part flow into the Yellowstone River in Yellowstone National Park; streams on the southeast drain into the Clarks Fork of the Yellowstone, which flows north through Wyoming into Montana; and the streams on the northern portion flow north directly to the Yellowstone River in Montana.

Because the Beartooth Plateau is so flat on top, communities of trees, grasses, sedges, and wildflowers have been able to develop. They evolved intriguing and complex ways to cope with their harsh environment of wind, cold, short growing season, and intense summer sunlight followed by intense cold and snow in winter. But one characteristic these organisms don't have is much resistance to human influences. While their ability to withstand harsh climatic conditions is impressive, they do not recover well from our trampling or our wheels. Please appreciate them only from established trails and roads.

Up, Up, and Away. . . .

The road rises rather sharply from about 7,330 feet at the junction with Wyoming 296 to 8,900 feet at Beartooth Lake, 19 miles miles east of Cooke City. Most of the trees are characteristic high-elevation stands of spruce and subalpine fir, with some lodgepole pine and increasing numbers of whitebark pine.

About six miles east of the Wyoming 296 junction, two miles west of Beartooth Lake, a turnoff on the north side of the road to Clay Butte takes you up to 9,811 feet and a Forest Service fire lookout with maps identifying

Beartooth Butte from Clay Butte. The upper tree limit is determined by steep slope.

the peaks and ridges that surround you. Clay Butte, and Beartooth Butte 10,514 feet, immediately east of Clay Butte, are remnants of the sedimentary formations that once covered the entire top of the plateau. They were deposited under water, and contain fossils of animals that lived in the ocean. Now they are more than 10,000 feet above sea level.

Moist meadows and willow flats at the base of Clay Butte along the highway provide ideal moose habitat. Look for them early in the morning and late in the evening.

Pocket Gophers: Symbols of Instability

At Clay Butte, notice the networks of long mounds of soil that snake along the surface of the ground. These are tunnels made in winter by pocket gophers, one of the many smaller rodent residents of the high-elevation world. Their mounds are evidence that they don't hibernate, but scurry around beneath the snow, nibbling on plant roots.

In summer, pocket gophers expand their underground homes and pile the dirt outside the holes in great circular mounds. When snow covers the ground, they can't travel outside or pile soil in heaps. As they excavate for new roots to eat during the winter, they backfill their burrows under the snow, and these appear when the snow melts.

Wind scarps that frequently follow pocket gopher activity. Wind blows away unstable soil. Prevailing wind direction here is from the left.

The pocket gopher, Geomys bursarius, *is rarely seen because it stays underground. However, their long mounds on the soil surface indicate their widespread presence.*

The tunnels underground and the loosely piled soil in the mounds make for very unstable conditions; the tunnels eventually collapse, providing protective runways in the grass for smaller voles. However, before vegetation grows along the collapsed tunnels, the area is very susceptible to wind erosion. It provides a place for wind cavities and depressions called scarps —steep on one side, gentler on the other—to start on windward slopes. The ground instability can be seen at many meadow locations. It can take many years, with the short growing season of 35 to 70 days, to revegetate the ground.

Alpine Lakes

Beartooth Lake at the base of Beartooth Butte, about 21 miles east of Cooke City, is the largest lake visible from the highway. Most lakes have native grayling and introduced trout: brook, cutthroat, rainbow, and the rare golden trout. Trout were planted throughout the region beginning in the late 1800s, but habitat suitability was not always taken into consideration. Some lakes, such as these high-elevation glacial lakes, don't naturally support fish, even though many of them have suitable water depth, food supply, and spawning streams to support a breeding population; fish just never found a way to ascend the waterfalls. Other lakes are too barren to support the food chain necessary for fish, or are so shallow that they freeze to the bottom during the winter. Fish planting of the lakes is now done

One of the countless lakes on the Beartooth Plateau.

more thoughtfully by departments of fish and wildlife, which introduce fish into alpine lakes only if conditions are suitable for their survival.

Alpine lakes are extremely sensitive to pollution and to changes in water acidity. The lakes sit directly on igneous granite and metamorphic gneiss and schist rocks, which contain little or no limestone or other carbonate rocks that could buffer acidic pollution. Acid rain and snow threaten these pristine bodies of water, as does the toxic acid runoff from mining or oil and gas developments. The lakes are being studied in the wake of the 1988 fires to see if the heavy smoke particles caused any problems.

Approaching Timberline: Hummocks, Krummholz, Flag trees, and Other Strange Shapes

Between Beartooth Lake and the summit of Beartooth Pass, the tree stands become more spotty. Instead of extensive stands of forests, the trees tend to be in islands of various sizes. You are approaching upper timberline. Above timberline you will be in alpine meadows, where some trees can survive in protected patches but where large areas have no trees at all. This is alpine tundra.

Near Island and Long lakes, the soil and plants form hummocks, characteristic of cold regions. Movement of soil and rock in small convection currents under the surface of the ground makes little mounds of soil a foot or two high and the same in diameter, with depressions between them. Small willows or sedges grow on top of the mounds, and various kinds of mosses grow on the sides. They're fairly stable until the tops of the hummocks push above the top of the winter snow level. Then winter winds erode the willows or sedges off the top of the mound; they become unstable, and degenerate. A new cycle of little convection currents rebuilds the hummocks in slightly different places. This takes several years, depending on the size of the hummock.

As the road heads northeast from Island and Long lakes, spectacular switchbacks carry it through areas of bare granitic rock with little or no soil, and patches of trees that obviously look like they endure rough weather. The trees are stunted or have branches only on one side, or thick branch growth around the bottom, or crooked growth. This kind of tree form is called krummholz, a German word meaning crooked wood. The wind carries snow and ice particles that scour off the growing buds that produce branches, so none grow on the windward side of the tree. Trees with branches on one side are called flag trees.

Notice the thick branch growth around the bottoms of many of the trees. Since buds under the snow are protected from wind damage, they can grow luxuriantly during the spring and summer. The lateral branches on the ground can also establish roots and reproduce the tree sideways in a kind of growth called layering.

Islands of trees, bare rock, grassy areas, and July snow form mosaics near upper timberline.

149

Krummholz: growth of tree branches on one side, skirts of branches at the bottom. Timberline is near.

The main types of trees in the island and krummholz stands are whitebark pine, subalpine fir, and spruce.

West Summit Outlook

At Beartooth Pass, about 29 miles east of Cooke City and about 10,947 feet in elevation, is a visitor stop, the West Summit Outlook—a very good vista on a clear day. Climbing to the top of the ridge along the path gives you a view of Rock Creek Canyon to the northeast; Rock Creek runs down through Red Lodge. Looking the other direction, you see mostly the peaks of the Absaroka mountain range and other parts of the plateau.

Patterns in the Ground

This is a superb place to notice patterned ground, a characteristic feature of arctic and alpine landscapes. It is seen only in areas where soil is shallow, the temperature is never very far above the freezing point, and there is water in the soil, frequently from melted snow. Notice the patterns of rock on the ground by the parking lot. Some of the shapes are almost circular, others are more elongated. Convection currents of freezing, then thawing water in the soil move the soil and rock upward and sideways during spring and fall. Where the surface is rather level, the rocks are deposited in circles or polygons several feet in diameter. Where the surface slopes, water runs

150

downhill carrying the rocks with it. You can see these stripes on the hills in the switchback areas between here and Island Lake.

The patterned ground here is different from the hummocks at Island and Long lakes. Hummocks are smaller, not usually rocky, and covered with vegetation. The ground patterns can be several feet in diameter, with definite rims of rock at the peripheries and soil covered with grass and wildflowers in their centers. The convection currents here seem to be inactive now. The rocks appear black because of lichen growth, mostly *Umbilicaria* species. Lichens grow slowly, so their presence on rock means it is not moving very much.

Mountain Goats

Mountain goats occasionally appear along the road near Gardner Lake, about five miles west of the border between Montana and Wyoming, one mile below West Summit Outlook. Even if you don't see the goats, watch for tufts of their white hair blowing across the meadows; this is their winter coat, scrubbed off each spring by persistent rolling on the vegetation.

Mountain goats are not native to the Greater Yellowstone ecosystem; their historical natural range extended from southeastern Alaska to south-central Washington and into central Idaho and southwestern Montana. Twelve animals were introduced into the Snake River drainage in the southern part of the ecosystem between 1969 and 1971 by the Idaho Fish and Game Department. They were introduced in the Beartooth region in the 1940s. The introductions cause some concern, in part because mountain goats are known to damage delicate alpine plant life and soils, and in part because of the potential for mountain goats to compete with native bighorn sheep for food where their ranges overlap.

The mountain goat is not a true goat. It is really a type of antelope. Both males and females have straight, cone-shaped horns that grow continuously throughout life, and are never shed like deer or elk antlers. Mountain goat hooves are specially adapted for life on the rocks, with large, pliable pads that give them great traction and dexterity on rough terrain. Mountain goats usually stay at or above timberline and within reach of rocky outcrops where they can retreat from danger. In winter deep snows can force them to lower elevations, but they always stay close to the safety of rock cliffs.

Alpine meadows

Between West Summit Outlook and the switchbacks that lead down to Red Lodge, Montana, watch for beautiful development of alpine meadow vegetation. Rock fields and other areas that get battered by wind support an elegantly adapted growth form: cushion plants. They look like little pin cushions, three to five inches tall. The plants grow a tiny bit each year and are extensively branched; the roots of a cushion plant nine inches in diameter can be four to five feet deep in the soil. Mat plants are a little different in form, but no taller; they creep sideways and put down roots at intervals along the lateral stem.

The cushion plants—moss campion, phlox, alpine forget-me-nots—and mat plants—including clovers and alpine dryas—produce most of the vivid wildflower color during the few short weeks of summer. Other plants like alpine bluebells, potentilla, grasses and sedges, are miniature versions of their lower-elevation cousins. The flowers of these tiny plants stick up above the leaf mats and bloom profusely. The main pollinators are flies and ten different species of bees. The pollen of grasses and sedges is carried by the wind.

It might look like there is very little vegetation between the cushion plants, but soil is rarely bare. A cover of lichen and moss between most flowering plants helps prevent wind erosion. Where pocket gophers disturb the soil, however, the wind excavates fairly large pockets called scarps and blowouts that might take many years to revegetate. Eventually plants move in from the less steep side and stabilize the blowout.

In slightly more protected areas, the cushion plants yield to an amazingly dense turf of grasses and sedges, with *Geum* or *avens,* a member of the rose family. Again, the height of these plants is rarely more than six to eight inches. Most are perennial; in their short growing season, they produce more roots, leaf and stem tissue, flowers, and fruit.

Take a Closer Look: Clues in the Leaves

Stop at any roadside pulloff and examine the leaves of some of these alpine plants for clues about other ways plants cope with adversity. Some leaves are thick and succulent, a water-storage device that comes in handy where drying winds blow constantly. Other leaves and buds are hairy. Why the hairs? Perhaps they help reflect the intense sunlight, and also help insulate delicate plant tissue; perhaps the hairs also help protect against the persistent wind. Insects find it more difficult to nibble through thick hairs or lay eggs on hairy leaves, so this fuzzy surface might also give alpine plants an edge against them.

Life on the Rocks

Two types of good-sized gnawing animals live in rock piles in various places along this route. The easiest to see is the yellow-bellied marmot, a rodent similar to, but larger than its eastern cousin the woodchuck, or groundhog. Marmots eat the vegetation around rocks, and enjoy sunning themselves on rocks along the road. They hibernate in winter, so are active only from about June to September. Marmots have a high, shrill "chip!" sound that reverberates through the hills as you approach.

A smaller, more elusive creature is the pika, a relative of the rabbit. About the size of a guinea pig, pikas lack tails and have short rounded ears. They don't hibernate; instead they accumulate little haystacks, bunches of grass poked near cavities among the rocks and used as a winter food supply. During the summer, their daytime scurrying makes them visible to observing humans—and vulnerable to weasels and even hawks, if the pika strays too far from its secure rock pile. You can also spot a pika home by watching for orange, nitrogen-loving lichens, *Xanthoria* or *Caloplaca*, that reveal where the animals leave their droppings.

Pika

Other Alpine Animals

Many smaller rodents — voles, ground squirrels, and the pocket gophers introduced earlier—also live in this high-elevation world.

Some elk and bears cross the plateau in the summer, and deer are common around the high elevation ponds or around patches of trees that protect them from the wind. Most large animals cannot live in alpine areas for lack of food or shelter. Their homes are in more protected areas, but they cross the meadows to get from one feeding area to another.

The major bird of the plateau is the water pipit, a hardy little thing that nests on the ground. Watch for its bobbing appearance; it doesn't hop like other birds but walks, and when it flies it dips up and down. Many other birds feed and fly through this harsh environment. Watch for golden eagles, peregrine and prairie falcons, horned larks, Clark's nutcrackers, ravens with their coarse squawking, mountain bluebirds, rock wrens, white-crowned sparrows, and rosy finches.

Switchbacks

Switchbacks that lead downward to the Rock Creek Canyon and Red Lodge start 45 miles from Cooke City, 20 from Red Lodge, offering spectacular vistas. At one of the first pull-outs above the switchbacks, you see a good view of a krummholz island of spruce, subalpine fir, and whitebark pine north of the road. It exhibits the classic flag trees with scoured, dwarfed trees on the windward side of the island, and relatively normal trees on the protected lee side. Which way does the wind blow? Determining the age of these trees is difficult because they grow laterally along the ground, then upward.

Mats of *Dryas octopetala* or alpine dryad, a typical alpine and arctic tundra plant of the rose family, grow on the windward side of the island. It's difficult to overestimate the role of this plant in colonizing and stabilizing bare soil and gravel. Like many hardy colonizing species, it has root nodules containing nitrogen-fixing bacteria that help it survive in these poor soils.

Mining in the Mountains

Out of sight on the east side of the road is an old chromite mine, used during World War II. In the 45 years since this mine was abandoned, a few weedy species have recolonized the open pits, and lodgepole and whitebark pines have started to grow where they are protected from the wind by rock or mounds of soil. This slow recovery of sites disturbed by mining is a reminder of the fragility of high-elevation systems. Currently active platinum and palladium mines are lower on the Stillwater Plateau, the northernmost plateau of this area. Increasing proposals for mining or for oil and gas drilling in these high-elevation areas are creating concerns about water and air quality, and about long-term disturbance of fragile vegetation and soils.

Lichens

The bright yellow-green lichen on some branches and especially on old dead trees whose bark is gone is *Letharia* or wolf lichen. It grows in the Western U.S. and in northern Europe; it was once used as a wolf poison in Scandinavia, where it was mixed with rotten meat and finely ground glass. A gray-green lichen on branches is the genus *Usnea*; black hairy growth is the genus *Bryoria*, also known as old-man's beard.

Pines of Plateau and Plains

There are several pullouts on the switchbacks that lead down off the northeast corner of the plateau. Many of the trees, especially subalpine fir, show extensive branching or layering at their bases.

The major pine here is whitebark pine, but it gradually gives way to limber pine as elevation decreases. If at some stopping place along here you find good big woody cones, usually very sappy, the tree is limber pine; if the cone looks like it is disintegrating, with the seeds missing and many scales broken off, it is probably whitebark pine. The road descends along Rock Creek Canyon, where once again you are in limber pine and juniper trees, and the beginning of the Great Plains grassland. The trees along the creek are mostly spruce, Douglas fir, and lodgepole pine.

Upper Rock Creek Canyon between Red Lodge and Beartooth Plateau. This is a classic U-shaped glacially gouged valley.

Near Red Lodge, ponderosa pine appears. It lives throughout the West, except for most of the Greater Yellowstone ecosystem. It grows in rather open, park-like stands of large, well-spaced trees, on sunny slopes below the zone of dense spruce-fir forest. Everything about this tree deserves the name ponderosa: large overall size, huge five- to eight-inch needles in bundles of two or three, three- to five-inch prickly cones, and large thick plates in the mature bark. Stick your nose close to the orange bark for a distinct whiff of vanilla.

Red Lodge, Montana

Red Lodge is at an elevation of about 5,575 feet. Its total annual precipitation is about 25 inches, double that of Gardiner; over half the precipitation falls as snow. The Red Lodge Ski Area is on the slopes of the Beartooth Mountains, southwest of town.

At Red Lodge you can follow U.S. 212 northeast to Laurel and I-90, or take scenic Montana 307 northwest around the flanks of the Beartooth Range to Columbus and I-90 (see map 16: page 156); from I-90 you can proceed east to Billings or west to Bozeman.

MAP 16
U.S. 212, I-90
RED LODGE—BILLINGS

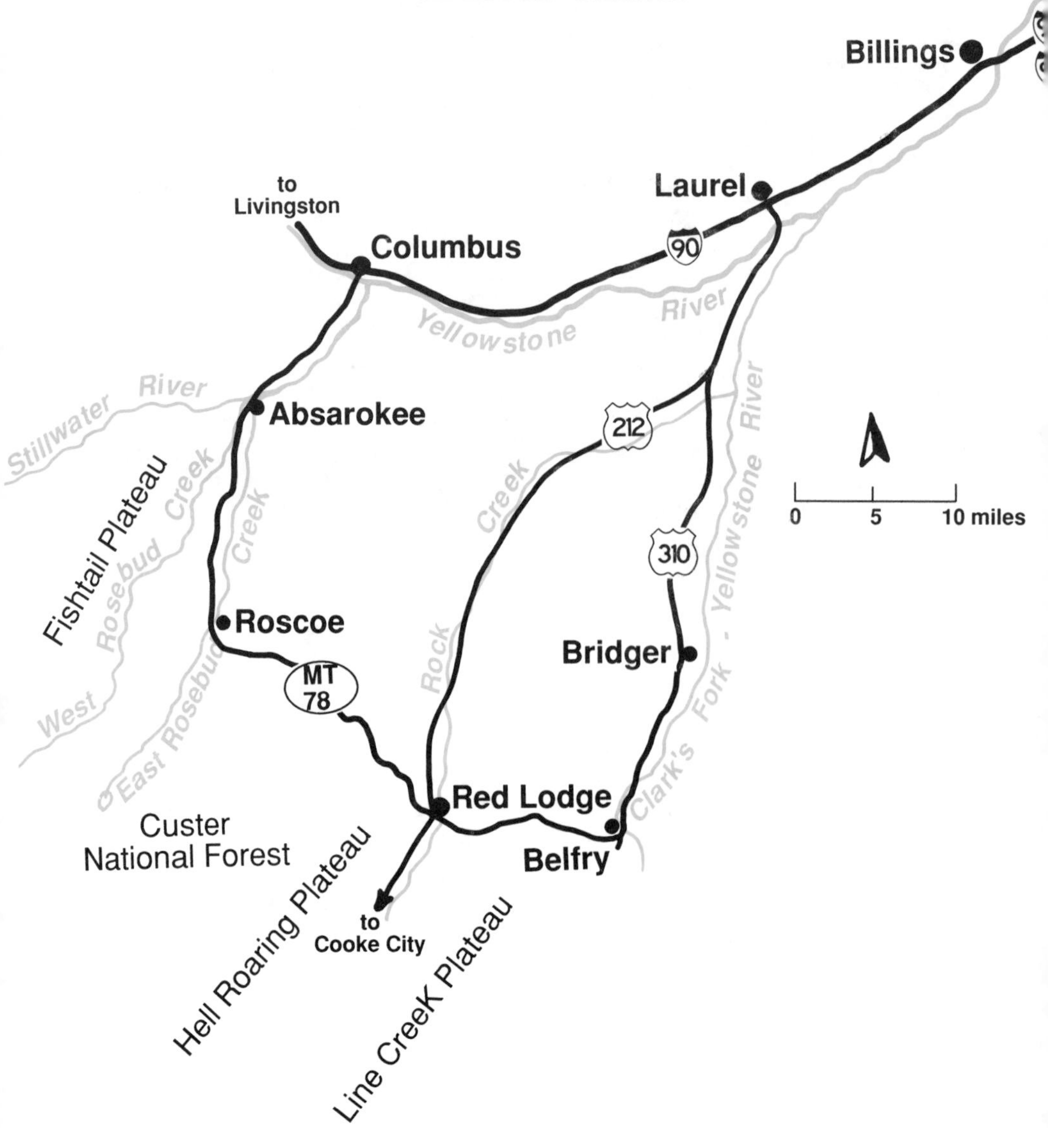

Billings

Laurel

to Livingston

Columbus

90

Absarokee

Stillwater River

Fishtail Plateau

Rosebud Creek

Creek

Yellowstone River

212

Creek

Rock Creek

310

Yellowstone River

Bridger

West

Roscoe

MT 78

East Rosebud Creek

Red Lodge

Clark's Fork - Yellowstone River

Belfry

Custer National Forest

Hell Roaring Plateau

to Cooke City

Line Creek Plateau

0   5   10 miles

U.S. 212, I-90
Red Lodge—Billings
60 miles/96km.

U.S. 212 follows the Rock Creek Valley northeast toward Interstate 90, then follows the Yellowstone River east to Billings, the largest city in Montana. The streamside vegetation is habitat for many whitetail deer, and ringtail pheasants live in the heavy cover. This area is agricultural, with many sugar beet fields, wheat, barley, and some corn. The hills on both sides of the valley are dry grassland and juniper-sagebrush-ponderosa pine, today used mostly for cattle grazing.

The elevation of Billings is about 3,500 feet, low enough to have growing seasons warm and long compared to areas farther west. About 28 percent of the 15 to 18 inches of annual precipitation falls as snow, compared to over 60 percent in the Yellowstone and Beartooth country. The Yellowstone River also provides irrigation water, so farming is important in the valleys.

Sugar beets are a major crop in the Yellowstone River Valley. Beets are rotated with wheat and barley to vary nutritional demands on the soil and to control beet disease organisms, especially roundworms called nematodes.

Sugar beets are in the same plant family, Chenopodiaceae, as red beets, spinach, chard, and weeds like pigweed, Russian thistle, goosefoot, and lamb's quarter. Sugar beets provide about 30 percent of the nation's sugar; the rest comes from sugar cane. The large white roots average between 15 and 20 percent sucrose, about the same sugar content as in cane. The largest beets usually do not have a sugar content as concentrated as medium-sized beets, so biggest is not best.

Beet seeds are planted in the spring, and harvest starts in earnest about October 1. Leafy beet tops can be used as cattle feed. The beets are trucked to local sugar factories along the rivers. It takes a lot of water to irrigate, wash, and process the beets to sugar, and to serve as settling ponds for some of the lime residue from processing. Molasses and pulp, by-products of the refining process, can be used in cattle feed. Other by-products are monosodium glutamate and potash fertilizer.

Field corn is grown in the Yellowstone River Valley, mostly as feed for local cattle and hogs. Both winter and spring wheat are grown, irrigated along the river as a non-irrigated dryland crops on higher slopes. Many farmers have contracts with beer companies for raising malt barley for brewing. When wet conditions late in the summer lead to unwanted germination of seeds while they are still on the plant, or other problems reduce the seed quality, the barley is used for cattle feed.

Ponderosa pine is the major tree species from the foot of the Beartooth Plateau north and east toward Billings and most of the rest of Montana. It shares the hillsides with Rocky Mountain juniper and grasses such as Idaho fescue, bluebunch wheatgrass, and Western wheatgrass. Cottonwoods and willows line the rivers.

Oil and natural gas fields surround Billings; refineries in Laurel and Billings process the oil.

An alternative route to Interstate 90, if you are headed west, is Montana 78, a winding, scenic road. This route skirts around the flanks of the Beartooth Plateau, up and down through ranch land, then along the East Rosebud Creek and Stillwater River from Absarokee to Columbus. Deer live in the thick cottonwood stands along the river. Active palladium and platinum mines are on the plateaus to the southwest.

U.S. 212, Wyoming 296
Chief Joseph Scenic Highway—Cody
70 miles/112 km.

The road leading southeast from the junction of U.S. 212 and Wyoming 296 is the Chief Joseph Scenic Highway. Part of this beautiful drive follows the Clarks Fork of the Yellowstone River, one of the wildest rivers in the lower 48 states. The river chisels away at what may be the deepest glacially eroded gorge in Wyoming. Most of the land along the road is privately owned; grazing cattle and horses abound along the entire route.

The Clarks Fork of the Yellowstone:
Truly a Wild and Scenic River

As you turn onto Wyoming 296 from the Beartooth Highway, the road starts out in sagebrush, with pockets of aspen, spruce, and lodgepole pine trees. To the southwest, the Shoshone National Forest — the country's first national forest — shows evidence of the 1988 Clover-Mist fire, which burned heavily on the steep upper slopes.

About six miles from the junction, the road crosses the Clarks Fork River. Its headwaters begin just inside Yellowstone National Park to the west; it flows southeast along this route for about 22 miles, then bends northeast and joins the Yellowstone River near Laurel, Montana. About 21 miles of this portion of the Clarks Fork River was designated by Congress as a Wild and Scenic River in 1990, becoming the first Wild and Scenic River in Wyoming and in the Greater Yellowstone ecosystem. This designation protects the river and its shores from development or disturbance, and preserves its wild character.

Along the course of the Clarks Fork is a great variety of plant communities, from the spruce-fir at its mountain headwaters to high-plains grassland vegetation at the canyon's lower end. The river drops more than 100 feet per mile in some spots, working away at the dramatic canyon northeast of the highway. The canyon attracts anglers, kayakers, hikers, and photographers, and provides habitat for mountain goats, native Yellowstone

MAP 17
U.S. 212, WYOMING 296
CHIEF JOSEPH SCENIC HIGHWAY—CODY

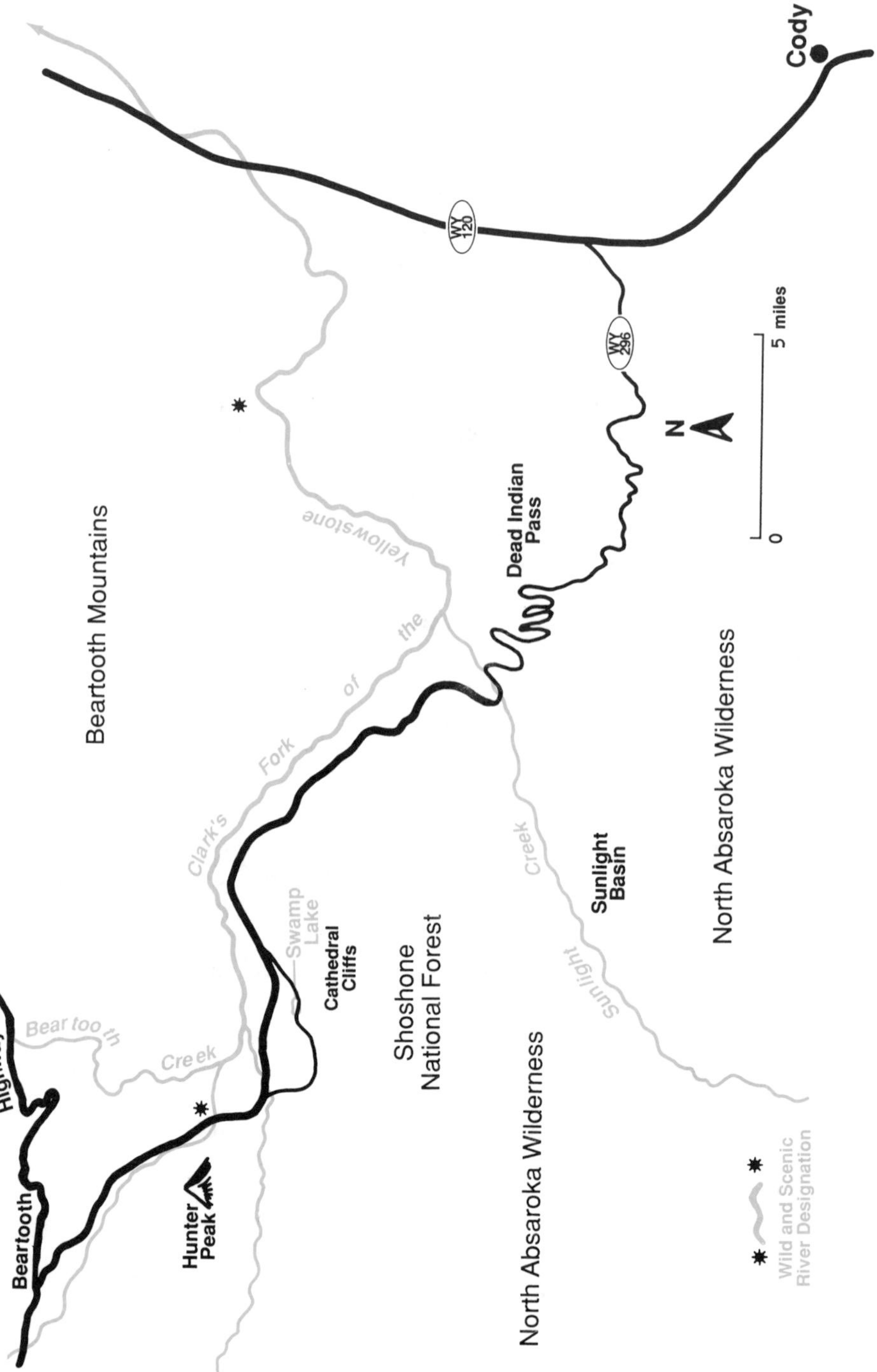

Cody

WY 120

WY 296

5 miles

N

0

Dead Indian Pass

Beartooth Mountains

Yellowstone

Clark's

Fork

of

the

North Absaroka Wilderness

Swamp Lake

Sunlight Basin

Cathedral Cliffs

Sunlight

Creek

Shoshone National Forest

Beartooth

Highway

Bear tooth

Creek

Hunter Peak

North Absaroka Wilderness

Wild and Scenic River Designation

Douglas fir sneaking into grassland in little damp depressions. Trampling by grazers forms small horizontal terraces in the grass.

cutthroat trout, grizzly bears, peregrine falcons, bighorn sheep, and numerous other wildlife species.

A Variety of Habitats

About nine miles southeast of the junction of U.S. 212 and Wyoming 296, notice the series of small ponds and marshy areas filled with thick sedges and cattails on both sides of the road; look for coots and ducks in spring, summer, and fall. To the west is the Swamp Lake Botanical Area, where a number of rare plants live, including some of the only bog plants in the ecosystem. A little farther on, mixed forests of aspen; Douglas fir and lodgepole pine with sagebrush undergrowth provide good habitat for mule deer.

About 20 miles south of the Beartooth Highway, Douglas fir and spruce begin to carpet the mountain slopes, while the nearby range remains open. Look back down the valley to the drier sagebrush grassland below.

Dead Indian Pass

About 33 miles from the Beartooth Highway, you reach Dead Indian Hill summit, 8,000 feet, and Dead Indian Pass. Through this pass, herds of migrating deer, elk, bison, and other wildlife in the past found their way from the mountains to the plains. Historical Indian tribes also found a

161

The Chief Joseph Scenic Highway linking subalpine forests on the Beartooth Plateau with grasslands of the Great Plains.

Lower timberline with limber pine and juniper in wetter spots among the grasses.

natural gateway between these two landscapes. Such migration corridors have always been critical to the survival of many species of wildlife and still must be taken into account when creating and managing parks and reserves.

A forest of pine and Douglas fir lines the road east of the pass, but you can begin to glimpse the immense Wyoming plains in the distance to the east. Red bands of sandstone and siltstone create an interesting landscape as you travel back down to sagebrush and juniper country. Notice the numerous grazing trails on the hillsides.

About 47 miles southeast of the Beartooth turnoff, at the intersection with Wyoming 120, the Chief Joseph Scenic Highway ends. The entire road is scheduled to be paved by 1996. You can turn north on Wyoming 120 toward Belfry, Montana; take a side trip on a dead-end road into the very base of the Clarks Fork Canyon. Or, turn south on Wyoming 120 and continue to Cody, Wyoming.

The Sagebrush Flats

The road now winds through flat, dry, rocky sagebrush grasslands, with large cottonwood trees marking the course of the Shoshone River. Though the sagebrush might look hostile and barren as you drive through, this actually is excellent habitat for many species, including cottontail rabbits, horned larks, Western jumping mice, and golden eagles, among others.

At Cody, the bright green lawns around the homes are a sharp contrast in late summer and fall to the brownish rust of the surrounding area. This is a dramatic example of the influence of added water in a normally arid area. Where does all the water come from to water the lawns? How would you expect removal of the water from its natural source to affect the plants and animals that depend on it for survival?

At Cody, circle west toward Yellowstone Park along U.S. 14-16-20 (see map 11: page 112).

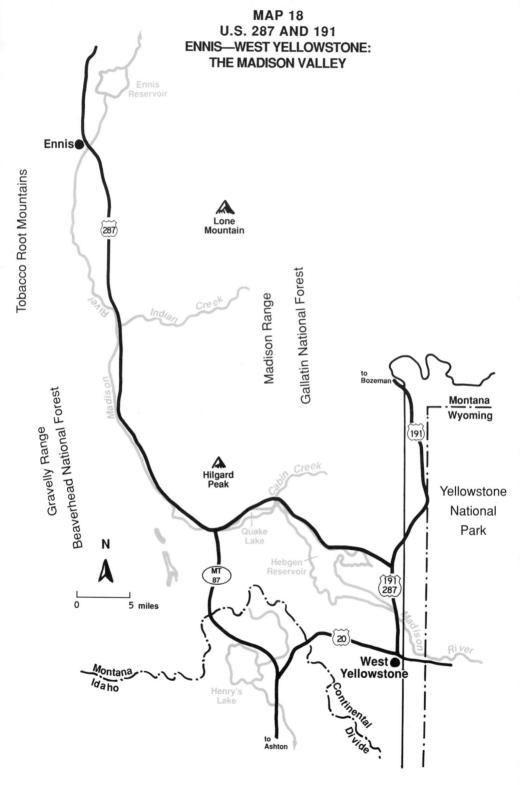

The Madison River Valley looking west toward the Tobacco Root-Gravelly mountain ranges. This is cattle country.

U.S. 287 and 191
Ennis—West Yellowstone:
The Madison Valley
73 miles/117 km.

Ennis, Montana

Ennis lies in the Madison River Valley, which reaches about 50 miles from the west side of the Madison Range to the east side of the Tobacco Root-Gravelly Range. Spectacular flat terraces rise like flights of steps from the Madison River to the mountains on either side.

If you approach Ennis on Montana 84 from Bozeman, you pass through beautiful Beartrap Canyon, part of which is a designated Wilderness Area managed by the federal Bureau of Land Management, one of the few Wilderness Areas in the ecosystem not in a national forest. The Beartrap area contains nesting sites for two endangered raptors, the bald eagle and the peregrine falcon.

Ennis Lake, on the east side of the highway north of Ennis, is a reservoir formed by the damming of the Madison River. Its shallow water provides excellent fishing for eagles and ospreys. Humans find the lake more suitable for wind-surfing.

The Madison River is a blue-ribbon trout stream, a popular recreation area.

From Ennis the road follows U.S. 287 south 40 miles along the Madison River to a junction with Montana 87.

The Valley: Where the Deer and the Antelope Play

The Madison Valley is deer, antelope, and cattle country. The grassy fields, heavily chewed by the domestic and wild grazers, extend from the river banks to the Douglas fir forests on the mountain sides. Alluvial fans are conspicuous all along the west flanks of the Madison range.

The valley is becoming more developed for tourism, with big game hunting and fishing for brown and rainbow trout. The wind blows here with great gusto, much as it does at Livingston, Montana (map 2: page 46), with air rushing off the Yellowstone Plateau.

Henry's Lake

About 40 miles south of Ennis, Montana 87 heads south into Idaho past Henry's Lake, a popular lake for large cutthroat, brook, and hybrid cutbow trout. Named for Andrew Henry, an early trapper, the area sports profuse aspen stands, an indication of abundant groundwater. Grasses and big sagebrush grow below and among the aspens.

166

A gravel road 12 miles south of the junction of Montana 87 and U.S. 287 leads 27 miles to the Red Rock Lakes National Wildlife Refuge in the Centennial Valley. The refuge is more easily accessed via U.S. 20 (see map 20: page 178). On clear days the peaks of the Teton Range are visible across Henry's Lake.

Three national forests abut this region: the Beaverhead and Gallatin forests in Montana, and the Targhee in Idaho. The state lines are drawn here along the Continental Divide in the Henry's Lake Mountains. Idaho is on the Pacific side and Montana is on the Atlantic side. Henry's Lake drains into the Henry's Fork of the Snake River, which meets the Snake farther south near Rexburg, Idaho, and proceeds to the Columbia River and the Pacific Ocean.

Highway 87 continues 18 miles past the Red Rock Lakes turnoff to a junction with U.S. 20 and U.S. 191. From that junction, you can travel north to West Yellowstone or south toward Macks Inn and the southern reaches of the ecosystem.

The Madison River Valley looking toward the Henry's Lake Mountains. Cottonwoods, willow, and last year's great mullein stalks line the river.

Quake Lake, technically Earthquake Lake, formed in 1959. The mountainside that slipped and dammed the Madison River is visible in the background.

On Shaky Ground

Greater Yellowstone is a geologically dynamic area. A massive earthquake in 1959 was a dramatic reminder that one is on shaky ground. About 45 miles south of Ennis on U.S. 287, stop at the Earthquake Area Visitor Center for explanations and pictures of the enormous Madison Slide. It buried an unknown number of campers and formed Quake Lake, as a chunk of the mountain slid all the way down one valley wall and part of the way up the other.

Dead trees in Quake Lake are typical of those drowned by reservoirs. Their roots can't get oxygen when the soil is flooded, so they can no longer do the required pumping of ions and sugars for root nutrition; the roots die and so do the trees.

Notice that part of the slumped mountainside visible from the visitor center has trees on it; most are lodgepole pine. Some of the trees were carried down on the massive slide; others have recolonized bare soil. The mountainside that remains, however, is apparently too steep for easy recolonization; melting snow and water run fast down slopes like this, making it difficult for seedlings to get established.

The fault scarp, formed during the 1959 earthquake, at Cabin Creek Campground.

Hebgen Lake

Just east of Quake Lake, Hebgen Lake is a reservoir on the Madison River, impounded behind a small concrete and earth dam built for power. The dam, about five miles east of the visitor center, held perfectly during the 1959 earthquake. At the Cabin Creek picnic area near the dam you can see remnants of the fault scarp, a little cliff that rose as the earth moved during the earthquake. Most of the obvious evidence of that earthquake is now covered by plants along this stretch of road, but the extent of fault movement can still be seen at Cabin Creek. The Madison Range rose, while this valley dropped.

Conifer stands along the road are nearly all Douglas fir. Look for stripes running down the mountain that are bare of trees; they mark the tracks of repeated avalanches, which prevent tree growth. The large aspen stands on the northeast slope farther up the road indicate areas of groundwater readily available to the trees.

About 15 miles east of the visitor center, U.S. 287 merges with U.S. 191. Head north to travel through the Gallatin Canyon to Bozeman (map 1: page 36), or south to complete this route into West Yellowstone.

MAP 19
WEST YELLOWSTONE—ASHTON

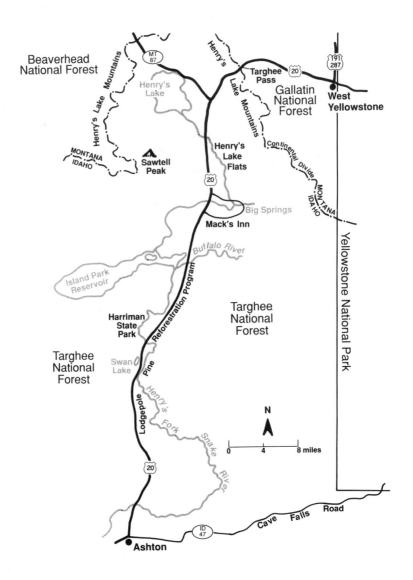

U.S. 20
West Yellowstone—Ashton
55 miles/88 km.

U.S. 20 crosses Targhee Pass between Montana and Idaho, from the Missouri River drainage system of the Madison River to the Columbia River drainage system of the Henry's Fork of the Snake River. About 12 miles west of West Yellowstone, Montana 87 branches to the northwest, past Henry's Lake and over Raynold's Pass to Ennis in the Madison River Valley.

Henry's Lake

Henry's Lake is a popular fishing area on Henry's Lake Flat, where amazing winds blow ground blizzards in winter. The lake is known for its spectacular fishery, which includes rainbow, cutthroat, and cut-bow (rainbow-cutthroat trout hybrids) often 20 to 30 inches long. The lake is shallow, and by mid-summer large weed banks begin to fill in, allowing insects, leeches, and fresh-water shrimp to proliferate. All that food enables the fish to grow to such impressive size.

Just south of the lake is a turnoff to the west on a good gravel road for Red Rock Lakes National Wildlife Refuge, a great trip through the beautiful Centennial Valley to the nesting grounds of Greater Yellowstone's rare trumpeter swans (map 20: page 178).

Along the main road heading south, watch along the flats for grazing sandhill cranes and antelope. The road follows the Henry's Fork of the Snake River, again a very popular fly-fishing stream. Brown and rainbow trout live in the river, brook trout and kokanee salmon in the tributaries. The substantial winter snow cover makes this a popular area for snowmobiling and cross-country skiing.

Big Springs (4.5 miles)

A short side trip to the east at Macks Inn takes you to Big Springs, where groundwater that seeps into the ground on the large ridge to the east in Yellowstone Park emerges at 92,000 gallons per minute. The resident population of large rainbow trout in this incredibly clear, cold (52 degree) water can easily be seen at the bridge. Their diet now consists in part of bread and popcorn furnished by visitors on the bridge, poor nutrition for wildlife.

The fish population was decimated during the winter of 1988-89, apparently by disease, but now seems to be recovering. Rainbow trout were stocked for many years into lakes and streams throughout the ecosystem, and in many cases have replaced or hybridized with the native cutthroat trout that once abounded.

A new footpath along the stream includes directories to the many bird species that live here.

National Forests and National Parks: "Mission Impossible" ?

Beginning about eight miles from West Yellowstone, U.S. 20 travels mostly through the Targhee National Forest, for more than 40 miles. This stretch illustrates a major difference in objectives and activities between the U.S. Forest Service and the National Park Service. The focus here is on insect infestation and forest management.

In many areas of the Greater Yellowstone ecosystem, the pine bark borer has affected the lodgepole pine populations. The mission of the Park Service is to maintain things in a condition as pristine as possible — no cutting, no removal of dead trees, no spraying, no replanting of vegetation. Insect infestations are recognized as a part of the natural scheme and generally left to cycle themselves out of business.

The Forest Service has traditionally followed a more crop-oriented, husbandry type of management goal. National forests are formally charged with maintaining forests for multiple use, including wildlife habitats, recreation, scenic value, ecological value, timber production, mineral and oil exploration, and so forth. In practice most are managed primarily for timber production, whether or not this is the best use of a particular forest. This dictates very different management methods than those used by the Park Service. These in turn may differ from the missions and goals of other landowners, including the Bureau of Land Management, the wildlife refuges, the states, and the private landowners.

These management and mission differences among various interests create difficulties in managing land at the ecosystem level, where the resource cuts across political lines. The clash of the missions between the

Aerial view of boundary between Yellowstone Park on the left and a logged clear cut in Targhee National Forest on the right. —Richard Marston photo

Park Service and Forest Service is obvious both from the road here and from the air. The boundary of Yellowstone National Park with its thick lodge-pole pine forest contrasts sharply with the adjacent Targhee National Forest, which cut most of the trees.

Habitat Fragmentation

Certain kinds of timber management are incompatible with some other forest uses. For example, clear-cutting, the most widely used timber practice in the Rockies, can conflict with protection of significant wildlife habitat. Some wildlife species, such as the pine marten and the pileated woodpecker, can survive only in the interior portions of a large forested area. This is partly because predators, competing species, or conditions like sunlight, heat, or human activity that are intolerable to some wildlife species, exist mostly around the edges.

Some species like skunks and jays that can deal with these edge conditions are likely to thrive after a large clear-cut. But inner forest animals might be pushed farther into the remaining patch of forest, stranded on a kind of island. Unable to cross the foreign open area habitat to another patch of forest, their small and isolated populations can suffer a variety of genetic and other problems and decline drastically. The same phenomenon can affect any wildlife species that becomes isolated from others of its kind by some kind of barrier or hostile surroundings.

Timber production and wildlife protection can sometimes be achieved at the same time. Problems can be minimized if logged acreages are reasonably small, if logging is done in a way that avoids disturbance during sensitive nesting periods, if critical patches of trees and shrubs are left for wildlife, and if road construction is limited. But large-scale clearcutting and road-building can interrupt whole populations and interfere with migration routes for many species, especially large or sensitive animals like grizzly bears. This kind of habitat fragmentation can seriously disrupt a wildlife population and lead to its decline.

More sensitive timber objectives and practices are being considered for this and other forests around the ecosystem. These efforts reflect an acknowledgement that perhaps the best and wisest use of Greater Yellowstone forests is not simply timber production but rather protection and enhancement of the wildlife and recreational values.

Lodgepole Reforestation Program

The Lodgepole Reforestation Program demonstrated along this route illustrates the intensive management approach of the Forest Service to areas with insect damage to trees. Trees killed or damaged by pine bark borers provide the bulk of the timber harvested by the Targhee National Forest, which provides the bulk of the timber cut in the ecosystem. Here, for demonstration purposes, some skeletons of dead trees were left standing.

A series of road signs points out several aspects of reforestation: insect-killed treees, plots of trees replanted or naturally reforested in 1960, plots replanted periodically since 1980, and plots that are ready to be planted. Notice that the ground to be replanted retains its natural vegetation; most plots contain a combination of planted and naturally reseeded trees. Leaving the ground unplowed simulates the natural situation to an extent, leaving essential microorganisms in the soil as intact as possible.

A stop at one or more of these plots will give you some idea of the rate of growth of lodgepole pines at this 6,200-foot elevation with its cold climatic regime. Since trees are usually planted at the age of one to two years, add one or two to the age listed on the signs. You can also estimate the age of young trees by counting the whorls of branches coming off the main trunk; this will be a slight underestimation, but it works for a ballpark figure.

In any case, you probably will be surprised at how slowly these trees grow on the Yellowstone Plateau. Notice, too, that most of the replanted areas have trees that are well spaced, and their branches are full nearly to the base of the trees. This looks very different from a naturally reforested lodgepole site, where millions of seedlings take hold and compete with each other to form the typical doghair stand of closely spaced, tall, thin trees. Compare

Lodgepole pine reforestation in the Targhee National Forest, as shown in photos from 1990. Signs are about five feet high. Between 1960 and 1985, the trees grew about 20 feet in height and four inches in diameter.

what you see along here with older, undamaged stands along this route and throughout the ecosystem.

Pine Seedling Growth

It is possible for anyone to plant native tree or wildflower seeds and eventually obtain the mature plant. However, most of the plants of this climate need a winter for seeds to germinate and grow. In the field they get plenty of winter naturally; you can simulate winter and get seeds from native plants to germinate by keeping seeds damp in a refrigerator for at least a month, then planting them.

Apparently, biochemical changes or changes in the seed coat or embryo occur during a cold period to allow the seeds to germinate. Germination and growth are slow, at least a month for the cold period or stratification, then a month or so for germination. You will have a little pine seedling two to three inches tall with many cotyledons, not true leaves, for a few weeks, then the true leaves will branch out of the growing stem tip.

Dropping Off the Plateau

All the routes leading from the Yellowstone Plateau follow the pattern of descent from high elevation conifer forests to dry grassland. As you drop down off the Yellowstone Plateau, the usual change from lodgepole pine to Douglas fir to juniper-limber pine to sagebrush-grassland is compressed to about one to two miles; there is nothing subtle about this change on this stretch of road. As you wind down, notice the wind-battered aspens, particularly east of the road.

Ashton: Potato Country

Ashton is on U.S. 20 a few miles above the confluence of the Falls River and the Henry's Fork of the Snake River. The elevation of Ashton is about 5,260 feet, in a natural grassland; the area is mainly agricultural. Idaho potatoes are the primary crop. Others include sugar beets, wheat, barley, and alfalfa.

Ashton-Cave Falls (28 miles)

From Ashton you can take a good gravel road — Idaho 47 then Forest Service 582, the Cave Falls Road — east and northeast through lovely aspen groves among the lodgepole pines. About one mile inside Yellowstone Park, a foot trail takes you to two waterfalls: Cave Falls on the Falls River, and Bechler Falls, about a mile farther on the Bechler River. These rivers drain the isolated southwest corner of Yellowstone, both eventually emptying into the Snake River. Different trails lead through soggy

Bechler Meadows and then up to the Pitchstone Plateau, a rarely visited portion of the park (see map 14: page 136).

At Ashton, head southeast on the Teton Scenic Highway to Jackson, Wyoming and Grand Teton National Park (map 21: page 184), or continue south on U.S. 20 to Idaho Falls, Idaho (map 22: page 186).

**MAP 20
RED ROCK LAKES AND
THE CENTENNIAL VALLEY**

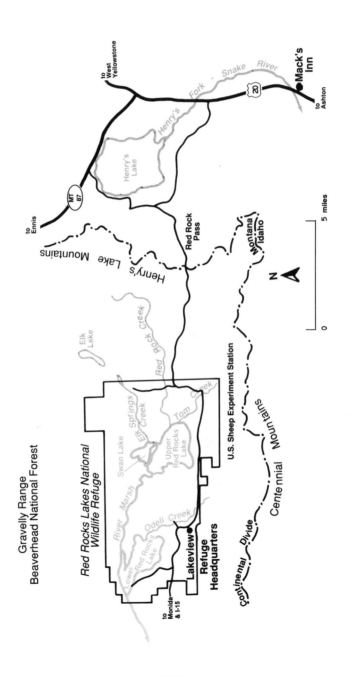

Avalanche track in Centennial Mountains visible from Upper Red Rocks Lake.

Red Rock Lakes and The Centennial Valley
approximately 60 miles round-trip from U.S. 20

From U.S. 20 about 15 miles west of West Yellowstone, Montana, a turnoff onto a good gravel road to the west leads to the Red Rock Lakes National Wildlife Refuge; the trip is about 29 miles one way, in the Centennial Valley. Red Rock Lakes is also accessible from Montana Highway 87 (map 18: page 164).

The Spectacular Centennial Mountains

One of the few mountain ranges in the Rocky Mountains that run east-west, the Centennial Mountains separate the Snake River plain of Idaho from the spectacular Centennial Valley in Montana. The range provides unusually rich wildlife habitat, a fine Douglas fir community on the southern slopes, and a critical corridor for migrating wildlife, including grizzly bears. The wildlife refuge was established in 1935, mostly to protect the rare and beautiful trumpeter swan.

The road winds through cattle ranches, magnificent aspen groves, and some lodgepole pine stands. The mountain sides of the Centennial Range south of the valley are covered with Douglas fir, and contrast dramatically with the rounded sagebrush-covered foothills of the Gravelly Range to the north.

179

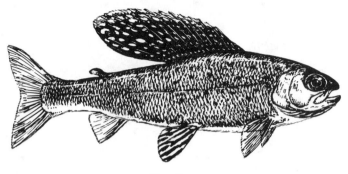

Grayling

Several lakes and marshes in the 40,300-acre refuge are protected as nesting sites for the trumpeter swan; these lakes and marshlands depend on heavy snow captured by the nearby timbered slopes and rocky basins. Moose also abound here, as do 18 species of resident and migratory ducks and geese, sandhill cranes, ospreys, and bald eagles; about 237 other species of birds come through in their seasons. The refuge is one of the few remaining places that support a native population of Montana grayling, a trout-like fish whose original habitat has almost entirely disappeared.

This valley has a fierce winter. Most birds and other animals don't hang around past fall. The few areas that usually remain open in winter do support a large wintering population of trumpeter swans.

Endangered Special Profile:

Trumpeter Swan, *Cygnus buccinator*

Wingspan: up to 8 feet

Weight: 20 to 30 pounds

Diet: mostly aquatic plants—up to 20 pounds per day!

Special needs: solitude, and up to 150 acres of territory per family

Trumpeter swan

Trumpeter swans, the world's largest waterfowls, once ranged over much of the United States. But by 1935, when the Red Rock Lakes National Wildlife Refuge was established for their protection, fewer than 100 remained in the continental United States, all in the Greater Yellowstone region. The species then appeared to be in danger of extinction.

With the protection provided by the refuge, the trumpeter population began to recover. By the 1950s it had increased to about 600 resident swans. An additional 1,000 or so swans nest in Canada and migrate to the Centennial Valley for the winter.

Their troubles are hardly over, though. In 1986 only 366 non-migratory swans were counted in the Greater Yellowstone area. Although the Canadian populations of trumpeter swans appear to be increasing, they are also at-risk since they spend the winter with the resident population.

The Trumpeter swan was never formally declared an endangered species because when the Endangered Species Act was passed in 1973 it looked like the swan population was recovering. But the fluctuating status of the resident trumpeter swan population is troubling. Declines in recent years may have been caused in part by:

- Fluctuating water levels controlled by the Island Park dam. This sometimes permits the shallow water to freeze, which eliminates the critical open water areas.

- Activities in the watershed, including grazing and phosphate mining in the Centennial Mountains. These may be increasing the amount of silt in the lakes and marshes, causing them to fill in.

- Possible changing ecological conditions following the 1959 earthquake.

- Increased human activity on the refuge, especially in winter. This may be causing birds to abandon critical open water areas.

- Possible inability of the refuge and nearby areas to support more than about 400 trumpeter swans. Should numbers of swans increase too much in this small area, crowded conditions could lead to disease and other problems, and force biologists to seek additional wintering grounds in other areas where water stays open all winter.

Cooperative efforts are under way with federal and state agencies and local landowners to create, enhance, and protect swan habitat. Among these are recent attempts to trap and relocate a number of wintering trumpeter swans to other locations in Idaho and Wyoming, with the hope that they will go back to these new locations in coming winters.

Resource Partitioning: Your Nest or Mine?

Three species of buteo hawks live in the Centennial Valley. These are large, chunky birds with long broad wings and fanned tails; all are small-mammal hunters, generally very similar in lifestyle and habitat needs.

In spite of their similarity, the buteos in the Centennial Valley don't seem to compete directly for resources such as food and nest sites. According to researchers, each bird achieves its goals in a slightly different way. The way they divide up the nest sites, which are scarce in this nearly treeless valley, is a good example of resource partitioning.

The ferruginous hawk is the largest of the three. A prairie bird that likes open areas, the ferruginous hawk nests on rock outcrops or flat on the ground in late April, when tasty ground squirrels have emerged from hibernation. They also commonly nest at the top of willow shrubs along the streams that provide a commanding view of the surrounding area. Their huge nests are built mainly of sagebrush twigs and lined with sagebrush and willow bark. About 12 nesting pairs of ferruginous hawks live in the valley.

Swainson's hawks are the smallest of the three, and the most common. They begin nesting almost three weeks later than ferruginous hawks. Their nests are smaller, about two feet in diameter, made of willow and sage, and tucked inside dense willow bushes rather than on top. This gives them less of a commanding view, but they have more spaces for nesting than ferruginous hawks.

Red-tailed hawks are intermediate in size between the other two, and the least abundant, with only about 10 nesting pairs. Some 65 percent of the redtails nest high in clumps of aspen trees along the drainages and sometimes in the Douglas fir along the slopes. Though they nest around the same time as the ferruginous hawks in late April, their choice of nest sites is clearly distinct. Their nest materials also differ: mostly aspen and some sagebrush twigs, lined with fresh aspen sprigs or sagebrush bark.

Refuge Headquarters

When you reach refuge headquarters, stop for a map and further information. The best route out of the refuge is the way you came in, but other gravel roads are open in fair weather. One leads north to Henry's Lake; another leads west to Monida and I-15.

Idaho 32 and 33; Wyoming 22
Ashton—Jackson: Teton Scenic Highway
68 miles/109 km.

From Ashton, you can head southeast on the Teton Scenic Highway to Jackson, Wyoming. Take Idaho 47 into the Ashton city center, then take Idaho 32 toward Driggs, where you pick up Idaho 33 to take you down the western side of the Tetons. This side of the range rises more gradually than the east side, but still provides a dramatic and ecologically interesting approach.

The first 20 miles or so pass through farm land where potato silos give a clue to the major crop that has displaced the native vegetation. Even in this predominantly agricultural area, microclimates on north slopes, gullies, and other non-agricultural spots allow growth of small groves of sagebrush and grass, aspens, Douglas fir, and other native vegetation.

As you approach Driggs, then Victor, the country changes from high dry valley grassland to mountain foothills, then rises to the spectacular Teton Pass. The road up and over Teton Pass leads you from the usual grassland-aspen-cottonwood communities, 6,390 feet at the base of Teton Pass, through lodgepole pine, then subalpine fir and spruce forests, 8,431 feet at the summit. The summer meadows stage a tremendous display of wildflowers. Road grades on both sides of Teton Pass often exceed 10 percent.

Potato barn typical of many seen along roads around Ashton and Idaho Falls.

MAP 21
IDAHO 32 & 33; WYOMING 22
ASHTON—JACKSON:
TETON SCENIC HIGHWAY

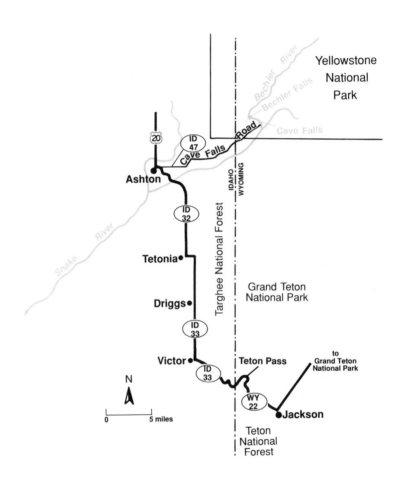

Climbing to Teton Pass. Farmland gives way to Douglas fir, to spruce, and finally to subalpine fir as elevation increases.

On the west side of the pass the Douglas fir and spruce-fir forests are lush; on the east side, you descend through drier lodgepole pine habitat. The valley floor east of the Grand Tetons is in the rain shadow of the higher mountains to the west. As the air climbs to go over the Grand Tetons, it drops its moisture closer to the summit, mostly on the windward west side, resulting in the forest patterns you see. Air descending into Jackson Hole, about 6,230 feet; is drier, and lodgepole pine is again the major tree.

At Jackson, the major town in the Jackson Hole valley, take U.S. 26-89 south and loop back west to Idaho Falls (map 23: page 190); or U.S. 26-89-187 north to Grand Teton National Park and points east and north (map 25: page 198); or U.S. 187-189 south to Pinedale, Wyoming (map 24: page 194).

MAP 22
U.S. 20
ASHTON—IDAHO FALLS

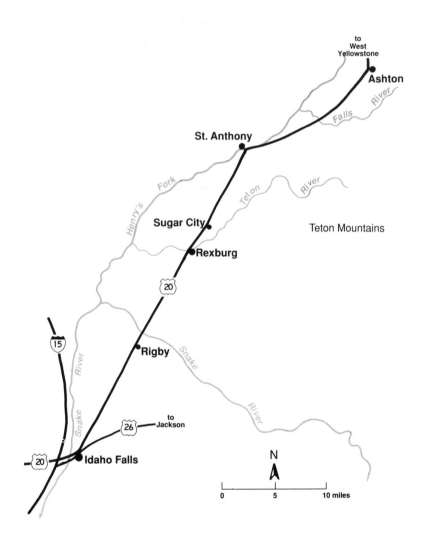

to
West
Yellowstone

Ashton

St. Anthony

Sugar City

Rexburg

Teton Mountains

Henry's Fork

Teton River

20

15

Rigby

Snake River

Snake River

to
Jackson

26

20

Idaho Falls

N

0   5   10 miles

186

U.S. 20
Ashton—Idaho Falls
52 miles/83 km.

Ashton is in a natural sagebrush grassland on dark basalt flows. Its major business is agriculture, with beef and dairy cattle, wheat, and barley in addition to the renowned Idaho potatoes. The fields are irrigated and provide the usual western view of green wet agricultural lands along valley bottoms contrasting vividly with the dry brown non-irrigated lands above them.

Irrigation water from the streams is controlled by reservoirs on the streams west of the Tetons. At Rexburg, 20 miles south of Ashton, the local museum has a dramatic exhibit of the flood resulting from the collapse of one of those dams, the Teton Dam, in 1976.

The road generally follows the Henry's Fork River, which flows into the Snake River north of Idaho Falls. The city's name comes from waterfalls on the Snake River.

Numerous potato barns on this road and others near Ashton and Idaho Falls indicate the prominence of this crop. On a worldwide basis, potatoes are the fourth major food crop behind wheat, corn, and rice. With their excellent nutritional content of proteins,carbohydrates, vitamins B and C, potassium, iron, and magnesium, potatoes are being encouraged as a food crop in much of the world.

Potatoes are in the same plant family, Solanaceae, as tomatoes, tobacco, peppers, nightshade, and petunias. The part we eat, the tuber, is an enlarged end of an underground stem. Potato farmers plant not potato seeds, but seed potatoes. These are small entire potatoes or parts of potatoes that contain the eyes or buds in the axils of small leaf scars on the tuber from which new roots and leaves grow. Potato diseases are easy to spread, so farmers are careful to plant certified virus-free potatoes.

Cool summers with a little more than 100 frost-free days in this area are nearly perfect for growing potatoes. They seem to grow best when soil temperatures do not get above 75 degrees Farenheit, and when the soil is light-textured, well drained, and well aerated.

Potato barns are built to provide optimum storage conditions: low temperature for less respiration and growth so they don't sprout, high relative humidity to prevent drying out, and dark so green chlorophyll does not form in the skin.

The toxin in green parts of the plant family to which potatoes belong is solanine, an alkaloid or bitter-tasting substance that can be poisonous if eaten in large amounts. Wild relatives of potatoes contain enough solanine to repel Colorado potato beetles, but cultivated potatoes do not. Some strains of wild potatoes are also more resistant to fungal attack than cultivated ones because of fast plant antibiotic reactions to disease-causing fungi such as the one that caused the infamous Irish famine in the 1800s. Breeding programs are trying to develop domestic potatoes that have some of the resistant compounds and reactions of wild relatives.

Russet potatoes are the baking kind, red or white skinned are boiling potatoes, and other potatoes are for processing into chips, fries, and other prepared products. Differences in cooking techniques and results stem from different properties of starches in the potato varieties.

Fields of potatoes are rotated with wheat and barley, partly to vary nutritional demands on the soil and partly to control diseases that come from organisms in the soil.

From Idaho Falls, U.S. 26 heads east toward the Tetons, with two alternative roads as described on the Idaho Falls-Jackson route (map 23: page 190).

Grazing cattle and sheep are an integral part of the Western landscape. High-elevation grasses have a higher protein content than those at lower elevations.

U.S. 26
Idaho Falls—Jackson
102 miles/163 km.

About 19 miles east of Idaho Falls on U.S. 26, the flat land starts to roll. Wheat fields and potato fields and the distinctive potato barns dominate the landscape until the hills get too steep; then extensive aspen stands with associated rose and chokecherry shrubs and two kinds of sagebrush, cover the lower hills. The aspens are the dominant vegetation cover all the way through Swan Valley.

At Swan Valley, you can choose one of two routes into Jackson. The northern road, Idaho 31 and Wyoming 22, rises up through the aspens and Douglas fir to the spruce and subalpine fir forests of Teton Pass. Teton Pass at an elevation of 8,429 feet is more than 3,000 feet higher than Swan Valley.

The southern route from Swan Valley follows the Snake River, which originates high in the wilderness at the Yellowstone Park border. The road skirts the Palisades Reservoir and passes through parts of the Caribou, Targhee, and Bridger-Teton national forests.

Palisades Dam is primarily for controlling irrigation water for arid eastern Idaho; it also has a power plant and provides recreation facilities. The roadside signs tell you to watch for eagles and osprey that feed on the native cutthroat trout. The neighborhood also supports moose, deer, elk, and black bears.

MAP 23
U.S. 26
IDAHO FALLS—JACKSON

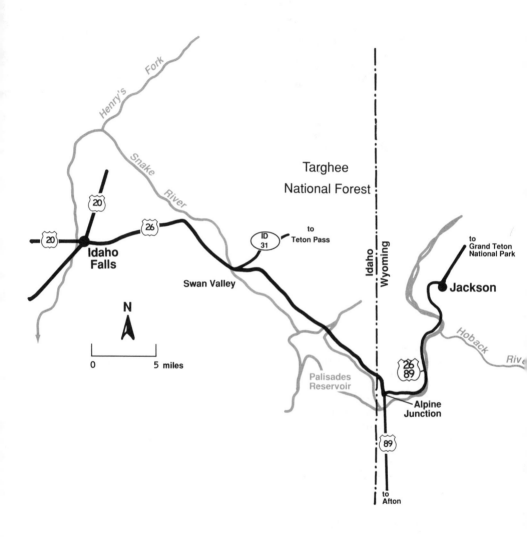

190

Palisade Lake, a reservoir for irrigation water, some power, and recreation facilities. This is eagle country.

Bald eagle

Eagles

Bald eagles in this area belong to one of three populations in the ecosystem. This group is the Snake Unit; the birds nest and hunt along the Snake River and its tributaries in Wyoming and eastern Idaho.

The bald eagle is tied critically to riparian and wetland areas, which provide its only year-round habitat. Here it finds important prey such as fishes, waterfowl, and small mammals. On rivers such as the Snake, eagles concentrate on runs and pools that provide year-round foraging, though they depend seasonally on riffles where prey fishes spawn and feed. On reservoirs such as the Palisades and lakes such as Jackson Lake, eagles need dependable shallow areas and wetlands, with tall trees nearby on which to perch and watch for fish.

A Kinder, Gentler Climate

Lodgepole pines are massive here compared to those in Yellowstone Park; this is a sure sign of more moisture and milder climate than higher up on the Yellowstone Plateau. Again, the aspens are everywhere. The tall shrubs are chokecherry, serviceberry, and Rocky Mountain maple, with some smaller gooseberry bushes.

Through the Canyon

At Alpine Junction, U.S. 26-89 heads north through a canyon cut through the little Snake River Range by the Snake River.

East-facing hills, on the same side of the canyon as the road, are covered with lodgepole pine, Douglas fir, and juniper. West-facing hills on the other side are dry; grass grows on their gentler slopes. This is the prevailing pattern in this region: trees on eastern and northern slopes where moisture is more abundant; grasses and associated shrubs and wildflowers on the warmer, drier southern and western exposures. Snow, if it stays at all on these steep slopes, melts very quickly during winter thaws.

Cottonwoods and willows share space with spruce on the flats along the rivers. An abundance of cones hanging from the upper branches of the spruce trees give some of them a brown-topped appearance.

You enter Jackson, Wyoming, through South Park, once prime elk habitat now being commerically developed.

In Jackson, head north for Grand Teton National Park and points north in the ecosystem (map 25: page 198); south for Pinedale, Wyoming (map 24: page 194); or west over Teton Pass (map 21: page 184) to Driggs and Ashton, Idaho.

The Green River Valley with the Wind River Range on the east side.

U.S. 189-191
Jackson—Pinedale
81 miles/130 km.

The route southeast from Jackson to Pinedale starts in Jackson Hole. It drops a bit into the broad valley of the Green River, and follows it to Pinedale, at the eastern side of the valley. The road starts in the Snake River drainage of the Columbia River and goes into the valley of the Green River, which drains into the Colorado River, which finally empties into the Sea of Cortez.

Between Jackson and Hoback Junction, 15 miles to the south, you're closely surrounded by the mountains — the Snake River Range on the west and the Gros Ventres on the east. After the Snake River cuts west about eight miles south of Jackson, you then follow the Hoback River through Hoback Canyon at the northern end of the Little Hoback Range.

So, who's Hoback? All these Hobacks are named after John Hoback, one of the first American commercial trappers in Jackson Hole, along with John Colter, 1810-1813.

MAP 24
U.A. 189-191
JACKSON—PINEDALE

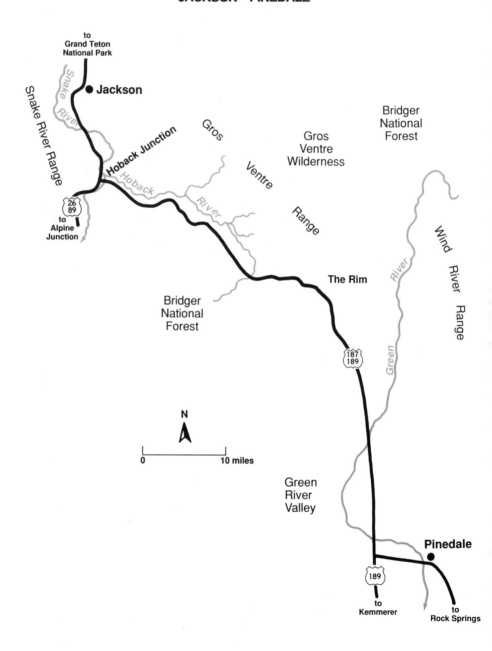

to
Grand Teton
National Park

● Jackson

Snake River

Snake River Range

Hoback Junction

Gros

Gros
Ventre
Wilderness

Bridger
National
Forest

Ventre

Hoback

26
89

River

Range

Wind River Range

to
Alpine
Junction

The Rim

River

Bridger
National
Forest

Green

187
189

N

0   10 miles

Green
River
Valley

Pinedale ●

189

to
Kemmerer

to
Rock Springs

Extensive aspen stands occupy the sunny slopes above the sagebrush.

Vegetation and Vistas

Big, dry, grassy hills to the east face the warm afternoon sun and prevailing westerly winds. Contrast them with the tree-covered slopes to the west which face east to the cooler morning sun. The trees are Douglas fir, lodgepole, and limber pines, mixed. The river banks are lined with the usual cottonwood, willow, and spruce.

Mountains visible to the east where the valley opens up a bit southeast of the Hoback Canyon are the Wind River Range. It reaches from near Dubois, Wyoming, more than 100 miles south to beyond Lander. The Wind River Mountains contain the highest point in Wyoming, Gannett Peak, 13,804 feet, and many other magnificent peaks and alpine areas. Although Pinedale is in a valley, it is at a 7,178 foot elevation, nearly 900 feet higher than Jackson. Residents report that gardening is generally a discouraging activity. This is definitely high, dry country. South of Pinedale, the early wagon trails crossed the Continental Divide where the mountains are less formidable than farther north and south.

Aspen Clones

As the view opens up, you see extensive aspen stands on the low hills on the east side of the road. Aspens grow at least occasionally from seeds blown from one hill to another. However, once established, numbers of trees in aspen stands increase substantially from new shoots growing from underground root systems. Since many trees all developed from one original tree,

195

they are nearly genetically identical: clones. One aspen stand, or clump, or clone, is genetically dissimilar to an adjacent stand. In the spring, aspen stands green up at various times. In autumn, the leaves turn their wonderful gold and fall off at slightly different times in separate stands. This non-identical timing identifies distinct clones.

Mule deer

Into Pinedale

About 50 miles southeast of Jackson, the road leaves the Bridger-Teton National Forest at The Rim; the vegetation changes also from mostly lodgepole pine forest to open aspen and sagebrush hills, then expansive sagebrush-grassland into Pinedale.

This valley and surrounding mountains are excellent big game country — elk, deer, and pronghorn antelope abound. For about seven years in the middle 1800s, trappers and mountain men met each summer to sell their beaver pelts and buy supplies for the next winter's trapping activities. They of course also whooped it up a bit, and the Upper Green River Rendezvous was a notorious regional social event. Jim Bridger, for whom many mountains, passes, and forests in this neck of the woods are named, was one of the most colorful storytellers; his tall tales of Yellowstone country entertained his friends around evening campfires.

A general view of Jackson Hole, looking east toward the Gros Ventre Mountains. Aspens and conifers prefer the deeper soil of moraines; grass and sagebrush cover the flat valley floor.

U.S. 26-89, 191
Jackson—Moose Junction
12 miles/19 km.

Jackson Hole is a 400-square mile valley surrounded by rugged mountain ranges; early trappers called any such mountain-encircled valley a hole. This hole was used by Indians for centuries and by trappers beginning in the early 19th century for its abundant beaver, marten, and other valuable furbearers. John Colter was probably one of the first white men to see this area when he was sent here in 1807 by Manuel Lisa, his second boss in the West, after Lewis and Clark.

Ring Around the Valley
The west side of this famous valley is bordered by the 40-mile long Grand Teton range, which includes part of Grand Teton National Park and the Targhee National Forest in Idaho, and the Teton National Forest in Wyoming. On the southeast are the Gros Ventre Mountains, and on the northeast is the Absaroka Range that extends from Dubois, Wyoming, through Yellowstone Park, to Livingston, Montana. The Hoback Range is on the south, and the Snake River Range is on the southwest corner of the valley.

Aren't we in the Rocky Mountains? Yes, but . . . the general Rocky Mountain chain extends from Alaska to Central America and from the western boundary of the Great Plains to the Great Basin region on the west.

197

MAP 25
U.S. 26-89-191
JACKSON—MOOSE JUNCTION

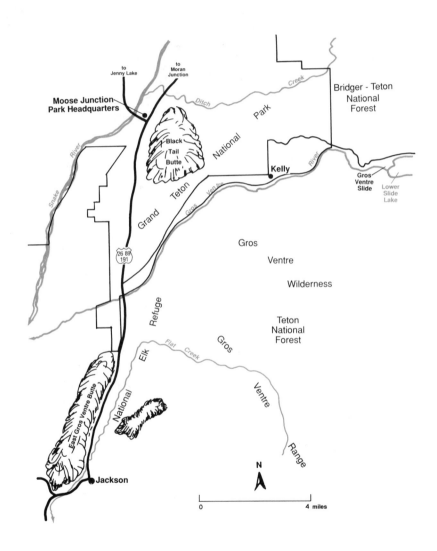

to
Jenny Lake

to
Moran
Junction

Ditch

Creek

Bridger - Teton
National
Forest

Moose Junction
Park Headquarters

River

Black
Tail
Butte

National

Park

Grand

Teton

Kelly

River

Gros Ventre

Snake

Gros

Gros
Ventre
Slide

Lower
Slide
Lake

26 89
191

Gros

Ventre

Wilderness

Teton
National
Forest

Refuge

Elk

Flat

Creek

Gros

East Gros Ventre Butte

National

Ventre

Range

Jackson

N

0   4 miles

The Rocky Mountains consist of many smaller ranges of mountains separated by valleys of various sizes. The general uplift of the region happened between 140 and 60 million years ago, but some ranges are younger.

The Tetons are among the youngest mountains on the continent, less than 10 million years old and still rising about a foot every 500 years — a lot for a mountain! The entire landscape before you has been sculpted and manipulated by glaciers, faults, landslides, and other geological activities, some of which are still active.

National Elk Refuge

North of Jackson, the National Elk Refuge is prominent east of the road for about six miles. The lush cattails, dark green sedges, and grasses identify this as an area that's a bit submerged during the growing season.

Here some 7,500 elk — about half of the entire Jackson Hole population — spend the winter. Beginning around late October or early November, the herd migrates from high elevations to lower, less snow-covered ground, seeking winter food.

In the days before settlement, the elk summered in the high country, then migrated down to winter in the valleys: Jackson Hole in the south, Gallatin and Yellowstone valleys in the north and west, Shoshone Canyon east to Cody. The amount of forage available in any spot would help determine how many elk stayed there; the herd would spread out over the entire valley. Availability of food in winter and cover for protection from the cold and wind were major natural population regulators.

Now, fences, cattle, and other human uses of the region have truncated traditional migration routes. Elk still move down out of the high country for the winter, and still need to eat, but the available winter range is severely restricted. As far back as the turn of the century, local ranchers began feeding elk in winter to make up for the lack of natural range. An official government feeding program began in Jackson Hole in 1909, and the elk refuge was established in 1912.

Although it provides a safe haven from human disturbance and harrassment, the refuge is far too small to support such large numbers of elk. They have no opportunity to spread out and by early spring much of the vegetation has been consumed. In mid-winter the natural range is supplemented with alfalfa hay pellets.

To Feed or Not to Feed

Artificially fencing and feeding wild populations of elk does cause controversy. Fish and game officials in Montana do not feed elk in winter, but the state of Wyoming has done so for many years. Individual ranchers and landowners in both states are free to do so anytime; and in many communities private feeding continues through the winter.

Those who favor such feeding programs often stress the humanitarian idea that helping wildlife through the winter is desirable. Another justification is that thwarting the natural trend for winter deaths among deer and elk keeps game populations higher for hunting.

Arguments against feeding point to the increased risk of disease and behavioral complications in abnormally dense groups of animals. Approximately half of the elk on and around the refuge, for example, are thought to be infected with brucellosis, which threatens cattle. Another problem often connected with artificial feeding is that it limits natural population control. This can lead to overpopulation and potential damage to the range. It also limits the critical winter and early spring food supplies that many predators such as the grizzly bear depend on, and can also change normal migration activities.

Gros Ventre River (approx. 13 miles)

About seven miles north of Jackson, the Gros Ventre Road turns off U.S. 89 and travels east for about 13 miles, through the village of Kelly, to Lower Slide Lake, the site of the massive 1925 Gros Ventre landslide.

At first the road threads between Grand Teton National Park and the National Elk Refuge; it follows the Gros Ventre River, with its banks lined with water-loving cottonwood trees and patches of spruce and willows. Contrast this moist riparian community with the drier sagebrush flats on the west side.

Watch for antelope amid the sagebrush; their white rump patches are alarm signals for each other, and clues to their presence for us. The pronghorn can run about 30 to 60 miles per hour and can bound 12 to 20 feet—excellent adaptations for escaping predators in the wide open spaces where they spend most of their time.

Along the Gros Ventre River you can also see stands of common juniper. Relatively few animals inhabit the juniper community, in part because juniper isn't very tasty. Deer sometimes wander in and out in winter, and chipmunks and marmots hang around areas with rocky outcrops. The Townsend's solitaire, a slender gray bird related to the thrush, prefers these open juniper areas; look for this quiet, shy bird perched on the outermost or top-most branch of a small tree along the edge of a clearing.

About a mile north of Kelly, turn east to stay on the Gros Ventre Road. At the intersection, you can also go straight ahead, back around to the main road north of Moose Junction and to the Teton Science School.

About two miles east of the previous intersection, you drive into the Bridger-Teton National Forest. Cottonwoods line the river, and the moister slopes are covered with a mixed forest of lodgepole pine, Douglas fir, spruce, and subalpine fir. Mule deer find this a favorable habitat, as do moose down on the moist lowlands and elk higher on the hillsides; bighorn sheep can sometimes be seen on the reddish hillsides. Beavers live along the river valley.

A massive landslide in 1925 at the edge of the Gros Ventre Wilderness created interesting ecological complications. Many trees that grew high on the mountain on the south side of the river slid down to river level on the moving chunks of earth. Though most older trees were killed by this traumatic transplant, many younger trees survived. They moved vertically down the mountain with their roots still in place, and continued to grow at their new, much lower, location. New trees have since grown on the landslide. The rocky talus slope now provides ideal habitat for pikas, chipmunks, mice, and marmots.

About six miles from the last turnoff, watch for a roadside pull-off with information about the landslide and a short interpretive trail that takes you up onto the shoulder of the slide. From there you can drive another seven or eight miles on a gravel road to the Crystal Creek Campground, or turn around and return to Kelly and Grand Teton National Park.

At Moose Junction, turn west to take the Jenny Lake-Teton Park Road along the base of the mountains to Jackson Lake Junction (map 26: page 202), or stay on the main road to Moran to travel north through the center of the valley (map 28: page 214).

MAP 26
TETON PARK ROAD
MOOSE—JACKSON LAKE JUNCTION
VIA JENNY LAKE

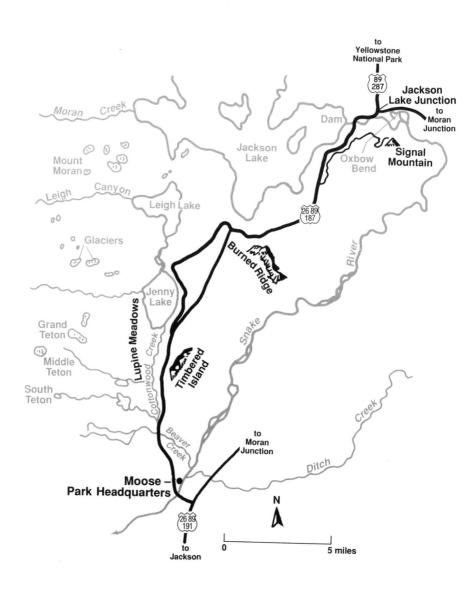

Teton Park Road:
Moose—Jackson Lake Junction via Jenny Lake
approximately 20 miles/32 km.

This road is under reconstruction as of this writing in 1992, so consult your current park map for the exact route. Generally the Teton Park Road takes you along the western edge of Jackson Hole, along the base of the Grand Teton Mountains, to the Jackson Lake junction. Short one- and two-way side roads lead close to Jenny and Leigh lakes. A side road about four miles south of Jackson Lake Junction takes you to the summit of Signal Mountain, where you can view the ecological pattern of nearly all of Jackson Hole.

No Room at the Top: The Timberline

Its route close to the base of the Teton Range makes this road superb for viewing the mountains. The ruggedness of these mountains demonstrates some of the factors instrumental in establishing an upper timberline on high mountains. No trees grow above timberline.

If the tops of the mountains here were lower, say 9,000 feet, and if the slopes were not so steep, then trees could grow to the top. But some of these peaks reach to 12,000 to 13,000 feet; at that elevation daytime temperatures are low and the growing season is too short for trees to form wood. Plants receive only enough sun and heat to grow a little, maybe make some flowers for reproduction, get hardened for winter, and call it a year. Nearly all are perennials.

The general vegetation pattern—grass and sagebrush on the flats and tree stands of lodgepole pine and subalpine fir—holds true here. Engelmann and blue spruce and subalpine fir grow in wetter spots along streams, frequently with willows and cottonwoods. Lodgepole pine, Douglas fir, subalpine fir, spruce, and whitebark pine ascend in that approximate order up the Teton slopes to timberline.

Near timberline, the wind- and weather-battered trees take on the twisted-wood shapes called krummholz, typical of trees at high elevations.

High elevation trees stay short; if they stay covered with snow in winter they are protected from winds and drying sun. In addition, some slopes are so steep that rock and soil keep washing and sliding downhill; if seedlings do try to get started, their roots wash or slide out from under them. Notice that tree growth tends to be on more convex slopes, where less water and soil move. Where slopes are too high and too steep, tree growth stops altogether.

The treeline here is one determined by both high elevation and steep slopes. On other routes, you can see examples of edaphic timberlines, determined by soil and slope. Edaphic treelines can occur at much lower elevations than the treelines you see here.

Richard Shaw, author of plant and flower books of Yellowstone and Teton national parks, has recorded 216 plant species living in alpine, or above timberline, habitats. Most are dwarfed because of special adaptations that allow them to live in the harsh conditions of high elevations. For descriptions of these kinds of plants, see the Beartooth Plateau (map 15: page 142), which has broad flat surfaces where large meadows can develop more easily than here in the jagged Tetons.

Timberlines on the Grand Tetons. Notice trees on lower convex slopes where less snow collects.

Bighorn sheep, black bears, moose, deer, and elk roam around the Tetons. Grizzlies are possibly expanding their range southward into Grand Teton Park from Yellowstone Park, though there are no reported matings or cubs yet. Smaller creatures include pocket gophers, pikas, marmots, and flower pollinators like bees and flies.

At Jackson Lake, turn east to Moran Junction and points south and east (map 27: page 206), or north toward Yellowstone Park (map 14: page 136).

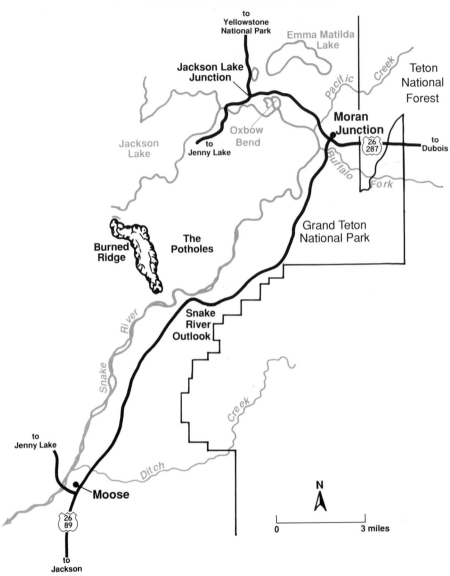

MAP 27
U.S. 89, 191, 287 AND
U.S. 26-89, 191
JACKSON LAKE JUNCTION—
MORAN JUNCTION—MOOSE JUNCTION

to
Yellowstone
National Park

Emma Matilda
Lake

Teton
National
Forest

**Jackson Lake
Junction**

Pacific
Creek

**Moran
Junction**

26
287

to
Dubois

Oxbow
Bend

Jackson
Lake

to
Jenny Lake

Buffalo
Fork

**The
Potholes**

Grand Teton
National Park

**Burned
Ridge**

Snake
River

**Snake
River
Outlook**

Creek

to
Jenny Lake

Ditch

Moose

N

26
89

0   3 miles

to
Jackson

206

Varied habitats make the Oxbow bend of the Snake River an ideal place to watch for animals and birds.

U.S. 89, 191, 287
and U.S. 26-89, 191
Jackson Lake Junction—
Moran Junction—Moose Junction
18 miles/29 km.

Great Blues

Watch about 3½ miles north of Moran Junction for the turnout at the Oxbow of the Snake River. This is an excellent place to look for eagles and ospreys fishing nearby, and to see great blue herons and trumpeter swans, which feed here. Watch carefully for tall, long-legged herons standing or slowly stalking along the shallow river shores. Their nests are harder to see, even with binoculars: look for large stick structures high in the trees in the distance across the river. Human traffic along the Snake River below Jackson Lake appears to have caused a decline in nesting; only about three nests are active now, and these are hidden in a secluded corner of the Oxbow no longer used by floaters. Great blue herons build their nests close together in a colony, always in or near a wetland, which provides their diet of fish.

Canada geese, many species of ducks, white pelicans, and other waterfowl also find the quiet Oxbow and the other lakes and streams of Jackson Hole important feeding and nesting areas. Common loons may be seen in spring and fall as they pass through on the way to wintering areas.

Pelicans

One of the largest North American birds, the white pelican is unmistakable. Its huge white body and long yellow bill with the drooping pouch for catching and holding fish makes this bird look almost like a cartoon on lakes and ponds and rivers. Their ungainly appearance is transformed into pure grace, however, when pelicans lift off for flight, cruising and gliding with head held back and bodies propelled with strong, slow wingbeats.

Pelican

Pelicans are social birds that nest in colonies, usually on traditional island sites. The nests are built close to water, providing access to this bird's diet of trout, minnows, suckers, and even crayfish and salamanders. A pelican can capture a fish up to two feet long and eat as much as four pounds of fish each day.

Pelicans that feed here at the Oxbow and throughout the ecosystem are from a nesting colony of about 400 nests in the southeast arm of Yellowstone Lake. Although this colony appears to be fairly stable thanks to strong protection efforts, the pelican is considered a species of concern. Breeding colonies are very sensitive to disturbance, sufficient additional habitat for foraging for fish is vulnerable, and eggshells have exhibited signs of thinning probably as a result of pesticide poisoning.

Diversity Begets Diversity

Conifers growing near the road include pines, Douglas fir, spruce, and subalpine fir. Deciduous trees include cottonwoods and aspens. Shorter willows and shrubs are also present. At the hands-and-knees level, grasses and forbs or wildflowers provide food and cover for a diverse community of insects and invertebrates, small mammals and reptiles, and countless microorganisms that tie the entire web together. The variety of textures and

The general vegetation pattern of Jackson Hole: sagebrush and grass are on the gravelly flats; lodgepole pine, subalpine fir, and spruce populate the glacial moraines.

sizes of the vegetation thus gives many different species of birds and other wildlife the chance to occupy different niches in the forest. Anything that destroys or disturbs the structure of plant communities affects the animal residents as well.

At Moran Junction, turn south to Moose, Wyoming, or east to Dubois, Wyoming (map 28: page 214).

The main route through Grand Teton National Park slices through the wide open sagebrush of Jackson Hole, following the naturally carved route of the Snake River. Mid-summer travelers might get an impression of a baking, barren landscape along the road, but the valley actually contains a rich, complex, and fascinating tapestry of life forms woven into a unique setting.

The Valley Communities

The flat valley floor, about 6,500 feet above sea level, has relatively poor glacially deposited soil — coarse, dry, and shallow. Water drains out easily, so it can't support many trees except along waterways, in scattered glacial potholes filled with rich organic material, and on the hills and ridges left by the glaciers. These little islands of trees, as ecologist Tim Clark calls them, can provide a critical oasis for animals, sheltering them from intense sunlight in summer and from harsh winds and deep snow in winter.

Microclimates exist in many forms: not only as islands of trees, but stands of sagebrush among the grasses, or patches of lichens on rocks. All these spots can provide moisture, shade, and protection from wind or weather for animals of all sizes, from bison to beetles. Stop at a roadside pulloff and explore some small or large islands where the habitat differs from its surroundings.

The Sagebrush Landscape

Grass and big sagebrush are the dominant plants throughout much of the valley. Though the sagebrush landscape looks harsh and inhospitable, it is actually a complex and lively community. Over 120 plant species live on the Jackson Hole sagebrush flats, including 20 species of grasses and some half dozen shrubs, in addition to the occasional pockets of trees.

These provide habitat for numerous animal species, including ground squirrels, white-footed mice, chipmunks, an occasional jackrabbit, and maybe a few badgers. Elk, bison, pronghorn antelope, and coyotes are among the larger animals of the sagebrush flats. Many birds live here, including the Western bluebird, often seen sitting on fenceposts; the sage grouse; chipping and vesper sparrows; and several raptors. Some of these species, notably the sage grouse, depend on this harsh sage habitat and cannot survive without it. In early evening, watch for bats and nighthawks zipping around, chasing flying insects.

Most of the ridges are glacial moraines, long piles of debris dumped directly from glacial ice. Because the moraines hold more water than the valley floor soils, they can support a forest community. They are generally covered with lodgepole pine forests and subalpine fir, with some Douglas fir or spruce; underneath the trees, grasses and shrubs take hold.

Aspens

The aspens of Jackson Hole provide spectacular gold splashes in the fall, especially in dry autumns. They grow in large stands where elk grazing has been light, where fires have been allowed, and where ground water is in good supply. Aspen in Jackson Hole can form two different kinds of communities: open stands on dry hillsides with poorer soils, and dense stands on moister, richer, flatter terrain.

In the western United States, aspens generally sprout from underground roots, occasionally from seed, and grow in full sunlight. Research since the fires of 1988 has found that aspen seedlings are now growing in some burned areas where sufficient moisture is present. Some ecologists are convinced that early suppression of fire here and in Yellowstone Park encouraged the growth of lodgepole pine and Douglas fir; these conifers

Young spruce growing in the shade of the older aspens at Moran Junction. In time, the aspens will disappear, and spruce will dominate.

have created too much shade for abundant aspen growth. This in turn may have enabled browsing elk and moose to eat whatever aspen shoots do pop up. Whatever the exact cause or interacting causes, some biologists feel that fewer aspens grow in Jackson Hole now than at the turn of the century. In some stands, near the Moran Post Office, for example, conifers are growing among the aspens; these aspen stands are changing to conifer stands, a natural phenomenon referred to as succession.

Just Snaking Along

Watch about seven miles north of Moose Junction for the turnoff on the west side of the road called Snake River Overlook. This is a good place to stop and view the river valley below—a broad ribbon of water and greenery in the valley floor dominated by sagebrush.

The Snake River originates high in the Teton Wilderness Area near the southeast corner of Yellowstone National Park. It flows into Jackson Lake, where a dam regulates the water level, then south through Jackson Hole. The river swings west into Idaho, then north through agricultural land until it joins the Columbia River on its way to the Pacific Ocean. Along the way through Jackson Hole, several other rivers also feed into the Snake: the Lewis River coming down from Yellowstone Park; the Buffalo Fork, which drains the mountains northeast of the valley; the Gros Ventre, which drains the mountains to the east; and the Hoback, which drains the areas southeast of Jackson Hole.

211

One of the most important and heavily used rivers in the West, this section of the Snake meanders along in braided channels from Jackson Lake to the south end of the valley. The slower-moving backwaters in this part of the river provide critical habitat for many aquatic animals such as beavers and river otter. Native cutthroat trout live throughout the river, and feed on aquatic insects, invertebrates, and small fish. Osprey, eagles, and other wildlife depend on the trout, completing a complex food web that revolves around the ever moving river.

Dense cottonwoods, willow stands, and Engelmann spruce line the riverbanks, providing excellent riparian habitat for moose and deer. Spotted sandpipers are abundant along the shoreline of the Snake River. Other diving and wading birds also abound, especially in spring and fall.

The river supports a mix of plant comunities and animal habitats that change constantly as currents shift. Spring floods from melting snow pack in the mountains enriches the floodplain area with sediment and nutrients. Riparian corridors such as this are among the most heavily used and critically needed areas for all kinds of wildlife throughout their life cycles.

At Moose, continue south to Jackson, Wyoming (map 25: page 198), or head back via Jenny Lake to Jackson Lake and points north (map 26: page 202).

U.S. 287, 26
Moran Junction—Dubois
54 miles/86 km.

A varied and fascinating drive, this route rises from a broad sagebrush valley at Moran Junction in the northeast corner of Jackson Hole, through mixed forests of lodgepole, spruce, and subalpine fir on the hillsides, to rich old-growth forests at Togwotee Pass. South of the pass, the road descends along the Wind River into stark badland country at Dubois, Wyoming.

The road follows the northwest end of the Wind River Range, with the southern end of the Absaroka Range visible to the north. The Absaroka Mountains reach about 170 miles from the east side of the Yellowstone Valley near Livingston, Montana, past the Beartooth Mountains, and along the eastern boundary of Yellowstone Park nearly to the Wind River. They include parts of the Custer and Shoshone national forests.

Jackson Hole

Throughout Jackson Hole, sagebrush dominates the valley floor; cottonwoods and willows follow the Buffalo Fork River, which starts on the slopes below Togwotee Pass. Aspens pinpoint moist areas on the hillsides, and often provide a dramatic spectacle of gold in autumn.

Going up: to Togwotee Pass

Along the climb to Togwotee Pass (pronounced Tog-o-tee), undulating alpine meadows provide rich habitats for moose, deer, and bears. Willow and sagebrush create a patchwork of texture on the gentle slopes. You see more evidence of moisture on the west side of the pass than on the east side.

A National Forest overlook on the west slope of Togwotee Pass provides a view west to the Grand Tetons. Mount Randolf and Gravel Mountain rise in the foreground. These are the southern boundary of the half-million-acre Teton Wilderness. Two important rivers originate in this wilderness area: the Yellowstone and the Snake. The Snake River flows into the Columbia and on to the Pacific Ocean; the Yellowstone River joins with the Missouri and then the Mississippi to empty into the Gulf of Mexico. Part of the water supply for much of the western half of the country starts right here, at the pinnacles of the Greater Yellowstone ecosystem. Protecting the watersheds of rivers from siltation, pollution, diversion, or other disturbance is one of the prime reasons wilderness areas are established.

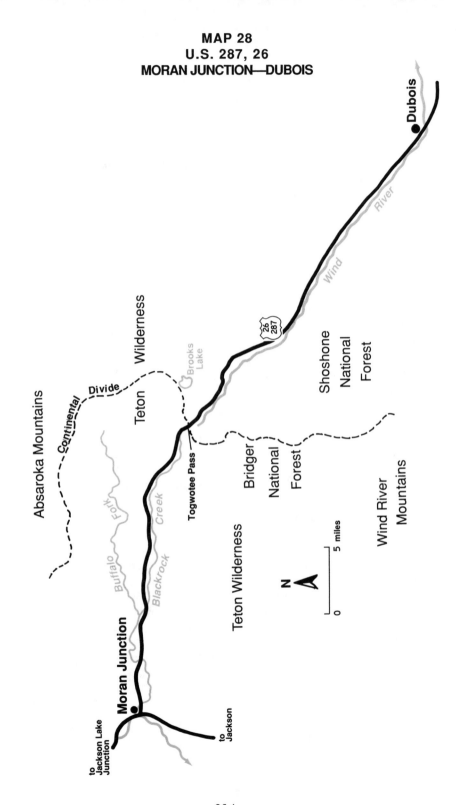

MAP 28
U.S. 287, 26
MORAN JUNCTION—DUBOIS

Wilderness and Wild Lands

This road passes from a national park through two national forests, the Bridger-Teton and the Shoshone. The road is flanked in the distance on either side by three wilderness areas, and ends up in private land in and around Dubois, where there is scattered Bureau of Land Management land as well. Much of the federal land between the Wilderness Areas is managed as roadless areas by the U.S. Forest Service, a designation that provides temporary protection until formal Wilderness status has been decided. Some people have suggested that this entire area be more formally protected as a wilderness linkage area, connecting the separate pieces of official Wilderness and the national parks to create something of a macroreserve. This would be especially significant for large, roaming animals like the grizzly bear, which are sensitive to disturbance and need large expanses of habitat.

Grizzly Country

Around the pass are whitebark pine trees. This pine is a high-elevation conifer that provides an important fall food source for grizzly bears when cone crops are good, about every five to seven years. The seeds are high in fat and quite large, and provide top-quality nutrition for bears going into winter sleep. Red squirrels play an important role in stashing huge piles of whitebark seeds which bears sometimes raid; see map 9: page 100 for details.

This area marks an eastern region of known occupied grizzly bear habitat in the Greater Yellowstone ecosystem, an area in which grizzlies appear to be expanding their range in recent years. A single adult grizzly bear might cover 100 square miles or more in the course of a summer, and during that time each grizzly must avoid other bears, as well as human disturbance. Nearly 90 percent of a grizzly's diet is plants, and the bear must forage or search for food where they are available. These areas are not always within prescribed park boundaries; a recent study by the Interagency Grizzly Bear Study Team revealed that the Greater Yellowstone grizzly population occupies a combined territory of about 9,000 square miles, only about 3,500 of which lie within Yellowstone National Park.

A bear often will exhaust a food supply in one area early in the season, move on to another area as a different crop ripens, and find itself very far from the start at the end of the year. Female grizzlies with cubs move in different circles than the males, since male grizzlies often attack and kill females and young; so the overall habitat needed by a population of grizzlies is enormous.

At the Peak of the Pass: Old Growth Forests

Togwotee Pass, almost 20 miles east of Moran Junction, crosses the Continental Divide at 9,544 feet. As many as 10,000 years ago, Indians and

High elevation trees: subalpine fir, at left, with a "skirt" of dense branches; a small lodgepole pine and larger spruce are to the right.

the herds they pursued found this to be a natural passage from the areas of Yellowstone Park and Jackson Hole into the Great Plains.

As you approach and travel past the pass, a mature spruce-fir forest begins to dominate the scene. This forest has many of the ecological characteristics of much older forests often called old growth, a term which refers to more than just old trees. Characteristics of such forests include: large standing trees; a dense overhead canopy; many layers of growth— from tiny ground covers to shrubs and trees of all sizes; and on the ground, lots of dead trees and debris, called coarse woody debris. Because of their diverse habitat types, these kinds of forests support a varied assortment of wildlife species such as bears, moose, owls, squirrels, voles, pileated woodpeckers, and pine martens. Many of these are closely tied to the special ecological characteristics of old growth for their survival.

The pine marten, for example, a member of the weasel family about the size of a housecat, is found most often in old-growth forests. In spring, the hollows of dead trees provide nesting areas, and later the higher branches in the thick conifers provide safe refuge for young martens. Deep in the coarse woody debris live populations of voles and other small rodents, which form the primary source of food for martens in spring, summer, and fall.

In winter the marten has its most critical need for old-growth conditions, for the coarse woody debris sticking up through the snow provides entrances to the world under the snow. There the marten can find voles huddled up for the winter, providing a concentrated and energy-efficient food supply, as well as critical insulation from the cold and wind. The marten needs to eat high-energy foods and find ways to get out of the cold, because its fur is not high quality insulation and its body doesn't accumulate as much fat for the winter season as other mammals do. So access to snug piles of debris under the snow in an old-growth forest is a limiting factor for survival of this attractive and valuable furbearer.

Old-growth forests provide not only habitat for a wide variety of wildlife species, but essential ecological services as well. The rich accumulations of debris on the forest floor absorb and retain moisture, for example, filtering and regulating water flow and preventing erosion and flooding. Nutrient cycles and energy flow are woven in complex webs within and around mature forests, affecting not only the forests themselves but all the habitats that surround them as well.

Wildlife species associated with old-growth forests are often used as indicator species for the forest. If the spotted owl in the ancient forests of the Pacific Northwest or the pine marten in Rocky Mountains should be found to be declining, that would be seen as an indication that the forest might be declining in health as well. Thus the attention paid to such indicator species is not only to protect the particular species itself, but more broadly to ensure that the integrity of the habitats needed by that species remains intact.

Summer Snow

Visitors to high country are often charmed, surprised, or upset by deep snow in June on such places as Togwotee Pass. One's perspective depends on one's home range. This snow is absolutely essential for sustaining agriculture along western river valleys, and preservation of good mountain meadow and forest communities is vital for naturally regulating water availability in the valleys of the arid West. July and August are usually extremely dry months, with very little rainfall; the slow melt of the snow provides water for irrigation through the summer. Dams are built for further water regulation, flood control, and storage of irrigation water.

The native plants of meadows—grasses, herbs, lichens, mosses, sedges —help the melting snow seep into the soil rather than run off quickly, and tree cover shades the soil so it loses its snow more gradually. Plant roots of all kinds, and invisible plant and animal creatures of the soil, make the soil porous, further helping to regulate water movement.

Going down...

About 20 miles west of Dubois, the road descends into lower elevations. Lodgepole pine and aspen trees begin to provide habitat for mule deer and moose, as do the broad patches and fingers of willow which reach into the landscape wherever soil moisture is abundant.

Young spruce and fir trees are growing in the shade of the lodgepoles, and in time, perhaps 200 to 300 years, will probably be the climax tree species in these lower forests, just as they do higher up. Some past disturbance such as a fire or perhaps logging probably opened this area to the sun-tolerant lodgepole seedlings. You can still see young lodgepoles coming up and thriving in the open areas along the roadside.

Badlands

In the eight miles north of Dubois, grayish sagebrush is prominent on both sides of the road; notice the moisture-loving willow shrubs and cottonwood trees on the south side, marking the course of the Wind River

Krummholz spruce at top of Togwotee Pass. Snow in June is an important source of summer water for the lower elevations.

Moose habitat: low wet areas with willow among spruce and subalpine fir.

through the plain. The north-facing slopes on the south side of the road support thicker forests on their upper slopes compared to the drier slopes with sparser tree cover on the north side.

The south-facing slopes have less snow in winter; so they provide valuable winter range for large herbivores such as deer, elk, and bighorn sheep in the Dubois area. These are also the first areas to provide fresh green forage in the spring. The cooler north-facing slopes are valuable in summer as refuges from the heat.

Gradually, the broad plain on the north, with dry rolling hills behind, gives way to a striking badlands topography.

Dubois is in the Wind River valley at about 6,917 feet in elevation, in a harsh, dry, alkaline landscape dominated by sagebrush. Treeless badlands topography on the north contrasts dramatically with the broad flood plain of the Wind River on the south.

Notice how the shadier, cooler, moister north-facing slopes on the river side support far more vegetation than the hot, dry, sunny south-facing badlands. Examples of this phenomenon abound throughout the ecosystem; the intense sunlight that beats on south-facing slopes for most of the day dries out the air and the soil, making conditions difficult for plant life in the already arid West. Visitors from cooler and moister areas of the country will find that this is different from their home areas, where sunny south slopes often provide a more hospitable microclimate for plant life than cold, damp north slopes.

Selected Readings

General Ecology

Alexander, Taylor R. and George S. Fichter. 1973. *Ecology*. Golden Press, New York.

Brewer, Richard. 1979. *Principles of Ecology*. W. B. Saunders Company, Philadelphia.

Clark, Tim W. *Ecology of Jackson Hole, Wyoming: A Primer*. T. W. Clark/Paragon Press, Salt Lake City, Utah.

Glick, Dennis, and Mary Carr, eds. 1991. *Environmental Profile of the Greater Yellowstone Ecosystem*. Greater Yellowstone Coalition, Bozeman, Montana.

Greater Yellowstone Ecosystem

Clark, Tim and Ann H. Harvey. 1988. *Management of the Greater Yellowstone Ecosystem: An Annotated Bibliography*. Northern Rockies Conservation Cooperative, Jackson, Wyoming.

Glick, Dennis and Mary Carr, eds. 1991. *Environmental Profile of the Greater Yellowstone Ecosystem*. Greater Yellowstone Coalition, Bozeman, Montana.

Little, Charles E. 1987. *The Challenge of Greater Yellowstone*. Wilderness 51 (179): 18-56.

Reese, Rick. 1984. *Greater Yellowstone: The National Park and Adjacent Wildlands*. Montana Magazine, Inc., Helena, Montana.

Schullery, Paul. 1988. *Mountain Time*. Simon and Schuster, Inc./Fireside Books, New York.

Tixier, J. S. 1986. *The Greater Yellowstone: An Introduction to an area and its issues*. Western Wildlands 12(3): 2-6.

The Wilderness Society. 1987. *Management Directions for the National Forests of the Greater Yellowstone Ecosystem*. The Wilderness Society, Washington, DC.

Geology and Climate

Adams, George F. and Jerome Wyckoff. 1971. *Golden Guide to Landforms*. Golden Press, New York.

Fritz, William J. 1985. *Roadside Geology of Yellowstone Country*. Mountain Press, Missoula, Montana.

Love, J. D. and John C. Reed. 1984. *Creation of the Teton Landscape: The Geologic Story of Grand Teton National Park*. Grand Teton Natural History Association, Moose, Wyoming.

Keefer, William R. *The Geologic Story of Yellowstone National Park*. *Geological Survey Bulletin #1347,* reprinted by Yellowstone Library and Museum Association,1987.

Lageson, David R. and Darwin R. Spearing. 1988. *Roadside Geology of Wyoming.* Mountain Press Publishing Company, Missoula, Montana.

Rhodes, Frank. 1977. *Golden Guide to Geology.* Golden Press, New York.

Vegetation Patterns

Arno, Stephen F. and Ramona P. Hammerly. 1987. *Northwest Trees*. The Mountaineers, Seattle, Washington.

Arno, Stephen F. and Ramona P. Hammerly. 1984. *Timberline: Mountain and Arctic Forest Frontiers*. The Mountaineers, Seattle, Washington.

Brockman, C. Frank. 1968. *Trees of North America*. Golden Press, New York.

Clark, Tim W. 1981. *Ecology of Jackson Hole, Wyoming: A Primer*. T. W. Clark/paragon Press, Salt Lake City.

Clark, Tim W. and Ann H. Harvey. 1989. *Rare, Sensitive, and Threatened Species of the Greater Yellowstone Ecosystem*. Northern Rockies Conservation Cooperative, Jackson, Wyoming.

Despain, Don, Douglas Houston, Mary Meagher, and Paul Schullery. 1986. *Wildlife in Transition: Man and Nature on Yellowstone's Northern Range*. Roberts Rinehart, Boulder, Colorado.

Duft, Joseph F. and Robert K. Moseley. 1989. *Alpine Wildflowers of the Rocky Mountains*. Mountain Press Publishing Company, Missoula, Montana.

Murie, Olaus. 1979 edition. *Nature Guide to Jackson Hole*. Teton Bookshop, Jackson, Wyoming.

Pielou, E. C. 1988. *The World of Northern Evergreens*. Comstock Publishing Associates/Cornell University Press, Ithaca, New York.

Shaw, Richard. 1976. *Field Guide to Vascular Plants of Grand Teton National Park and Teton County, Wyoming*. Utah State University Press, Logan, Utah.

Shaw, Richard. 1981. *Plants of Yellowstone and Grand Teton National Parks*. Wheelwright Press, Ltd., Salt Lake City, Utah.

Willard, Bettie E. and Chester O. Harris. 1969. *Alpine Wildflowers of Rocky Mountain National Park*. Fifth edition. Rocky Mountain nature Association, Estes Park, Colorado.

Zwinger, Ann and Beatrice E. Willard. 1986. *Land Above the Trees: A Guide to American Alpine Tundra*. Harper & Row/Perennial Library, New York.

Wildlife

Clark, Tim W. and Ann H. Harvey. 1989. *Rare, Threatened, and Endangered Species of the Greater Yellowstone Ecosystem*. Northern Rockies Conservation Cooperative, Jackson, Wyoming.

Clark, Tim. 1981. *Ecology of Jackson Hole, Wyoming: A Primer*. T. W. Clark/Paragon Press, Salt Lake City.

Craighead, Karen. 1978. *Large Mammals of Yellowstone and Grand Teton National Parks: How to Know Them, Where to See Them.*

Cundall, Alan W. and Herbert T. Lystrup. 1987. *Hamilton's Guide to Yellowstone National Park.* Hamilton Stores, Inc., West Yellowstone, Montana.

Despain, Don, Douglas Houston, Mary Meagher, and Paul Schullery. 1986. *Wildlife in Transition: Man and Nature on Yellowstone's Northern Range.* Roberts Rinehart, Boulder, Colorado.

Follett, Dick. 1985. *Birds of Yellowstone and Grand Teton National Parks.* Roberts Rinehart, Inc., Boulder, Colorado.

Johnsgaard, Paul A. 1982. *Teton Wildlife: Observations by a Naturalist.* Colorado Associated University Press, Boulder, Colorado.

McEneaney, Terry. 1988. *Birds of Yellowstone.* Roberts Rinehart, Boulder, Colorado.

Murie, Olaus. 1979 edition. *Nature Guide to Jackson Hole.* Teton Bookshop, Jackson, Wyoming.

Perry, Bill. 1972. *Yellowstone Wildlife.* U.S. Government Printing Office, Washington, DC, stock #2405-0474.

Raynes, Bert. 1984. *Birds of Grand Teton National Park and the Surrounding Area.* Grand Teton Natural History Association, Jackson, Wyoming.

Schullery, Paul. 1988. *Mountain Time.* Simon & Schuster, Inc., New York.

Scott, M. Douglas and Suvi A. Scott. 1988. *Yellowstone and Grand Teton Wildlife.* Wheelwright Press, Ltd., Salt Lake City, Utah.

Streubel, Donald. 1989. *Small Mammals of the Greater Yellowstone Ecosystem.* Roberts Rinehart, Boulder, Colorado.

Weaver, John. 1986. *Of Wolves and Grizzly Bears.* Western Wildlands 12(3):27-29.

Bibliography

Adams, George F. and Jerome Wyckoff. 1971. *Golden Guide to Landforms. Golden Press,* New York.

Alexander, Taylor R. and George S. Fichter. 1973. *Ecology.* Golden Press, New York.

Alt, David D. and Donald W. Hyndman. 1986. *Roadside Geology of Montana.* Mountain Press Publishing Company, Missoula, Montana.

Alt, David D. and Donald W. Hyndman. 1972. *Roadside Geology of the Northern Rockies.* Mountain Press Publishing Co., Missoula, Montana.

Arno, Stephen F. and Ramona P. Hammerly. 1987. *Northwest Trees.* The Mountaineers, Seattle, Washington.

Arno, Stephen F. and Ramona P. Hammerly. 1984. *Timberline: Mountain and Arctic Forest Frontiers.* The Mountaineers, Seattle, Washington.

Brewer, Richard. 1979. *Principles of Ecology.* W.B. Saunders Company, Philadelphia.

Brewster, Wayne G. 1986. *Cogs and Wheels: Meditations on an ecosystem.* Western Wildlands 12(3): 7-11.

Brock, T. D. 1978. *Thermophilic Microorganisms and Life at High Temperatures.* Springer-Verlag, New York.

Brockman, C. Frank. 1968. *Trees of North America.* Golden Press, New York.

Clark, Tim W. 1981. *Ecology of Jackson Hole, Wyoming: A Primer.* T.W. Clark/ Paragon Press, Salt Lake City, Utah.

Clark, Tim W. and Ann H. Harvey. 1988. *Management of the Greater Yellowstone Ecosystem: An Annotated Bibliography.* Northern Rockies Conservation Cooperative, Jackson, Wyoming.

Clark, Tim W. and Ann H. Harvey. 1989. *Rare, Sensitive, and Threatened Species of the Greater Yellowstone Ecosystem.* Northern Rockies Conservation Cooperative, Jackson, Wyoming.

Craighead, Karen. 1978. *Large Mammals of Yellowstone and Grand Teton National Parks: How to Know Them, Where to See Them.*

Cundall, Alan W. and Herbert T. Lystrup. 1987. *Hamilton's Guide to Yellowstone National Park.* Hamilton Stores, Inc., West Yellowstone, Montana.

Despain, Don. 1977. *Forest Successional Stages in Yellowstone National Park.* Information paper #32, Yellowstone National Park, National Park Service, U.S. Dept. of Interior.

Despain, Don. 1973. *Major Vegetation Zones of Yellowstone National Park.* Information paper #19, Yellowstone National Park, National Park Service, U.S. Dept. of Interior.

Despain, Don. 1983. Nonpyrogenous climax lodgepole pine communities in Yellowstone National Park. *Ecology* 64(2): 231-234.

Despain, Don, Douglas Houston, Mary Meagher, and Paul Schullery. 1986. *Wildlife in Transition: Man and Nature on Yellowstone's Northern Range.* Roberts Rinehart, Boulder, Colorado.

Duft, Joseph F. and Robert K. Moseley. 1989. *Alpine Wildflowers of the Rocky Mountains.* Mountain Press Publishing Company, Missoula, Montana.

Follett, Dick. 1985. *Birds of Yellowstone and Grand Teton National Parks.* Roberts Rinehart, Inc., Boulder, Colorado.

Fritz, William J. 1985. *Roadside Geology of Yellowstone Country.* Mountain Press, Missoula, Montana.

Galbraith, Alan F. 1986. Headwaters of the West: The Yellowstone Ecosystem. *Western Wildlands* 12(3): 12-13.

Glick, Dennis, and Mary Carr, eds. 1991. *Environmental Profile of the Greater Yellowstone Ecosystem.* Greater Yellowstone Coalition, Bozeman, Montana.

Gruell, George. 1986. The importance of fire in the Greater Yellowstone Ecosystem. *Western Wildlands* 12(3): 14-18.

Holland, David G. 1986. The role of forest insects and diseases in the Yellowstone Ecosystem. *Western Wildlands* 12(3): 19-23.

Houston, Douglas B. 1971. Ecosystems of national parks. *Science* 172: 648-651.

Johnsgaard, Paul A. 1982. *Teton Wildlife: Observations by a Naturalist.* Colorado Associated University Press, Boulder, Colorado.

Keefer, William R. *The Geologic Story of Yellowstone National Park.* Geological Survey Bulletin #1347, reprinted by Yellowstone Library and Museum Association, 1987.

Lageson, David R. and Darwin R. Spearing. 1988. *Roadside Geology of Wyoming.* Mountain Press Publishing Company, Missoula, Montana.

Little, Charles E. 1987. The Challenge of Greater Yellowstone. *Wilderness* 51 (179): 18-56.

Love, J. D. and John C. Reed. 1984. *Creation of the Teton Landscape: The Geologic Story of Grand Teton National Park.* Grand Teton Natural History Association, Moose, Wyoming.

McEneaney, Terry. 1988. *Birds of Yellowstone.* Roberts Rinehart, Boulder, Colorado.

Marschall, Mark C. 1990. *Yellowstone Trails: A Hiking Guide.* The Yellowstone Association for Natural Science, History, and Education, Inc., Yellowstone National Park, Wyoming.

Marshall, Kent G., Dennis H. Knight, and William J. Barmore, Jr. 1979. *An Indexed and Annotated Bibliography on the Ecology of Grand Teton National Park.* University of Wyoming/National Park Service Research Center.

Mattson, David J. and Daniel P. Reinhart. 1987. *Grizzly Bear, Red Squirrels, and Whitebark Pine: Third Year Progress Report.* Report to the Interagency Grizzly Bear Study Team, Bozeman, Montana.

Murie, Olaus. 1979 edition. *Nature Guide to Jackson Hole.* Teton Bookshop, Jackson, Wyoming.

Penn, Bradley G. 1986. Multiple use in the Yellowstone Ecosystem: Oil and gas exploration. *Western Wildlands* 12(3): 24-26.

Perry, Bill. 1972. *Yellowstone Wildlife.* U.S. Government Printing Office, Washington, DC, stock #2405-0474.

Pielou, E. C. *The World of Northern Evergreens.* 1988. Comstock Publishing Associates/Cornell University Press, Ithaca, New York.

Raynes, Bert. 1984. *Birds of Grand Teton National Park and the Surrounding Area.* Grand Teton Natural History Association, Jackson, Wyoming.

Reese, Rick. 1984. *Greater Yellowstone: The National Park and Adjacent Wildlands.* Montana Magazine, Inc., Helena, Montana.

Rhodes, Frank. 1977. *Golden Guide to Geology.* Golden Press, New York.

Schullery, Paul. 1980. *The Bears of Yellowstone.* Yellowstone Library and Museum Association, Yellowstone National Park, Wyoming.

Schullery, Paul. 1988. *Mountain Time.* Simon and Schuster, Inc./Fireside Books, New York.

Schullery, Paul. *Road Guide for the Four-Season Road from Gardiner to Cooke City Through Yellowstone National Park.* Yellowstone Library and Museum Association, Yellowstone National Park.

Scott, M. Douglas and Suvi A. Scott. 1988. *Yellowstone and Grand Teton Wildlife.* Wheelwright Press, Ltd., Salt Lake City, Utah.

Shaw, Richard. 1976. *Field Guide to Vascular Plants of Grand Teton National Park and Teton County, Wyoming.* Utah State University Press, Logan, Utah.

Shaw, Richard. 1981. *Plants of Yellowstone and Grand Teton National Parks.* Wheelwright Press, Ltd., Salt Lake City, Utah.

Streubel, Donald. 1989. *Small Mammals of the Greater Yellowstone Ecosystem.* Roberts Rinehart, Boulder, Colorado.

Tixier, J.S. 1986. The Greater Yellowstone: An Introduction to an Area and Its Issues. *Western Wildlands* 12(3): 2-6.

Varley, John D. and Paul Schullery. *Freshwater Wilderness: Yellowstone Fishes & Their World*. 1983. The Yellowstone Library and Museum Association, Yellowstone National Park, Wyoming.

Weaver, John. 1986. Of Wolves and Grizzly Bears. *Western Wildlands* 12(3):27-29.

Wilderness Society. 1987. *Management Directions for the National Forests of the Greater Yellowstone Ecosystem*. The Wilderness Society, Washington, DC.

Willard, Bettie E. and Chester O. Harris. 1969. *Alpine Wildflowers of Rocky Mountain National Park*. Fifth edition. Rocky Mountain nature Association, Estes Park, Colorado.

Zwinger, and Beatrice E. Willard. 1986. *Land Above the Trees: A Guide to American Alpine Tundra*. Harper & Row/Perennial Library, New York.

Glossary

abiotic: non-living. Abiotic components of an ecosystem include air, water, rock, etc. Compare to biotic.

adaptation: a characteristic that helps an organism survive under particular conditions.

adiabatic cooling: cooling of an air mass as it rises to get over high land and expands; the cooled air tends to drop moisture.

adiabatic warming: warming of an air mass as it drops in elevation; the warmed air tends to hold moisture.

aerobic: using oxygen.

alpine: refers to areas of mountains above the limit of tree growth, or to the organisms living there.

amphibians: animals with backbones that lay eggs in water, usually have a larval stage, and need moist skin for gas exchange. Salamanders, frogs, and toads are amphibians.

anaerobic: without oxygen.

andesite: a medium-colored volcanic rock with iron and magnesium. Absaroka volcanic flows were of andesite, forming soil richer than that from rhyolite. Compare to rhyolite.

aquatic: refers to a watery environment, or to organisms that live primarily in water.

autotrophic: "self-feeding," or photosynthetic; organisms such as green plants and algae that can convert sunlight into food. See also producer.

backcountry: remote areas more than 250 yards from paved roads and more than a half mile from facilities; in Yellowstone National Park, backcountry is managed as wilderness and requires a permit for camping.

bedrock: solid rock exposed at or near the surface.

biodiversity: see diversity.

biogeochemical cycles: the various nutrient circuits such as the water cycle, the carbon cycle, the nitrogen cycle, and others. Biogeochemical cycles involve both biotic and abiotic elements of the ecosystem and keep essential materials circulating within the system.

biota: all the species of plants and animals occurring within a certain area.

biotic: refers to life, living.

bog: a special type of wetland ecosystem where organic matter accumulates as peat.

browser: an animal, such as deer or elk, that eats twigs or shoots of shrubs, trees, or woody vines. (Compare to grazer.)

buteo: a type of hawk with broad wings for soaring and circling high in the air. Buteos found in the Greater Yellowstone include the red-tailed hawk, the ferruginous hawk, and the swainson's hawk.

cache: a stash of food. Also called "midden."

caldera: a large, basin-like depression with steep sides formed by the explosion or collapse of a volcano.

canopy: the uppermost layer of a forest consisting of crowns of trees or shrubs; also called overstory.

carbonate: rocks such as limestone that contain carbon and oxygen in combination with sodium, calcium, or other elements.

carnivores: meat-eating animals. See also consumers.

carrying capacity: the maximum number of a species that can be supported indefinitely by available resources in a given area; symbolized by "K".

climax community: The kind of community that would probably occupy a site indefinitely if there were no disturbances or changes in the climate or soil.

cold drainage: the settling of cold air into low places such as the mouth of a canyon, displacing the less dense warm air. A good example in the Greater Yellowstone can be seen at Pine Creek Campground in Paradise Valley.

chlorophyll: green pigments in plants that are needed for photosynthesis.

community: a group of plants and animals occupying a particular area; usually implies that the members of the community interact with one another to some degree.

competition: the demand of two or more organisms for some resource (food, shelter, space, etc.) that exceeds the immediate supply of the resource.

consumers: animals that consume vegetation and/or other animals. Compare to producers.

continental divide: the invisible line which divides waters that flow east to the Gulf of Mexico and the Atlantic Ocean from waters that flow west to the Pacific Ocean.

convention: the mass movement of warmed air or liquid to or from the surface of an object. Usually used in reference to "convection currents," where water and air move in vertical circular patterns in soil or atmosphere.

copepod: a microscopic crustacean eaten by fish.

cordillera: a system of mountain ranges, for example, the Rocky Mountains.

cotyledons: the primary leaf of the embryo in seeds; there is one cotyledon in monocots like grasses and lilies, two cotyledons in dicots like aspen trees and geraniums; conifers like pines and spruce have many cotyledons, making their very young seedlings look like the ribs of an umbrella.

crustaceans: invertebrate animals, related to insects, that have a hard external skeleton and many pairs of appendages; shrimp and copepods are aquatic examples, sowbugs and pillbugs are terrestrial examples.

cushion plants: herbaceous perennial plants that have a dense mass of short stems and many leaves, found in harsh alpine areas; examples include alpine forget-me-not, phlox, moss campion.

decomposers: organisms such as fungi and bacteria that absorb nutrients from non-living organic material including corpses, fallen leaves, and body wastes; the nutrients are converted into inorganic forms which can be re-used by plants and animals.

desiccate: to dry out.

detritus: pieces of dead organic matter.

diversity: variety; usually refers to the number and abundance of species in a community.

drainage basin: on a large scale, the largest natural drainage area or subdivision of a continent, where water drains from its origins in the mountains into a major river system; within the Greater Yellowstone Ecosystem are drainage basins for the Yellowstone-Missouri, the Snake-Columbia, and the Green-Colorado river systems. The term is also used for smaller subdivisions, such as the Madison River drainage.

detritivores: consumers that eat detritus.

ecology: the study of the relationships of organisms to their environment and to one another; from the Greek "oikos," meaning "home."

ecosystem: all the living organisms in a given area, and the nonliving parts of their environment with which they interact, all functioning as an ecological unit.

edaphic: referring to soil and its properties that influence living organisms; one of these properties would be the capacity to hold water.

edge: refers to the edge of a forest, where trees give way to shrubby thicket and herbaceous areas.

endangered: according to the Endangered Species Act of 1973, a species that is in danger of becoming extinct in all or a significant portion of its range.

endemic: refers to organisms that are native to and found only in a certain country or region. Pronghorn antelope are endemic to North America, for example; they evolved here and are not found in the wild anywhere else in the world.

environment: the surroundings of an organism; "environmental" often refers to conditions or issues that affect the ecology and the environment of particular organisms, including humans.

enviornmental impacts statement (EIS): an examination of the potential environmental effects of a proposed action, required for federal projects by the National Environmental Policy Act.

erosion: the process by which rocks and soil are loosened and worn away from the surface through actions of wind, water, ice movement, etc.

eukaryote: an organism whose cells have a true nucleus; algae, fungi, plants, and animals are eukaryotes. Compare to prokaryote.

eutrophic: refers to bodies of water that are rich in mineral nutrients and organic materials and therefore extremely productive; usually used in reference to polluted waters with excessive amounts of nutrients which may lead to oxygen deficiency. Compare to oligotrophic.

exclosure (also enclosure): an area fenced to exclude certain kinds of organisms; there are several roadside examples of exclosures in Yellowstone National Park where elk and other browsers are being excluded from willow stands.

exotic: refers to any organism that is not native to the area where it occurs; "introduced." Brown trout, for example, are exotic fishes from Europe that have been introduced into Greater Yellowstone rivers and streams.

extinct: completely disappeared from the earth, such as the passenger pigeon; no individuals of the species remain alive anywhere. Some species such as the California Condor are called "extinct in the wild," though a few individuals are alive in captivity.

extirpated: disappeared from a particular part but not all of its range; some individuals of the species can be found elsewhere in the wild.

fauna: a collective term to include all the kinds of animals in a region.

fingerling: a young fish, in the "teenage" stage between fry and adult.

flag trees: trees found at timberline whose branches are removed from the windward side by the drying effects of wind and by physical damage from wind-carried ice, soil, and snow.

food chain: a sequence of specific organisms from producers to consumers, each feeding at a different trophic level. In an example of a simple food chain, for example, grass is at the lowest level, the rabbit that eats the grass is at the next higher level, and the fox that eats the rabbit is at the high end of the chain.

food web: the elaborate interconnected network of food chains showing who eats whom in an ecosystem.

forage: unharvested plant material that is available as food for domestic or wild animals; used both as a verb and a noun.

forb: an herbaceous plant that is not grass and is not grass-like; includes plants that are commonly referred to as weeds and wildflowers.

fragmentation: breaking apart formerly large expanses of habitat into small pieces isolated from each other by some barrier that certain organisms can't cross.

fry: a newly hatched fish.

galleries: elaborate tracks and trails left in the inner bark of a tree by beetle larvae feeding on young cells full of water and sugars.

genera: plural of genus; a group of related species. Lodgepole and whitebark pines, for example, are two species in the genus *Pinus*; the genus *Pinus* and the genus *Abies* (firs) are two different genera.

glacial erratic: a rock deposited by glaciers which is of a different type than the underlying bedrock on which it is dropped.

grazer: an animal that feeds on grasses and forbs, such as pronghorn antelope. Compare to browser.

groundwater: subsurface water that fills pores and spaces in the rock below the surface.

greenhouse effect: the warming of the earth due to atmospheric accumulation of carbon dioxide, which absorbs infrared radiation and slows its escape from the earth.

habitat: the specific place that is occupied by an organism, population, or community, including all of the environmental conditions such as water, climate, and soil.

habituation: a simple kind of learning where an animal begins to ignore stimuli that are frequently repeated, allowing the animal to conserve time and energy. Coyotes that frequently encounter humans with food, for example, begin to ignore the urge to flee and become habituated or oblivious to human presence.

headwaters: the origin of a stream or river, frequently composed of many small streams that come together.

herbaceous: refers to non-woody plants that die back to the ground each year; grasses and forbs, in contrast to woody shrubs and trees. Herbaceous annuals grow, flower, and produce seed in one year; herbaceous perennials overwinter as resistant underground parts such as bulbs and rootstocks.

herbivores: organisms that eat plants; elk and grasshoppers are examples of herbivores.

heterotrophic: "other-feeding," not photosynthetic; animals (and parasitic plants) are heterotrophs because they must use organic material from other organisms as food.

hibernation: a physiological state that permits survival during long periods of cold and lack of food; metabolism and body temperature drop, and heart and respiration rates slow down.

highlined: refers to trees whose bottom layers have been heavily browsed by ungulates, leaving a tree shape that looks something like a lollipop.

home range: the area around an animal's established home, over which the animal travels in the course of its normal daily activities.

homoiotherm: an animal able to maintain its body temperature at an approximate constant level regardless of the temperature of the environment; "warm-blooded." Compare to oikilotherm.

hybrid: a cross between parents with different genes or between two species.

hydrology: the science dealing with water and snow.

inbreeding: the mating of closely related individuals, usually reducing the genetic variability of a population and resulting in genetic problems.

indicator: an organism or species or community that serves to indicate the presence of certain environmental conditions. The pine marten, for example, is closely associated with old-growth type forests, and is used by several national forests in the Greater Yellowstone as an indicator of the presence of old-growth forest.

indigenous: refers to an organism that is native, not introduced; cutthroat trout, for example, are indigenous to the Greater Yellowstone Ecosystem.

inflorescence: the flower cluster in plants, including the flowers, bracts, and stems.

insectivores: insect-eating animals or plants, such as the shrew and the venus fly-trap.

interaction: any relationship between organisms (such as grazing, competition, or predation) or between organisms and the environment (such as the wilting of a plant from drought, or the migration of elk as a result of snow depth).

invertebrates: animals without a backbone, such as insects and crustaceans.

krummholz: scrubby, stunted trees found at timberline in the mountains.

"K": symbol for carrying capacity.

K-selected: refers to a reproductive strategy where a population or species produces relatively few offspring each of which has a good chance of surviving; most large mammals such as grizzly bears are K-Selected. Compare to R-selected.

larva: in some animal life cycles, a free-living but sexually immature form which may be different from the adult in morphology, nutrition, and habitat. The larval form of a butterfly, for example, is the caterpillar.

layering: the ability of many trees at timberline in the mountains to reproduce when their branches touch the ground, take root, and become a separate tree.

lichen: a symbiotic, specific relationship between an alga and a fungus which results in an organism that is different from either of the original partners; the presence of algae allows lichens to be autotrophic.

limiting factor: a factor that limits growth or activity of an organism because the factor is scarce or unavailable; nitrogen is a limiting factor for many organisms because it is unavailable for use until converted to a special form by bacteria.

mesic: having medium moisture content; compare to xeric and aquatic; aspens in the Greater Yellowstone Ecosystem are found in mesic conditions.

metabolism: all of the chemical processes that go on in an organism; "basal metabolism" is the rate at which an organism at rest expends energy.

microclimate: local climatic conditions, different from nearby conditions because of the effects of other factors. Examples might include the north side of a mountain, where moisture and temperature conditions are different from the south side because of the effects of slope, aspect, soil, etc.

midden: see cache.

mixed forest: a forest composed of trees of two or more species.

montane: refers to mountains.

moraine: an accumulation of gravel, boulders, and dirt deposited by a glacier; especially visible in Jackson Hole.

morphology: the form, structure, and development of an organism; also can refer to the texture and structure of soils.

mosaic: patchwork pattern of vegetation types; produced by fire, soil of different types, trees of different ages, insect activity, etc.

multiple use: the policy of using a resource in several ways, such as the use of national forests for timber, forage, water supplies, game and nongame wildlife habitat, wilderness, and recreation.

mycorrhizae: the symbiotic relationship between fungi and the roots of certain plants, important in nutrient uptake by the plant; "fungus-root."

niche: the ecological role of an organism in the environment; also refers to the specific part or smallest unit of habitat occupied by an organism. The little brown bat, for example, occupies the nocturnal-flying-insect-eating niche in its environment, and occupies the under-the-bark niche of a tree trunk habitat.

old-growth: refers to a forest with certain ecological characteristics, including large-diameter trees, dead and dying snags, coarse woody debris on the forest floor, and many canopy layers.

oligotrophic: refers to ponds and lakes that are low in basic nutrients for plant growth; high-elevation ponds usually are oligotrophic; compare to eutrophic.

omnivore: an animal that eats both plant and animal foods; grizzly and black bears are omnivores. See also consumers.

overstory: see canopy.

patterned ground: the patterning of rocks, soil, and vegetation into various geometric shapes, especially polygons, circles, and lines or stripes, by convection currents in the soil; common in certain high-mountain landscapes.

pheromones: small, volatile, airborne chemical signals that function in communication between animals and influence physiology and behavior.

pH scale: a measure of hydrogen ion concentration ranging from 0 to 14, with 7 being neutral, 0 having high hydrogen ion concentration and called acidic, 14 having low hydrogen ion concentration and called basic.

phloem: the tissue in plants that conducts foods such as sugar and other organic nutrients; the innermost bark of trees.

photosynthesis: the production of sugars from carbon dioxide and water by chlorophyll in plants and algae, using sunlight for energy and producing oxygen as a by-product.

pioneer community: the initial community in succession, usually made up of plants and animals that can tolerate or thrive in bright sunlight and harsh conditions.

plankton: floating or weakly swimming microscopic animals (zooplankton) or plants (phytoplankton) in lakes, ponds, and streams; form the bases of aquatic food chains.

poikilotherm: an animal that lacks the ability to control its body temperature and so maintains a body temperature roughly the same as that of the environment; "cold-blooded." Frogs and other amphibians and snakes and other reptiles are poikilotherms. Compare to homoiotherm.

population: a group of interacting individuals of the same species occupying a particular area at the same time.

predators: animals that attack and eat other animals.

prey: an animal that is killed and eaten by another; some people also consider plants to be prey, since they are killed and eaten by animals.

primary consumers: herbivores; animals that eat producers. Elk, bison, zooplankton, and grasshoppers are primary consumers.

primary succession: succession that begins on a bare area such as a lava flow, where no plants or animals previously existed.

prokaryote: a single-celled organism that doesn't have a nuclear membrane. Compare to eukaryote.

producers: organisms such as green plants and algae that can use the sun's energy to make organic substances from inorganic material through the process of photosynthesis. See also autotrophic.

production: storage of energy in the form of plant organic matter such as leaves and stems.

R-selected: a reproductive strategy where a population or species produces large numbers of offspring, only a few of which have a good chance of survival; fish which lay thousands of eggs are examples of R-selected animals. Compare to K-selected.

rain shadow: refers to an area in which little or no rain falls because it is located to the leeward side of a mountain or range whose opposite side is exposed to moisture-laden winds. Gardiner, Montana, is in the rain shadow of the Gallatin Mountains, for example; eastern Wyoming is in the rain shadow of Rocky Mountain ranges.

range: (1) refers to the extent of the geographic area in which an animal or plant occurs; (2) in the West also refers to land covered with plants that is suitable for grazing; (3) also refers to separate mountain units, such as the Gallatin Range, the Absaroka Range. See also home range.

raptor: a predatory bird with curved, sharp claws adapted for seizing prey; eagles, owls, and hawks are raptors.

resource: "natural resource" can refer to land, forests, minerals, water, and other natural features used by humans for their survival. Also refers to habitats and their components used by all organisms for their survival.

rare: occurring in only one or a few small populations and therefore potentially vulnerable to extinction.

rhyolite: a light-colored volcanic rock, low in iron and magnesium, not very fertile for plant growth. Many Yellowstone volcanic flows are rhyolite. Compare to andesite.

riparian: refers to land bordering a stream or lake, usually with trees and shrubs like cottonwood and willow.

ruminant: an even-toed ungulate that lacks upper incisor teeth, has a multi-chambered stomach, and chews its cud, such as deer, cattle, and elk.

scarp: a depression, cliff, or slope that's steep on one side, gentler on the other.

secondary consumers: carnivores and omnivores; animals that eat herbivores.

secondary succession: the kind of succession that takes place after part or all of the existing vegetation in an area is destroyed. Most forest succession after fire is secondary.

sedge: a grass-like plant found usually in wet places. The stem is triangular ("sedges have edges"), while grass stems are round.

sedimentary rocks: rocks formed from pebbles, sand, and clay in rivers, lakes and seas; usually forms distinct layers, such as sandstone and limestone, and is often rich in fossils.

sedimentation: the process of depositing materials in bodies of water.

sensitive: easily disturbed by human activities.

seral: refers to "sere," the series of stages that follow one another in ecological succession; species or communities in the sequence prior to climax are called seral.

serotinous: refers to "late opening," such as certain cones of lodgepole pines which remain on the tree for several years without opening.

siltation: the deposition of water-borne sediments in bodies of water, caused usually by a decrease in the velocity of the moving water.

sinter: deposits mainly of silica and calcium carbonate left by evaporation around geysers and hot springs. Most sinter in the Yellowstone area is geyserite, mainly silica. Travertine, calcium carbonate, is at Mammoth Hot Springs in Yellowstone Park.

species: a particular group of organisms which have similar anatomical and genetic characteristics and have the ability to interbreed and produce fertile offspring.

stand: a general term for an aggregation of plants, usually trees, that are more or less uniform in composition and habitat conditions.

stomates: minute openings found in the epidermis of leaves which allow for carbon dioxide to enter and oxygen to leave the plant.

subalpine: refers to the region or zone in mountains below the treeless alpine region; characterized in the Greater Yellowstone by coniferous forests of spruce and fir.

subnivean: under-the-snow.

succession: the replacement of one kind of community by another kind; the progressive changes in vegetation and animal life which may culminate in a climax community.

symbiotic: an association between two or more species which benefits both species; examples are mycorrhizal fungi and tree roots (see mycorrhizae), lichens, and parasites.

talus: piles of rock fragments at the base of steep slopes or cliffs.

taxon: a category of living things, such as species or genus.

territory: the area occupied by an animal and defended against intruders.

threatened: under the Endangered Species Act of 1973, any species or subspecies likely to become endangered in the foreseeable future in all or part of its range.

timberline: the upper limit of tree growth in mountains.

topography: a general term to include characteristics of the ground surface, such as hills, slopes, valleys, etc.

trailhead: the starting point for a hiking trail.

travertine: calcium-carbonate limestone formed when water evaporates; a kind of sinter at Mammoth Hot Springs in Yellowstone.

trophic level: feeding level; at the lowest level are producers, at the next level are herbivores, at upper levels are carnivores and omnivores. Crossing all levels are decomposers.

tuff: a porous rock formed of volcanic ash and cinder.

tundra: the treeless or alpine region, characterized by low shrubby or mat-like vegetation and bare areas.

turnover: mixing of layers of water in lakes in spring and fall; cool water sinks, warmer water rises. Important in distributing minerals.

undergrowth: the shrubs, seedlings, sapling trees, and herbaceous plants in a forest.

ungulate: a mammal with hooves, such as elk, deer, bison, and antelope.

vascular cambium: plant cells that give rise to wood (xylem) and inner bark (phloem) in woody plants and trees.

vascular plants: plants that have specialized tissue, xylem and phloem, that conducts water, sugar, and nutrients in the plant.

vegetation: the plant cover of an area.

vernal: refers to the season of spring.

vertebrate: an animal with a spine; mammals, birds, reptiles, amphibians, and fishes are vertebrates.

watershed: the total area of land above a given point that contributes water to a river or stream; see also drainage basin.

wilderness area: an area of federal public land designated by the Wilderness Act of 1964 in which organisms and geological and ecological processes are undisturbed by humans; also refers to areas not officially designated as Wilderness but managed for wilderness characteristics, such as backcountry areas within national parks.

xeric: refers to dry habitat; cacti are found in xeric conditions. Compare to mesic and aquatic.

xylem: woody plant tissue that conducts water and minerals from the roots to the rest of the plant.

Index